THOSE TOURISTS ARE MONEY:
THE ROCK'N'ROLL GUIDE TO CAMDEN

Ann Scanlon

First published in Great Britain in 1997

Copyright © Ann Scanlon 1997

*The author has asserted her moral rights in accordance with the
Copyright, Designs and Patents Act 1988*

ISBN: 0 9531029 04

*Printed and bound by
Antony Rowe Ltd, Chippenham, Wiltshire*

*Published by
Tristia, PO Box 14479, London, SW16 6ZP*

For Myles Scanlon

*Who hung out in Camden
when it was an Irish town*

By the same author

THE POGUES: THE LOST DECADE

Contents

Acknowledgements

Grateful acknowledgement is given to the following
for permission to reproduce lyrics:

McALPINE'S FUSILIERS
Dominic Behan © Harmony Music Ltd
11 Uxbridge Street, London W8 7TQ

YOU JUST CAN'T WIN
Words and music by Van Morrison © 1965 Carlin Music Corp
All rights reserved — used by permission

GARAGELAND
Words and music by Joe Strummer and Mick Jones © 1977
Nineden Ltd/EMI Virgin Music Ltd
Reproduced by permission of IMP Ltd

A PAIR OF BROWN EYES
Words and music by Shane MacGowan ©1985 Perfect Songs Ltd

LONDON GIRL
Words and music by Shane MacGowan © 1986 Perfect Songs Ltd

THE BROAD MAJESTIC SHANNON
Words and music by Shane MacGowan © 1987 Perfect Songs Ltd
All three MacGowan songs reproduced by permission of IMP Ltd

SORTED FOR E's & WIZZ
Music by Pulp/Words by Jarvis Cocker © 1995 Island Music Ltd
47 British Grove, London W4
Used by permission of Music Sales Ltd
All Rights Reserved. International Copyright Secured

Line Drawings and Maps
by
Max Décharné

THANKS

To all the people who agreed to be interviewed for this book, and also to Brian Behan, Andrew Lauder, George Melly, Todd Parmenter, Bernie Scanlon, Big Pat and the late Eamonn Monaghan and Owen Mangan for their comments.

Thanks also to the photographers who supplied me with pictures, particularly my sister Mary and Paul Slattery.

Lots of love and thanks to my family, Max Décharné and Neil Perry.
And also to Dagsy, Leo Regan, Alison and Paul Dempsey, Susie Boone, Sue Castling, Glyn Busfield, Gerry O'Boyle, Terry O'Neill, Paddy and everyone at Bad Moon and Martin Clegg at Antony Rowe Ltd.

Love and special thanks to Shaun Phillips, who commissioned me to write a feature on Camden Town for *Vox* in April 1994.

This book is for my father. It is also dedicated to the memory of Leo Finlay.

Introduction

Before you earn the right to knock a joint, someone once said, you have to love it a little while. Camden Town is one of those places that is easy to knock but even easier to love. Everyone's been here or knows at least something about it: the Market, the venues, the record shops, the pubs, the cafés, the Clash, Madness, The Pogues, Britpop.

Britpop. It sounds like the last stop, but it could never be a full stop. Camden has been a rock'n'roll town since London's first organised, all-night rave took place at the Roundhouse more than 30 years ago. When The Beatles and The Rolling Stones talked about building a joint studio and management office in the late summer of 67, they chose a canalside site in the heart of Camden Town. Their plans to build a rock'n'roll hotel and even a heliport to jet international bands straight up to Camden from Heathrow came to nothing, but other musicians continued to centre their dreams around here.

"No Elvis, Beatles or The Rolling Stones in 1977," Joe Strummer declared ten years later, as the Clash settled into a dilapidated warehouse mere yards from the site that those bands had once targeted, with plans to build a slightly less ambitious base of their own. In those days, Camden Town wasn't the rock'n'roll playground that it would later become. Back then, its main features were a few greasy spoon cafés, a couple of good record stores, a decent bookshop, lots of big, old Irish pubs and an expanding but still low-key market.

What set Camden apart, and continues to make it such an attraction today, is that it arguably has more rock'n'roll venues per square inch than any other place in the world. In the late-70s, Camden had the Roundhouse, Dingwalls, the Electric Ballroom and the Music Machine, all within a few minutes walking distance of each other, plus the Dublin Castle and various other pubs where bands could play live. "Because of all the rock'n'roll joints," says Shane MacGowan, "Camden and the North London area around it was very hip and musically sophisticated. The kids around Camden were into rockabilly first, they were into old soul first, they were into reggae first. As an audience, they were really hard to impress. If you could blow people's minds in Camden, you knew you really had something."

The Clash, Madness and MacGowan's band, The Pogues, are among those who did manage to impress crowds in Camden. The Clash played a row of great gigs at the Music Machine and the Electric Ballroom; Madness made their name during a Friday night residency at the Dublin Castle and The Pogues grew in popularity when their tin whistle player repeatedly bashed his forehead with a beer tray beneath the shadow of John F Kennedy's smiling portrait in the Camden Irish Centre. "The Pogues are the Camden jukebox of their own imaginations," the Irish journalist Bill Graham wrote in *Hot Press* in 1988, singling out Madness and the Clash as their London predecessors. "The three groups have in common that they are all truth-tellers not trivial pursuers of pop illusion, all based on raw, unfashionable and disenfranchised musics, all embedded into cultural diversity because they've actually *lived* it rather than purchased it to adorn their lifestyle."

The music of all three bands reflected the sounds that could be heard on the streets of Camden — whether it be reggae, bluebeat or traditional Irish music. The Irish, in particular, have had a very strong presence in Camden Town. Irish navvies were the first to arrive, descending in their thousands during the first half of the last century to build the London & Birmingham Railway line. Disgruntled by their terrible working conditions, the Irish made their voice heard by taking on the English navvies at the gates of the Roundhouse in 1846. The battle lasted for three hours and took the same number of police forces to quell it. Twenty Irish navvies were arrested and a long court case, known as The Trial Of The Roundhouse Rioters, followed.

However, it was not until the 1930s that the first big wave of Irish immigrants began to arrive in London and they, too, had to fight for a corner of it. At that time, the immigrant's search for accommodation would often end with an abrupt 'No Irish Need Apply' sign. There was one place where the Irish were always welcome, though, and that was at the Rowton House in Camden Town — the huge hostel for men, which was later renamed Arlington House and still provides accommodation for the homeless today.

The Irish felt at home in Camden Town, possibly because its main roads span out like a crucifix or a country crossroads. Consequently, many Irish immigrants settled down here, which in turn attracted even more of them to the area. "Camden Town was the Mecca for Irish people," says Bill Fuller, who opened an Irish ballroom on the High Street in the late-30s. "They lived in big Victorian lodging houses all around the town— there would be four or five Paddies in one room, God bless them."

The large number of single Irish men subsequently created the need for pubs where they felt comfortable. By the late-40s, a group of fiddle and flute players from the West Coast of Ireland had instigated the first regular weekly music session in London at the Devonshire Arms on Kentish Town Road, and from there the music spread to a handful of other Irish pubs on or around Camden High Street.

If the drinking hours weren't as generous as some people would have liked, then at least Camden Town enjoyed a few favourable hiccups in its licensing laws. For instance, there is a special privilege which allows certain people to sell alcohol or keep their premises open 24 hours a day — a right which dates back to July 1364 when Edward III signed royal letters allowing the vintners of London to sell wine by the glass or bottle without applying for a licence. By the late-50s, only nine of these licences were still in existence and two of them just happened to be in the possession of people who ran bars on Camden High Street.

THOSE TOURISTS ARE MONEY

Similarly, when the Dublin Castle pub on Parkway was given permission to keep its bar open until midnight six days a week, it was the first time that such a licence had been put into operation in this country. That was in 1970 and many of the other pubs in Camden Town subsequently applied for music and dance licences, which would also allow them to keep longer hours.

By this time, the Irish immigrants had been joined by Greek-Cypriots who opened up bakeries, kebab shops and late-night restaurants, and added more vibrancy to the area. The Irish continued to monopolise the pub trade, though, and by the early-70s half of London's 8,000 publicans were Irish. Some of them were extremely colourful characters and none more so than Michael 'Butty' Sugrue, who ran the Elephant's Head on Camden High Street in the 60s. Butty, from County Kerry, had originally been a circus strongman and was internationally renowned for his amazing feats of strength. The most famous of these was when he pulled a double-decker bus along a London street with just a rope gripped between his teeth. He was also able to lift chairs in this way and regularly entertained his customers at the Elephant's Head by lifting crates of Guinness between his teeth.

Butty was a passionate fan of boxing and one of his best friends was Jack Doyle, a heavyweight champion, singer, actor and playboy whose life motto was, "A generous man never went to hell" and who had squandered a £750,000 fortune by the time he was 30. Doyle was known as the Gorgeous Gael and had affairs with numerous beautiful women, including Carole Lombard and Diana Dors. However, the love of his life was Movita, a Hollywood actress who eventually left Doyle and began a ten year relationship with Marlon Brando, who was then at the height of his good looks and fame.

Brando wanted to marry Movita, but Doyle refused to divorce her. Brando went ahead and married her anyway and Doyle got to learn about it in his morning newspaper. Later, Brando decided that the wedding hadn't been such a great idea and came looking for Doyle to confirm that the boxer's marriage to Movita had never been annulled, which would allow him to derecognise his own union. Doyle was happy to oblige and took his mate Butty with him to have lunch with Brando in 1966, and they later met up again in London.

Brando was back in London in January 1971, to shoot *The Nightcomers*, and initially rented a flat near the Dorchester Hotel. Parties were organised in his honour, attended by the fashionable stars of the day, such as his neighbour Mick Jagger, Michael Caine and Joan Collins. However, rather than sticking to the Park Lane area of London, Brando went up to Camden Town in search of the kind of Irish pubs where Jack Doyle and Butty had spent so much of their time. He found one on the Kentish Town Road, where he hungout with an Irish machine driver called Dennis McLaughlin. Brando later got his chauffeur to deliver a bottle of whiskey to the Irishman's house telling him to keep in touch. Soon afterwards, Brando left a message with the pub landlord asking Dennis to call him at the studio in Cambridge where he was shooting the film. He then asked him to come up to the set and teach him to speak in an authentic Irish accent.

Richard Burton had been in the area a few months earlier to play a gangster in the film *Villain*, part of which was shot at the Assembly House pub beside Kentish Town Tube Station. Burton was on such a huge percentage deal that he estimated the film would earn him the price of a new Rolls Royce for each of the weeks he spent working on it. However, that didn't stop him from wandering down the road that led to Camden Town in between shoots, nor from showing up at a film festival at the Roundhouse, with Liz Taylor, during the same period.

Brando and Burton were not the only illustrious figures to walk these streets. Arthur Rimbaud, Dylan Thomas, Brendan Behan, Patrick Kavanagh, WB Yeats, Samuel Beckett — some of the greatest writers there has ever been — have either lived in or spent time in Camden Town. "Samuel Beckett hung around in Camden Square when he was working with Billie Whitelaw," says Suggs. "I know her step-daughter and she told me that she's got really vivid images of Beckett just sitting on a wall in the Square wearing a straw hat."

What drew those people to Camden Town is presumably the same thing that would later attract rock'n'roll mavericks from Strummer to Suggs to Jarvis Cocker. "Even before I moved down to London from Sheffield, I knew that I wanted to live in Camden," says Cocker. "And I suppose the main thing that attracted me to it was the fact that there were lots of pubs and places where I could go out. It wasn't like there was a great art gallery down the road and I could enrich my life, it was just that I wanted to go out."

Whatever it is about Camden, there is an *energy* here, an energy that you simply don't find in many other places. WB Yeats, great mystic that he was, must have picked up on some of that when he decided to hold Golden Dawn meetings in Camden. Someone who knows about such things explained that it is all down to ley-lines and that Camden Town is on the same one as Glastonbury. Certainly, the life, colour and festival atmosphere that can be found here every Sunday afternoon suggest that this is true — Camden Market is the closest thing that there is to a weekly Glastonbury Festival.

I grew up in an Irish pub in the north of England and the first time I became aware of Camden Town was when I realised that all the great songs on our jukebox came to us from a tiny record shop on Arlington Road. That shop, which was called Kay's, has long gone now but, in the 60s and 70s, it was one of the very few places in England which supplied Irish and country records to jukeboxes. Seven of my father's first cousins ran Irish pubs in North London and one of them had the Camden Stores on Parkway. I remember coming to Camden Town for the first time in 1979 with my mother and realising that Kay's,

THOSE TOURISTS ARE MONEY

the Camden Stores and Our Lady Of Hal's Catholic Church all stood together on the corner of Parkway and Arlington Road. The church, the pub and the music: just like an Irish town. Just as it should be.

That made Camden Town an even more romantic place to me — a romance that was reinforced by listening to the Clash's songs about London and later to The Pogues, who wrote so specifically about Camden. In 1987, I wound up getting a job on the music weekly, *Sounds*, which was based down the road in Mornington Crescent. Even then, Camden was a very different town to what it has become today. The choice of places to go in the early evening of an average night usually involved the Devonshire Arms, the Golden Grill, a French restaurant on the Kentish Town Road, the Russell Arms or the Halfway House. One night, a few months after moving to London, I broke this cycle by suggesting that we went for a drink at the Buck's Head pub on Camden High Street. It was a Friday night and there were just two old men in the whole place. I asked for a vodka and orange and a whiskey and ginger ale, which seemed like a simple enough order until I heard the barman asking the old man on one side of the bar to nip to the off-licence for a bottle of vodka, and then telling the other one to run out for some ginger ale. A full 15 minutes later, we finally got our drinks and went to sit on a couple of scruffy deckchairs which faced out onto the virtually deserted High Street. "Friday night," my friend Neil complained, "and we're sitting here staring at the state of this." For me, Camden Town was still a magical place and the old Buck's Head was very much a part of its downbeat appeal, but I knew he had a point. Close your eyes, I told him, and let's pretend we're on Sunset Strip.

Sometimes when I look at what has happened to Camden Town over the past five years, I can't help remembering that moment and wishing that we hadn't dreamed quite so hard.

Ann Scanlon, September 1997

THE ROCK'N'ROLL GUIDE TO CAMDEN

YOUR GUIDES

ALIE ALLERTON came to Camden Town to work at Rhythm Records, which was then known as Honest Jon's, in 1976. He has sold records to almost everyone who has made a great album or single in the past 20 years — and quite a few who haven't.

BARRY APPLEBY was one of the two men who brought the Rock On record shop to Camden Town in 1975. He is a man who's been there, done that and can probably tell you a questionable joke about it.

ROGER ARMSTRONG co-founded Chiswick Records in Camden Town in December 1975 and is a director of the reissue label that it evolved into, Ace.

MRS BELLAMY has run the family newstand in Camden Town Tube Station since 1973. She frequently sells music papers to pop stars, but rarely recognises them.

JOHN BEST started the PR company, Savage & Best, in the spare bedroom of his house in Camden Square on the first working day of 1990. He also co-runs a record label called Parkway.

MARY BYKER was the face and voice of Gaye Bykers On Acid. He now fronts Apollo 440 and once had coffee with Yoko Ono in Camden Town.

TED CARROLL started Rock On records on a market stall on the Golborne Road in August 1972 before opening a shop of the same name in Camden Town. He co-founded Chiswick Records in a room upstairs and is a director of the reissue label, Ace.

JARVIS COCKER is the lead singer of Pulp. He lived in Georgiana Street in the early-90s and once bought a ticket from some bloke who wasn't exactly mashed up but, well, he was from Camden Town.

ALO CONLON first came to Camden Town in the 50s. He has been the landlord of the Dublin Castle pub since 1976 and helped to break Madness by giving them a Friday night residency.

BAL CROCE is the former singer of The Sting-rays and the Earls Of Suave. He also started the Psychotronic video shop in Camden Town in 1989 and is the man who inadvertently turned the Good Mixer into one of the most popular pubs in the country.

PAUL CWYNARSKI joined the staff of the Rock On record shop in 1985 and worked there until it closed down in 1997. Camden Town just isn't the same without them.

DEMPSEY opened a stall at Camden Lock in 1976 and now runs a shop in the Market Hall. She is convinced that Camden Town changes people for the better.

JOE DILWORTH was born and bred in Camden Town. He is a photographer and was also the drummer in two local bands, the Mysterons and th'Faith Healers.

JOHN FITZGERALD took over The Brighton pub in Camden Town in 1957 and ran it for 12 years before moving up the road to the St John's Tavern in Archway.

BILL FULLER is one of the unsung heroes of rock'n'roll. He lives in Las Vegas and has shaken hands with Elvis.

THOSE TOURISTS ARE MONEY

NICK GARRARD is such an integral part of Camden Town that he named a record label after it. The former manager of The Meteors, he and his drinking mates were once memorably described in print as the 'subterranean psychobilly elite'.

FRANK GIROMANO grew up in the heart of Camden Town, above the Italian café that his family ran for 22 years. Some people have never gotten over the loss of it.

MIKE HART has worked at Compendium books on Camden High Street since 1983. He presides over one of the best music book sections to be found anywhere and is happy to point people in the direction of Nelson Algren.

JESSE HECTOR started hanging out in Camden Town when his band, the Hammersmith Gorillas, recorded for Chiswick. He still believes it's the centre of the rock'n'roll universe.

MIKE HURLEY was as surprised as anyone when the Good Mixer became the most mediated pub in the land. He and his wife Pat plan to leave Camden Town at some point in the future and pass their famous pub onto their daughter.

ANDREW JAMES's family ran the Devonshire Arms when it was the only rock'n'roll pub in Camden Town. He opened the Engine Room in 1991 and its Tuesday night Pop Quiz has played a significant role in revitalising the far end of the Chalk Farm Road.

PADDY JAMES worked at the Record & Tape Exchange in Camden Town for several years before one of his customers asked him to run the record label, Vinyl Japan. He also DJ'd at the Electric Ballroom for many years.

JAMES JOHNSTON is the singer of Gallon Drunk, one of the archetypal Camden Town bands. They immortalised many of the best aspects of it in a song called *Arlington Road*.

ALAN JONES is an ex-music journalist who was inspired to move here after reading David Storey's *Flight To Camden*. He's been selling records in Camden Town since the late-70s and now runs Out On The Floor on Inverness Street.

BEN JONES grew up in Camden Town and started working on his father's record stall when he was just ten-years-old. He has DJ'd at the Camden Palace, organised warehouse parties and has had more good nights round here than he can remember.

SYLVIA KEOGH was one of the original stall holders at Camden Lock Market and still dreams of opening an all-night diner in Camden Town.

PHILIPPE KORPAR-MIGRENNE came to Camden Town from his native Normandy in 1979 to visit Rock On records and have a drink in the Devonshire Arms. He immediately realised that he never wanted to live anywhere else.

STEVE LAMACQ is a Radio 1 DJ and music journalist who first came to Camden Town on a regular basis to flog his fanzine, *A Pack Of Lies*, at Dingwalls' Monday night club, the Panic Station.

LEMMY, the singer of Motorhead, hung out in Camden Town, and most other parts of London, for three decades before deciding to spend the 90s in LA. As soon as he saw the palm trees and swimming pools he wondered why he hadn't done it sooner.

THE ROCK'N'ROLL GUIDE TO CAMDEN

SHANE MacGOWAN was the singer/songwriter of The Pogues but has now swapped them for Popes. He has, quite literally, spent several years of his life in the bars and restaurants of Camden Town.

MOUSE is the former singer of Red Hot & Blue who started the famous Saturday rock'n'roll session at Dingwalls. He ran three other rocking clubs in and around Camden Town but got sick of travelling on the Northern Line in 1996 so he moved to Germany.

FRANK MURRAY has numerous Camden Town connections. He sold records in Rock On, opened the Electric Ballroom and managed The Pogues, initially from the back bar of the Devonshire Arms and later from an office on the Kentish Town Road.

VINCE POWER first came to Camden Town as a teenager in the mid-60s. As the head of the Mean Fiddler Organisation, he now owns nine bars and venues in London, one of which is the Jazz Café on Parkway.

RICK ROGERS was the press officer for Chiswick Records and later sealed the link between 2-Tone and Camden Town by managing The Specials from an office on the Kentish Town Road.

ANDY ROSS is the man who would have discovered Blur in Camden Town, only the bouncer at Dingwalls wouldn't let him jump the queue so he had to do it in Islington instead. He is a former Disco Zombie, an ex-music journalist and is now the MD of Food Records.

NICK ROUMANA has managed Holt's, the most famous shoe shop in Camden Town, since his grandfather, Alan, died in 1994. Fortunately, he has inherited his grandfather's extraordinary ability to remember customers' shoe sizes as well as their faces.

PHILL SAVIDGE briefly retired from the music business in order to write poetry but was persuaded to come to Camden Town to be one half of the PR company, Savage & Best, whose bands include Suede and Pulp.

SKI is an illustrator whose work has appeared on many record sleeves. He was one of the DJs at Camden Town's infamous Jungle Club and now does much the same thing at the Engine Room.

SUGGS is the most famous singer/songwriter to come out of Camden Town, but can no longer remember why Madness chose to hangout here in the first place.

VANGE is one of the most charismatic men in Camden Town and can usually be found serving good food to famous people at George & Niki's restaurant on Parkway. You name them, he's served them. Just don't expect him to be impressed.

ANNE WELLSTEAD was persuaded to come to Camden Town when she was a teenager and is still here as the co-director of the Electric Ballroom.

BRIAN WHEELER's first impression of Camden Town was, 'God help me if I ever end up in a place like this.' He has managed the Electric Ballroom since 1980.

CAMDEN HIGH STREET NORTH SIDE

"How many bloody shoe shops can you fit into one street? They should rename the whole thing Imelda Marcos Boulevard."
— Frank Murray, 1996

1. CAMDEN TOWN TUBE STATION

This is the most famous meeting point in the area, as sung about by Suggs in his 1995 single, *Camden Town*, and one place where you're almost guaranteed to see a pop star if you stick around long enough.

Once the site of St Pancras Workhouse, Camden Town Underground Station was opened in 1907 and, although it suffered bomb damage during the Second World War, it was repaired in its original red tiles. A traditional hangout for the homeless, one of Camden Town's most famous characters, a former Polish fighter pilot nicknamed Stanley, spent years living in a hole in the outside wall of the Tube until he was hospitalised and forced to live in a home instead.

2. FA BELLAMY & SONS NEWSAGENTS

Camden Town Tube Station, NW1. Telephone: 0171-267 0256

This newspaper and magazine booth in Camden Town Tube Station is one of the first places in London where you can buy copies of the weekly music press and is a Tuesday lunchtime stop-off point for the musicians who might be featured in them.

Mrs Bellamy, who took over the stall from WH Smith in 1973, endeared herself to local bands, like Madness, The Belle Stars and Deaf School, by letting them have a flick through the papers to see if they were worth buying. "When those bands started off, they didn't have any money, so I'd let them have a look to see if they were in that week," she says. These days, there are even more musicians hanging around Camden than there were in the early-80s, and the tradition of buying papers from Bellamy's has continued. "The first time I served Noel Gallagher," says Mrs Bellamy, "there were two young girls standing

CAMDEN HIGH STREET - NORTH SIDE

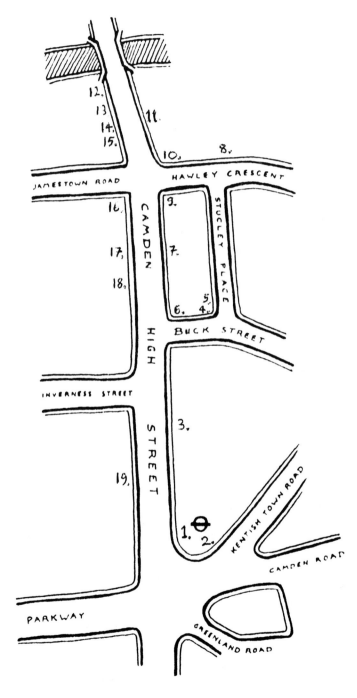

there with their mouths open, going, 'Give us a piece of paper quick!' and I was like, 'Whatever's wrong?' and they went, 'It's Noel!' I didn't even know who he was, but he signed his autograph for them. It's the young girls who draw your attention to these people, otherwise they just come and go, or I might occasionally think, 'Oh, he was on the telly.'"

The stall was given some kind of pop recognition when Stephen Duffy paid tribute to it in the opening lines of his 1995 single, *London Girls*, and Mrs Bellamy's nephew, Carl, who worked there at the height of Britpop, appeared in its accompanying video.

3. THE ELECTRIC BALLROOM
184 Camden High Street, NW1. Telephone: 0171-485 9006
Since the Electric Ballroom opened in July 1978, its stage has been graced by Sid Vicious, Philip Lynott, Iggy Pop, the Clash, Joy Division, Madness, U2, The Smiths, Nick Cave, The Pogues, Public Enemy and the Gallagher brothers. But the Ballroom was the centre of Camden Town nightlife in the days long before rock'n'roll.

It was first opened as a ballroom in the mid-1930s, mainly as a social centre for the large number of Irish immigrants who were coming to Britain to make up for the labour shortage during the Second World War. It was called The Buffalo — because that's what its aerial view was shaped like — and, at that time, the entrance was through an iron gate on the Kentish Town Road. For the first year or so, The Buffalo was run by an Irishman called Ginger Maloney and it had a reputation for being a very rough place, full of different tribes of fighting Irishmen. The police were constantly being called in to deal with late-night violence and, after one fight too many, it was closed down.

The Buffalo was saved, however, by another red-haired Irishman called Bill Fuller. He was a 20-year-old contractor and amateur wrestler from County Kerry, who had opened the St Patrick's Club, on Queen's Road in Bayswater, when he arrived in London three years earlier.

"The Buffalo had been closed down by the police, who had put a big lock on the gate," says Fuller, who still owns the Ballroom today. "So I went to the Chief Of Police in Holmes Road — he was an Inspector Harris and he was a hard man to bargain with — but I said, 'I'll make a deal with you: if you're ever called in to sort out a fight here, I'll put the lock back on the gate.' We'd get all the Connemara lads in, and they were all well used to fighting, those were wild days, you know.

"So I opened up The Buffalo in Camden Town — that was at the end of 1937, I think, or maybe 1938 — and I ran it myself. It was a small little place then and it was rough and ready, because I was breaking it in to see if I could handle the fights, but I handled them with these two fists [*holds them up and laughs*], these two fellas handled it all. You see that old gate on the Kentish Town Road? It's the same gate that has always been there, I never did away with it. I left it as a souvenir of the old days."

Fuller discovered that The Buffalo had previously been a

Masonic Lodge, which had a swimming pool and steam baths plus a large meeting room upstairs. He immediately cleaned the old ballroom up and started to make changes. But the real opportunity for expansion came in 1941 when Camden Town Tube Station was bombed, and both the back of The Buffalo and the small sidestreet beside it, which was called Dewsbury Terrace, were literally blown away. Bill Fuller took this as an opportunity to extend The Buffalo, rebuilding the back of the ballroom and creating a new dance floor on the site that was previously occupied by the row of terraced houses. "I bought the whole site then," says Fuller, "and, because I was a contractor with my own gang of men, I built The Buffalo up into a ballroom that could hold 2,000 people."

During the 1940s and 50s, Irish people came to Camden Town at the weekends, from all over London and from surrounding towns as far afield as Peterborough. The Buffalo didn't have a licensed bar, so everyone would drink in the pubs until closing time and then hit the ballroom.

"Irish fellas would come from all over for a night out in Camden Town," says John Fitzgerald, who took over The Brighton pub, on Camden High Street, in 1957. "They'd come here in holiday time and they'd get off at the station on a Thursday night and they probably wouldn't go back for a week and, when holiday time came again, they'd be in droves in Camden Town. They'd enjoy themselves for a week and they'd dance in The Buffalo and probably fall in love [*laughs*]."

Besides being one of the few late-night places where Irish people could meet in North London, The Buffalo was popular because of its great music. "In those early days, I always had good Irish music," says Bill Fuller. "It was mainly old-time waltzes, reels and jigs — tunes like *The Hornpipe* and *The Stack Of Barley*, which was a big one — and, after a while, the quick step came in. At first, I used to make up my own bands: I had a blind pianist called Billy and another lad called Tommy, who was half-Irish and half-Italian, who played the accordion."

By the late-50s, Bill Fuller was, quite literally, building a chain of ballrooms in England, Ireland and the United States, and he was also running a management and promotions company to provide live acts for his venues. Among those who worked for him in England were big band leaders, such as Ambrose, Geraldo, Jack Parnell and Joe Loss, and all of them regularly played at The Buffalo. "Joe Loss was one of my most famous bands," says Fuller. "He worked for me for years and was a very good friend of mine."

One of the singers with the Joe Loss band was Ross McManus, the father of Elvis Costello. Yet while it was the big bands that got The Buffalo crowds dancing, it was the Irish showbands, who began to emerge in the late-50s and early-60s, who really captured their hearts. The Clipper Carlton, from Strabane in Northern Ireland, are generally credited as being the first showband, but Bill Fuller gives that honour to the Irish big band leader, Mick Delahunty. "The Clipper Carlton were certainly one of the best Irish bands I've seen," he says, "but it was Mick Delahunty who had the first showband. He was kind of like Joe Loss and he was a great showman, probably one of the best ever."

Although he came from a different era to the Irish showbands, Mick Delahunty was supportive of the new, younger scene and helped to launch the career of The Royal Showband, by letting them open for him. Bill Fuller also did his bit for The Royal Showband, who were fronted by an Elvis-lookalike called Brendan Bowyer, by booking them into his ballrooms all over the world.

"I remember seeing The Royal Showband at The Buffalo," says Vince Power, who came to London as a teenager in the early-60s and would go on to build a Bill Fuller-style empire of his own with the Mean Fiddler Organisation. "The only reason I remember that show is because they came from Waterford, which is where I'm from. But I used to go to The Buffalo quite often — I saw lots of bands there, such as The Miami Showband and Big Tom. It was a place that filled up very quickly after the pubs closed, it would be full in five minutes. It was quite rough really, but it was one of the few places where the Irish would congregate, apart from the Galtymore in Cricklewood and the Garryowen in Hammersmith."

The greatest story surrounding The Buffalo concerns Jim Reeves, an Irish Catholic icon on a par with John F Kennedy and the Pope. In June 1963, Reeves had done a tour of Ireland and — unlike the showbands — had been shocked by the conditions he was expected to perform in. This included playing two venues each night, some of which were up to 50 miles of winding, Irish country roads apart, and, worse still, having to deal with a series of badly tuned pianos. Some of the dates were a complete disaster and Reeves was determined not to put up with such terrible conditions again.

Reeves was scheduled to play at The Buffalo in February 1964 but, according to Fuller, it never happened. "We had Jim Reeves booked in at The Buffalo but he never showed up," he says. "At the time, I was building a ballroom in San Francisco and I got a fellow called Philip Solomon to handle the tour. But Philip and Jim fell out, so Jim quit and he never played at The Buffalo. They sold all the tickets and Bill Foley, who was the manager, gave the crowd their money back, but they didn't want their money — they wanted Jim Reeves!"

The Jim Reeves story that has passed down through Camden Town legend is even better. "Jim Reeves was due to play at The Buffalo," says Frank Murray, who managed the Ballroom in the late-70s, "and there was just one thing on his rider: he insisted that the piano should be in tune. Irish ballroom promoters never quite grasped things like riders in those days, they just put the band up on the stage, expected them to play, took the crowd's money and went home. So when Jim arrived at The Buffalo, there was a piano but nobody had bothered to tune it. By this time, the ballroom was really crowded — it probably had rubber walls — but Jim's manager, or whoever, said, 'Jim's not playing.' So the manager of the ballroom and the staff took all of the money that they had in the cash box, went into the lane at the back of the building, loaded the cash into a manhole, secured everything that could be secured inside the ballroom, and then one of them got up on the stage and announced, 'Jim Reeves will not be playing tonight', before making a quick exit. The staff did a runner and just left the ballroom to the punters. Needless to say, there was a riot, as people started to demand their money back. The staff were off down the road and called in the police, who literally rode into the ballroom on horseback. I just have this great picture of mounted police riding into The Buffalo, with something like 2,000 Paddies going crazy because Jim Reeves hadn't shown up. It's cinematic."

The month after the Jim Reeves fiasco, The Manhattan Showband played at The Buffalo on St Patrick's Night. They were fronted by Van Morrison and had recently been formed from the ashes of his previous showband, The Monarchs. The band were invited to stay in a spare bedroom above The Buffalo and, the night before their own show, Morrison and guitarist Herbie Armstrong went to Studio 51 in Soho to see an R&B band called The Downliners Sect, who had long hair and played Jimmy Reed and Bo Diddley songs, and were exactly the kind of group that Morrison wanted to have.

Back at The Buffalo, Morrison and Armstrong sat in their little room drinking cider and Van played a song called *Could You Would You*.

"I thought it was incredible," Armstrong told the writer Steve Turner years later. "I had never known anyone who had written a song before." Exactly a month after their Buffalo show, Morrison's new band, Them, played for the first time ever at the Maritime Hotel in Belfast — *Could You Would You* was part of their early set, as was a song called *You Just Can't Win*, which contained a reference to Camden Town Tube Station.

In the 60s, three of the key ballrooms in Bill Fuller's chain were renamed The Carousel — these were The Buffalo in Camden, The Astoria in Manchester and a new one he had built in San Francisco [which would be leased out to the rock promoter Bill Graham in 1968 and renamed the Fillmore West]. By this time, entrance to the ballroom was from Camden High Street, rather than Kentish Town Road, and you can still see the red Carousel sign above the main door.

The Carousel continued to put on showbands, such as Big Tom & The Mainliners, Johnny McEvoy, Larry Cunningham, Brendan Shine and Dickie Rock, a romantic balladeer whose effect on women was powerful enough to inspire the universal mating call, "Spit on me, Dickie". It also showed hurling matches on large TV screens on Sunday afternoons and continued to be a major social centre for the Irish in London. "My aunt and uncle used to go dancing at The Carousel," says Shane MacGowan. "That's where they met, courted and got married in the mid-60s. Camden Town has always been a big Irish area with loads of pubs, all of which were Irish."

MacGowan's aunt and uncle are typical of the many Irish couples who met in The Carousel and The Buffalo before it. Many of them still come back here on Sunday mornings to search for the ghosts of their youth, retracing the steps that they once made across the dancefloor or to look around for the long gone mineral bar where he first bought her a drink.

In 1969, Bill Fuller asked a young woman called Anne Wellstead, who was working in one of his properties on the West Coast of Ireland, to take a job at The Carousel. She agreed to move to Camden Town, initially taking a room above the ballroom, and is still here as its co-director. A few years later some of the big rock names, including Paul McCartney's Wings, Led Zeppelin, Gary Glitter and a few of the new punk bands who were connected to the neighbouring Chiswick Records, used the ballroom as a rehearsal room. It was also popular with the local

> *"I was at primary school with this kid whose brother was in the police force and he'd tell stories about fights outside The Carousel. He said they'd be throwing people into the back of the police van, but the fight wouldn't get any smaller cos they'd be getting out of the front of the van and coming back and joining in the fight again." – JOE DILWORTH*

Greek community, who held wedding receptions here on most Sunday afternoons — and this is where George Michael's sister held hers.

In 1978, Bill Fuller got together with Frank Murray, the former tour manager of Thin Lizzy, and realised that his majestic old ballroom, with two-levels, three bars, an upstairs restaurant and glassed-in viewing areas, would make a great rock venue. Murray's intention was to model it on Bill Graham's Fillmore West, with no security and a good vibe, and make it the kind of place where famous musicians would be encouraged to get up and jam with other bands or even form a 'supergroup' for the night.

With this in mind, the Electric Ballroom opened on July 28, 1978, with the Greedies, who were the brainchild of Thin Lizzy's Philip Lynott and featured himself, Scott Gorham and Brian Downey; the Sex Pistols' Paul Cook and Steve Jones; Rainbow's Jimmy Bain plus Chris Spedding. Unlike many of the successful rock stars of the 70s, Lynott had quickly aligned himself with punk, befriending Cook, Jones and even Sid Vicious and Nancy Spungen, who were all frequent visitors to his home in Cricklewood. The Greedies closed their Electric Ballroom set with a mass jam through *Pretty Greedy*, an obvious take on the Pistols' *Pretty Vacant*, and a performance which partly inspired Sid Vicious to form the Vicious White Kids, who played a one-off show at the Ballroom two weeks later. The rest of the inspiration came from the fact that Sid needed a way of raising his and Nancy's air fares to America, which is why the gig was billed as 'Sid Sods Off'.

Featuring Sid on vocals, the Damned's Rat Scabies on drums, [who briefly had his own band The White Cats], plus original Pistols' bassist Glen Matlock and Steve New [who were both in the Rich Kids], they called themselves the Vicious White Kids. "It was a great band and the place was packed out with a really hip audience," remembers Shane MacGowan. "There were a lot of transactions going down — people joining groups, buying drugs, fucking each other in the toilets, you know, the usual stuff."

The set was largely made up of songs that the Pistols did, including *C'mon Everybody*, *Belsen Was A Gas* and *My Way*, which went down so well that the band ended up playing them twice. "All I remember is that Sid took up the role of lead singer without an instrument, and loved it," says Frank Murray. "He kept throwing Elvis shapes and grabbing his crotch — he was doing it years before Michael Jackson, believe me. He obviously hated being a bass player and this was his band. That's what I liked about it. It was as though he was living out his fantasy of being the singer and getting all the attention, while Nancy just squealed into the mike like a bad dose of feedback."

Fortunately, someone had taken the precaution of switching Nancy's microphone off before she sidled onstage. Less fortunately, she and Sid took a flight to New York a couple of weeks later, but were destined never to return.

Other bands who made early appearances at the Electric Ballroom include the Pop Group, Nico and Cabaret Voltaire, while the Greedy Bastards played another show in December, this time also including Bob Geldof in their line-up. "Both Greedies' gigs and the Vicious White Kids were big events," says Frank Murray. "And because the Ballroom opened with the Greedies, it became a favourite spot of visiting Americans — if Blondie or David Lee Roth were in town they would pop in — and Lemmy was always there. It became quite a place for people to hang out. The Clash rehearsed at the Ballroom for a week once and I also had Frank Zappa in for four days, which was great fun because I could just stand there and watch them as much as I liked."

However, the Electric Ballroom was forced to close down after about nine months, following severe objections to the noise levels from some local residents. It was given new soundproofing and reopened in July 1979, under a new manager, Terry O'Neill, who had previously run McGonagles, one of Bill Fuller's clubs in Dublin. The opening show was a 2-Tone evening, featuring The Specials, Dexy's Midnight Runners, Madness and The Selecter.

There were several more 2-Tone gigs at the Ballroom that autumn and on some occasions there were fights in the crowd or friction between the support band and the audience. This happened when Madness headlined over Echo & The Bunnymen and Bad Manners in October, and some skinheads prevented the Bunnymen from finishing their set. It was probably just as well that the Electric Ballroom had a policy of making everyone check their boots into the cloakroom as they entered the building. "Unfortunately, there were big fights at most of the early 2-Tone gigs, once they had grown to the Ballroom size, rather than the Nashville or Hope & Anchor," says Rick Rogers, who managed The Specials. "There was immediately an attraction to the right wing skinhead population, who would cause trouble, and sometimes it was caused by extreme left wingers who went there to fight the skinheads. It wasn't particularly either side, it was just one of the problems of the whole 2-Tone era. Despite the message that was being preached from the stage, there would always be opposing factions in the audience and very often there would be fights and people from the band would jump off stage to stop them."

Joy Division also played at the Electric Ballroom twice in 1979, once in August and again in October, when their set included early live performances of *Love Will Tear Us Apart* and *Atmosphere*. Shane MacGowan was among those in the audience mesmerised by Ian Curtis. "I saw Ian Curtis sing with Joy Division," he told Jon Wilde in 1994. "It was like a horror film. You were scared to go for a piss in case you missed something."

Other notable bands to play here during this period were Adam And & Ants, the B52's, Talking Heads, the Clash, who did a two-night stint here as part of their *London Calling* tour in January 1980, and Wire,

Ian Curtis at the Electric Ballroom, October 1979 [Paul Slattery]

who recorded half of their *Document And Eyewitness* live album at the Electric Ballroom the following month.

In 1980, Brian Wheeler, who had previously promoted gigs for Straight Music, became the new manager of the Electric Ballroom and has run it ever since. "This place was an eye-opener because it was always jam-packed and seemed like a complete madhouse to me," says Wheeler. "Most concerts that I'd been involved with were fairly well organised but, in this particular venue, it was always total mayhem and that was part of its appeal. It was laidback and seemed fairly indestructible so people could do what they wanted, within reason."

In the early-80s, dozens of influential bands played at the Electric Ballroom, including The Cramps, The Fall, The Only Ones, The Virgin Prunes, U2, the Sisters Of Mercy and Nick Cave, first with The Cavemen and later The Bad Seeds. The Smiths' first gig here is still remembered as an all-time great. "That was one of the best shows I've seen anywhere," says Brian Wheeler. "It was just one of those concerts that happens every once in a while. Most people had never heard of The Smiths at the time, so it was a bit of a surprise to me that we got a capacity crowd, but I guess word had already got around."

Another of the memorable shows was in August 1983 when Ace Records put together what was arguably the best R&B show to ever hit London, featuring Willie Egan, Chuck Higgins, Big Jay McNeely and Young Jessie. The same bill subsequently recorded studio sessions, which were later released as a live album on Ace. "I remember that gig at the Electric Ballroom," says Nick Garrard, "because I had been out on a drinking contest with Shane MacGowan the night before, and ended up needing stitches in my head. I was pilled out of my brain and couldn't stand because my legs were wobbly. So I sat in the cafeteria in a place where I could see the stage, and then Big Jay McNeely did his routine where he walks round the whole place and, of course, he makes a beeline for me because I've got this trilby on to hide where they shaved my head to put the stitches in. Anyway Big Jay ends up sitting on my lap — I was feeling like death at this point — and then this guy behind me takes my hat off and puts it on Jay's head. So I take it back and he does it again, so I have to hit him. The guy, not Jay."

In 1983, the Electric Ballroom became *the* place to be on a Saturday night when it started the Warehouse, which was a rockabilly club upstairs, while Jay Strongman played disco and funk downstairs. The Electric Ballroom was a legitimate place for the Warehouse which had grown out of various illegal clubs around North London, such as Dirtbox and Demob. "Loads of famous people came through the Warehouse when it first started," says Paddy James, who DJ'd with Jay Strongman at the Ballroom's Saturday night Crush Club for many years. "It was still hip for the first year that it went legitimate, because people didn't want that glammy, glitzy, Mecca-venue kind of vibe."

The Warehouse was the main reason why rockabillies originally

The Smiths backstage at the Ballroom, May 1983 [Paul Slattery]

hung out in Camden Town on Saturdays. "The first big rock'n'roll club around here was the Warehouse," says Mouse, who started the Saturday afternoon rocking sessions at Dingwalls three years later. "Dave Mahoney used to run the upstairs part with a guy called Steve Ross and, slowly but surely, more people started hanging out round here, because there was always something happening. After the Warehouse, we'd go down to the Scala at King's Cross and watch all-night movies. You could drink there, you could party there, you'd either get a Marlon Brando bill or a freak night — good days."

Unlike the divide between, say skinheads and mods, the Warehouse encouraged people to get into different kinds of music. "When Jay Strongman started at the Ballroom he played disco and funk but he would play rockabilly as well," says Ben Jones, who went to the Warehouse in the early days. "He'd whack on some of the big rockabilly tracks and everyone would jive. It was a brilliant, brilliant time because there was no differentiation between music."

One band who made themselves instantly unpopular when they played at the Ballroom were King Kurt, who encouraged their audience to shower them with raw meat. "I was aware of the general propensity of the crowd for throwing flour, offal and pigs' livers around the place," says Brian Wheeler, "but we decided that we'd simply confiscate anything like that as everyone came through the door. Unfortunately, people got wind of what was happening before they got to the front door and decided to unload whatever they had in the street, which resulted in all the neighbouring shops and offices being coated with flour and eggs and offal. We upset our neighbours in quite a big way. In fact, we got phone calls from a very long way away, for example, there was a Rolls Royce parked outside the station in Brighton that got completely covered in eggs and flour simply because a bunch of fans were on their way to London to see King Kurt at the Electric Ballroom and decided to offload their stuff early. The owner was extremely upset and expected us to pay for what he regarded as damage to his car."

In September 1985, the Jesus & Mary Chain played here, with Bobby Gillespie on drums. After they had played their usual 20-minute set, the band left the stage. The audience demanded an encore which they were never going to get. Some people threw glasses at the ceiling and smashed the strip lights, while others climbed onstage and started kicking over the amplifiers. At this point, some of the bouncers retaliated by waving microphone stands at certain sections of the audience and then dozens of police stormed into the Ballroom. It was hardly the Jim Reeves riot, but it was one of the more memorable gigs of the 80s.

Former Sisters Of Mercy Wayne Hussey and Craig Adams unveiled their new name, The Mission, at the Electric Ballroom in February 1986, after Andrew Eldritch [who was in the audience that night] stopped them from using their original name, The Sisterhood. Unfortunately, the banner failed to unfurl properly, announcing them to the stunned crowd as 'The Miss' before a roadie was quickly dispatched to pull down the other three letters.

The Mission are among the many bands who have recorded videos at the Electric Ballroom and it is also used as an occasional TV location. The most famous scenes to be shot here were in the 1986 film, *Hearts Of Fire*, a pretty atrocious account of a rock star, but one which nevertheless brought the lead character, Bob Dylan, to Camden Town for two days. "I was surprised that somebody of his enormity could just be like a regular Joe and walk around the streets and go into all the shops," says Brian Wheeler.

The Pogues used the Ballroom as their personal rehearsal room during the late-80s and played here in November 1987. Bill Fuller was intrigued enough by their records to fly over from Las Vegas for the occasion. "I've always loved Irish music, really good Irish music, and I still love it today," he says. "I'd travel thousands of miles to hear it."

Fuller insisted on cooking The Pogues a steak dinner in the Ballroom's upstairs restaurant before the show, which was a bit problematic for Shane MacGowan. "I wasn't going to say to Bill Fuller, 'I'm vegetarian', you know what I mean?" he says. "I had a lot of respect in his eyes — that would have turned me into a wanker in five seconds, so I said, "Thank you very much', and ate the potatoes and cabbage."

The Pogues, who were just about to release their big Christmas hit, *Fairytale Of New York*, made it worth Bill Fuller's time by playing a great show and Joe Strummer unexpectedly joined them for a rendition of *I Fought The Law* during the encore. Strummer later played guitar on The Pogues' US Tour that winter, a return to the stage which prompted him to form the Latino Rockabilly War band and do a Rock Against The Rich Tour the following summer. The tour stopped off at the Electric Ballroom and his set included everything from the 101'ers' *Keys To Your Heart* and the Clash's *Straight To Hell* to *Trash City*.

Public Enemy played at the Ballroom in 1988, on one of the last occasions when they would appear in such a small venue, as did the Red Hot Chili Peppers. Gaye Bykers On Acid specifically requested this as the venue for their major London gig, after releasing their 1989 LP, *Stewed To The Gills*. "I always remember going to other people's gigs at the Ballroom and thinking that I'd love to play there cos it's such a fantastic place," says Mary Byker. "It's faded grandeur, glamour gone wrong; it's lost in time somewhere. I remember when we went in to do our soundcheck, we were like, 'Yes, here we are — fuck the Town & Country, this is better, it's right in the middle of Camden.' But the gig was a disaster because the sound limiter went off and it cut all the backline out. Rat Scabies was there and he said afterwards, 'You should get me to produce one of your records.' And I'm like, 'Yeah, all right.' And he goes, 'What we'll do is we'll get some crates of beer, loads of cheap speed and we'll just lock ourselves in the studio for two weeks — that's exactly what you need to do.' And I remember thinking at the time, 'That is exactly what we *don't* need to do', but, looking back, he was right. To get a great record from that band, at that time, that's what we should have done, with somebody like him, who we all liked, because he was a punk."

In the early part of the 90s, live bands only played here occasionally — such as Elastica in February 1993 — and the Ballroom became best known for its Friday night goth disco Full Tilt and Saturday's house-oriented Crush Club. It is also renowned for its Sunday fashion market and its record fairs.

In 1996, the Ballroom not only reemphasised its Irish roots by hosting Tuesday night line-dancing sessions, but started putting on live bands again, such as Menswear and Lush. The most memorable gig of that year, though, was by Ocean Colour Scene, who played two nights here in May. On the second night, Liam and Noel Gallagher came on stage during the encore and sang three Oasis songs — *Live Forever*, *Wonderwall* and *Cast No Shadow* — and then were joined by Ocean Colour Scene for a mass rendition of The Beatles' *Day Tripper*.

4. VINYL EXPERIENCE
3 Buck Street, NW1.
This building is probably best remembered as Vinyl Experience, which had a motorbike permanently lodged in its front window in the late-80s, but it has a long history of being a record shop. It was originally called Playback, which was taken over in 1983 by Barry Appleby, who had been one of the founding partners of Rock On, but later decided to sell his share and set up his own record shop around the corner. He called it Sea Of Tunes, in honour of the chief Beach Boy. "I nicked the name from Brian Wilson's publishing company — I always thought it was a brilliant name because Wilson had a sea of tunes in his head," says Appleby, who bumped into his hero on the escalator of a Los Angeles shopping mall a couple of years after opening the shop.

Influenced by what he had seen in American record stores, Appleby left the albums in their sleeves, rather than keeping them behind the counter. "I used to stick them on the wall, as well as in the racks, and people would come in, take a record down, have a look at the vinyl and then buy it," he says. "Of course, someone would nick a couple of albums about once a month but, for what I sold, it was worth it. By then, reissuing was taking off, so I used to sell Gene Vincent albums and early Motown stuff in their original covers. I did some new records, but only bands like Black Flag — if people wanted Boy George or ABC records they could fuck off and get them in Woolworth's."

In the mid-80s, the shop changed hands a couple of times, specialising in funk and then reggae, before it became Vinyl Experience, which dealt in new and secondhand indie, psychedelic and rock'n'roll, and was a good place to exchange albums and singles for cash.

"I remember trying to flog some records in there when I was poor and needed money," says Jarvis Cocker. "I had this Byrds EP which was good, but it was a bit warped or it might even have had a fag burn on it. I could see that the bloke behind the counter was quite interested but, when he took it out, to see the condition it was in, he just looked at me and really tutted. It was a bit like, 'You shouldn't be attempting to pull the wool over my eyes' and I never dared go back in that shop again."

In the early-90s, Vinyl Experience changed hands and became Blah Blah Blah, who sold similar kinds of records, before being replaced by a film shop called Cult Videotheque and then falling empty.

5. PSYCHOTRONIC
3 Buck Street, NW1.

Downstairs from Vinyl Experience was a tiny basement which housed Psychotronic, which was *the* pioneering shop in the country for weird, sleazy and generally hard to find videos and exploitation film posters. It was a hangout for Gallon Drunk and Dave Vanian, and indirectly spawned the social scene that popularised the Good Mixer.

Psychotronic was opened by Bal Croce, the former singer of The Sting-rays, in 1988, who also started a video label, Mondo Movies, with his mate, Mark Isted. The shop was the only place where you could buy the sort of stuff that would later be seen on Jonathan Ross's *Incredibly Strange Film Show*, and it was Ross who helped to get Mondo Movies a distribution deal to put out their first releases, which were *Incredibly Strange Creatures Who Stopped Living And Became Mixed Up Zombies* and *Rat Fink A Boo Boo.*

In 1990, Bal went into partnership with Mike Delanian, the bassist in Gallon Drunk, who did early photo sessions on the roof of the shop and in the stairwell. By the summer of 1991, Psychotronic was rarely open, because Delanian was always touring and Bal was spending most of his time in the Good Mixer. "There was a point when I was seriously considering shutting the shop down," says Bal, "and saying to [Good Mixer landlords] Pat and Mike, 'Look, can I put a load of my videos up on the wall?' And I was just going to sit in the pub and hope someone would want to buy them. Later on, the guy who took the shop over from me actually did do his trading in the Good Mixer on a Saturday lunchtime. He used to go in there with a big suitcase and all these rare video buyers would go through them."

6. HARVEY FLOORBANGERS
202 Camden High Street, NW1. Telephone: 0171-284 1513

Ten years ago, as the Buck's Head, this was one of the most basic pubs in Camden, frequented by old men and a few locals who fancied a really quiet game of pool. Like many old-fashioned pubs around here, the Buck's had its hey-day in the 50s and 60s, when Irish labourers would pile in after work and spend the night drinking and singing; fighting and drinking. When Camden Market opened in the 70s, the pub

Oasis at the MTV studio, August 1994 [Paul Slattery]

became popular with traders and, for some reason, local comedians. It also continued the tradition of having Irish music at weekends.

"I used to pop into the Buck's Head on Fridays and Saturdays," says Frank Murray, who managed the nearby Electric Ballroom in the late-70s. "They'd have this three or four piece ceilidh band, dressed in tuxedos, playing away, and it was great because they'd have the snare drums, the saxophone, the accordion and sometimes the piano. Listening to that was definitely a change from the Ballroom."

At the end of the 80s, however, the Buck's Head became one of the first Camden pubs to be given a complete facelift, and was turned into a split-level bar and bistro. A few years later it was renamed Harvey Floorbangers, complete with a food bar called Nobby's Nosh Up and a massive mural on the outside wall. "I remember when they changed the Buck's Head," says Mary Byker. "I walked by one day and there was pumping techno blasting out and all these people standing on tables, with their backs against the glass windows, looking like they were about to come flying out at any moment. It was like this old boys' pub had suddenly turned into a massive rave."

7. TILLEY'S RESTAURANT
208 Camden High Street, NW1.

During the 80s, Tilley's Restaurant was one of Madness's favourite places in Camden. "George Tilley's was the ultra-cool restaurant to go to in Camden at the time," says Andrew James, who grew up in the Devonshire Arms just around the corner. "There wasn't a lot of room to move about in, but there was a good vibe and a very friendly atmosphere. There'd be George waiting on the tables and his mum in the kitchen — the food was fantastic, it was all home-made cooking. He had a great blues record collection, and you could go in and listen to Dylan and Little Feat. It also had a licence and George used to give free drinks to his regulars. He was a great character but he was probably too generous for his own good."

The Eurythmics also frequented Tilley's and invited George to add guest vocals to their 1983 single, *Love Is A Stranger*. By the end of 1984, however, the restaurant had been converted into an Indian restaurant called the Raj Mahal, which enjoyed a brief moment of pop glory when Madness shot the opening scene of the video for their 1985 single, *Yesterday's Men*, here.

8. MTV (EUROPE)
Hawley Crescent, NW1. Telephone: 0171-284 7777

When The Beatles and The Rolling Stones discussed the possibility of setting up a joint studio and management office, in the late summer of 1967, they chose this as their prospective site. In those days, it was occupied by a tumbledown brewery, whose canalside location made it particularly attractive to them. However, although Paul McCartney initially entertained ambitious plans of building a hotel here, and even a heliport, they came to nothing.

Now, as the home of *MTV (Europe)*, this building is a magnet for famous pop stars and visiting celebrities. Just about every band you care to mention has either done a live set or an interview here, including Iggy Pop, Happy Mondays, Metallica, Pulp, Paul Weller, The Prodigy, Nick Cave & Kylie Minogue, Radiohead, Eartha Kitt, Bon Jovi, Blur, Black Grape and Oasis. The latter did a pared-down live set in August 1994, with just the two Gallagher brothers, plus Bonehead at the electric piano, when they played *Live Forever* and gave *Whatever* its first TV airing, complete with a tribute to Manchester City in the closing lines.

MTV has also had its share of ex-pop star presenters over the years, including Miles Hunt, who lived locally and briefly became a presenter on *120 Minutes* after disbanding The Wonder Stuff, and Clare Grogan, the former singer of Altered Images.

The building itself was erected in 1982, by the independent breakfast television company TV-am, at a cost of £10 million. It was designed by Terry Farrell, complete with giant boiled eggs on the roof, and was highly controversial. It was scathingly referred to as "that Disneyland down the road" by the local writer Jonathan Miller, and how onlookers laughed when the great storm of 1987 caused a couple of the eggshells to fly off the roof and float down the Regent's Canal.

"TV-am was the first big media thing that happened round here," says Suggs. "I've been on there doing kung fu demonstrations at 6.30 in the fucking morning, in the days when that sort of thing was part of my life. They used to get Madness to do everything, cos they knew we lived just round the corner and could just about drag ourselves out of bed and go down there to have breakfast with the lovely Anne Diamond."

9. THE ELEPHANT'S HEAD
224 Camden High Street, NW1. Telephone: 0171-485 8043

Marlon Brando provided one of the magical moments in Camden's history when he called into the Elephant's Head for a drink — which may explain why the pub became the traditional hangout for London rockabillies on their way to Dingwalls on Saturday afternoons.

The pub took its name from Elephant Pale Ale, which was brewed on the banks of the Regent's Canal in the last century and had its bottling stores on Hawley Crescent. But, back in the mid-60s, when Brando would have first become aware of it, the Elephant's Head was run by an Irishman called Butty Sugrue, a famous strongman who entertained his customers by picking up full crates of Guinness with his teeth. In the years since Butty, the Elephant's Head has remained a traditional Irish-run pub and was the last one on this stretch of Camden High Street to be refurbished. The French barman plays in a garage band called The Squires and the pub recently introduced rocking sessions on Saturday afternoons.

10. FISH & CHIPS
226 Camden High Street, NW1.
This corner spot has a long history as a greasy caff. In the days before all-day drinking, it was one of the main places where rockabillies, complete with smuggled beer cans from the off-licence down the road, went on Saturday afternoons, while they were filling in the gap between Dingwalls closing and the pubs reopening. Now as a fish, chips, pizza and doner kebab shop, it is a late-night action spot, where people make a habit of fighting, throwing up or simply passing out.

11. COMPENDIUM
234 Camden High Street, NW1. Telephone: 0171-485 8944
Back in the late-60s, there were usually two reasons why young people came to Camden: one was the Roundhouse, the other was Compendium, which is widely regarded as one of the best bookshops in the world.

Opened in August 1968, by Nicholas Rochford and Diana Gravill, it originally occupied the ground floor of 240 Camden High Street. At that time, there were only two London bookshops — Better Books and Indica — which catered specifically for people who were interested in Beat literature and underground magazines, such as *OZ* and *IT*. By the early-70s, Compendium had outlived the other two bookshops and expanded its range of fiction and psychology books to also include poetry, art, architecture, surrealism, cinema, music, subculture and a women's section [the first of its kind in the country], which necessitated the move to the current premises.

In the early days, Compendium only had a small music section at the back of the shop, but it quickly became a Mecca for serious music fans. "Compendium was the only place where you could get all those great American rock mags like *Bomp*," says Barry Appleby, who became a regular customer in 1975. "They'd also have all these Dylan books, including bootleg copies of *Tarantula*. The guys who worked there, like Nick Kimberley, loved music as well, so you got to know them. We were after information, we wanted *facts*, and Compendium was the only place to get what we were looking for."

In 1976, the advent of punk brought a new generation of readers to Compendium, looking for hip literature or fanzines such as *Sniffin' Glue*. During this period, bands like the Clash began to frequent the shop — Joe Strummer once bought a copy of Jack Kerouac's *Visions Of Cody* here — and Lou Reed provided one of the best ever Compendium anecdotes when he came in and asked, in all seriousness, "Do you have any books on Lou Reed?"

Over the years, dozens of writers have made personal appearances at Compendium. But the greatest literary figure to ever walk through its door was probably William Burroughs, who did a couple of book signings here in the early-80s. "Meeting Burroughs was like meeting Jesus," says Paul Cwynarski, who went to a signing for

Cities Of The Red Night in 1982. "I got into him when I was 16 and I read *The Naked Lunch* seven times in a row, because it was the first book I'd ever read where I thought, 'This guy knows *exactly* what's in my head.' I'd read *On The Road* and I thought, 'This is lovely, it's so poetic', but Kerouac, bless him, can't get rid of that Catholic thing, and has such a rose-tinted view of everything, whereas Burroughs is a serious cat who gets into all these things and actually experiments with them. I saw a poster in the window of Compendium saying that Burroughs was doing a signing, so I went along with my little bag of books — I was the only teenager there and it was marvellous. I asked him to recommend some books and he told me to investigate Rimbaud, so I immediately went out and tried to find anything I could by him. I remember seeing a photo of Rimbaud for the first time — this shock of hair, this mad-looking cat who did it all in his teens — and I just thought, 'Fuck punk rock, these guys were doing it years ago.'"

In the 80s, Compendium's music section expanded quite dramatically and, among those who have made personal appearances at the shop, are Richard Hell, Henry Rollins, Lydia Lunch, Billy Childish and Nick Cave, who did signings for his collected lyrics, *King Ink,* in 1988, and, for his novel, *And The Ass Saw The Angel*, the following year. Most of these occasions went well, others not quite so.

"The worst signing we've ever had was John Densmore, who had just written his autobiography, *Riders On The Storm*," says Mike Hart, who has worked in Compendium since 1983 and is something of a literary guru to many of the regulars. "He had a real attitude — complaining that he'd been put too close to the cash-till when he did a signing at the Virgin Megastore the day before. What got me was that he'd written this book, which was all about The Doors, not about anything he's done since 1970, yet he had no charm whatsoever. Whereas the Grateful Dead's Mickey Hart — who had just published a book in the States called *Drumming At The Edge Of Magic* — turned up at about 11 o'clock in the morning and said, 'What do I do?'. There was a huge queue of Deadheads right around the block, but he did his best to try and chat to everyone before rushing off to do a soundcheck with the rest of the Dead at Wembley. Both he and Densmore were Californian drummers, but what a difference between the two of them."

Other American musicians to have visited the shop include Courtney Love, Thurston Moore and, best of all, Gene Vincent's Blue Caps, who turned up *en masse*, with their wives, looking for a copy of

> "Dennis Norden was in Compendium and a couple of kids came in and they noticed a Samuel Beckett book and they said, 'Samuel Beckett — that's a pub, in'it?' And Dennis Norden just pissed himself, well, he had a very wry smile." – MIKE HART

the hip rocking magazine, *Now Dig This*. Phil Kaufman, who did time with Charles Manson, tour managed The Rolling Stones and most famously disposed of Gram Parsons' ashes at the Joshua Tree, read from his book, *Road Mangler Deluxe*, when it came out in 1993.

"He talked for about 15 minutes and he was very funny," says Mike Hart. "Then there was a question and answer session with the inevitable enquiries about Manson. I think there are two things that Kaufman gets asked about, one is Manson, cos he knew him in the 60s, and the other is the Gram Parsons thing. His book is worth reading because it's an interesting life, he was road manager for people like Etta James as well as the Stones and Gram Parsons."

In recent years, Compendium has become a magnet for authors who have written books specifically about London, such as Iain Sinclair, the late Robin Cook, Martin Millar, Stewart Home and John Williams, who is a former Compendium employee.

12. GEORGE'S CAFE
208 Camden High Street, NW1.
Now a clothes shop, this was once an Italian caff called George's, which is where the Clash usually ate their breakfast when they were living and rehearsing on the Chalk Farm Road in the late-70s. "I still come to this café for my beans on toast. I don't want anything else," Joe Strummer told Caroline Coon after the band had signed to CBS in January 1977.

13. RHYTHM RECORDS
281 Camden High Street, NW1. Telephone: 0171-267 0123
Rhythm dates back to the beginning of the punk era and is now the oldest record shop in Camden. Originally called Honest Jon's, it was the second in a small chain of record shops owned by John Clare — he opened the first one in an old butcher's shop on the Golborne Road, in West London, in 1974, and got these premises a couple of years later when Compendium moved its occult book section across the road to 234 Camden High Street. "When we first came here," says Alie Allerton, who has worked in the shop since it opened, "we sold punk and jazz records, which was a strange mixture but it worked."

The building was ideal for a record shop, because the upstairs had been converted into a small recording studio called Keleidophon. The owner was David Vorhaus, an experimental American who recorded the cult space-rock album, *White Noise — An Electronic Storm*, here in 1968, while other bands, such as Chilli Willi, also made records at Keleidophon.

In the early-80s, John Clare and his partner Dave Rhino split their business into Honest Jon's and Rhythm Records — with the Camden shop taking the latter name. Over the years, they have expanded their range of records to include indie, hardcore, hip hop, 60s psychedelia, reggae, soul, country & western and easy listening. The main CD collection is kept upstairs and there are specialist and collectors' vinyl and CDs in the basement.

"There is probably hardly anybody who has made records of note in the last 20 years who hasn't been in this shop," says Allerton, whose customers have included Bob Dylan, Van Morrison, Robert Plant, the Clash and Oasis. "I remember Patti Smith coming into the shop and giving me some poetry when she was over here in the late-70s to play the Roundhouse, and if The Fall were in London they'd always buy records from us. I also remember Frank Bruno coming in and asking for a Paul McCartney record which was quite bizarre, but he's such a big bloke you certainly wouldn't argue with him, especially since he had his minder with him."

One of the most famous Rhythm stories involves The Lemonheads' singer Evan Dando, who turned up at the shop in the summer of 1994 and did an impromptu set, while wearing the late Kurt Cobain's coat. "Evan was off his trolley," says Allerton, "and asked one of the guys behind the counter if he could stand in the shop and play his guitar, which he proceeded to do. There were a few people in, and he was going on about his coat and showing everyone all the drugs that he had in his pocket."

The key to Rhythm's enduring appeal probably lies in the fact that they sell such a wide variety of music in such a tiny space. "We get De La Soul coming in, we get PM Dawn, we get Morrissey, we get Pulp — they all come in, because of the weird mixture that we sell," says Allerton. "You can buy some jazz albums, some 60s psychedelia, an R&B CD and a hip hop one. Do you really want to go down the West End and trawl your way through the big shops when you can come into this tiny little building and go round hoovering it all up?"

That statement might have been made somewhat redundant by the recent opening of a Camden branch of Tower Records, but people don't just come to Rhythm to buy records, they also come for specialist knowledge. "Alie at Rhythm was my psychedelic guru," says Paul Cwynarski, who worked at Rock On, another of Camden's specialist record shops. "I used to go to him and say, 'Who are Shiva's Headband, Alie?' And he'd go, 'Oh, you know, they're a Texas band, really tripped-out, not quite as trippy as the 13th Floor Elevators', and he'd know all their stuff backwards. It was because of him that I started buying loads of psychedelic and garage stuff."

14. CAFE TOTO
273-275 Camden High Street, NW1. Telephone: 0171-284 4499
Previously known as Fluke's Cradle, this is where Bob Dylan was photographed, wearing a top hat and drinking coffee, for the cover of his 1993 album, *World Gone Wrong*. Dylan had originally come to the café to shoot a video for his single, *Series Of Dreams*, a couple of years

earlier, with his friend Dave Stewart, who lived in Camden Town when he was in The Eurythmics.

"When I came back from my lunch break," says Mike Hart, who was working directly across the road in Compendium, "this woman I know from Glasgow, called June, was in the shop and she grabbed me and said, 'Dylan's over there' — she'd seen him in 66 and stuff. Anyway, she went over to the café and Dave Stewart noticed her and asked her to sit beside Dylan. So June was thinking, 'Oh, my God, I'm sitting beside Bob Dylan' and Dave Stewart goes, 'Just have a conversation' and she was sitting there and couldn't think of anything to say. So, in the end, she just said, 'Where did you get that earring, Bob?'"

During the 80s, this building was an indoor market, complete with an American soda bar. Now, as Café Toto, it has a very Parisienne feel, with wood panelling, a white-tableclothed dining area downstairs and a café/bar on the ground level, where they serve cocktails. But Bob Dylan has probably ensured that it is as Fluke's Cradle that this place will best be remembered.

15. SYD STRONG
271 Camden High Street, NW1.

Syd's is an old-fashioned barber shop, which became popular during the late-70s when the local Stiff acts, such as Madness and King Kurt, got their hair cut here — well, at least once. It's still a good place to pick up a pot of Black & White, the stuff that Elvis greased his quiff with.

16. OXFORD ARMS
265 Camden High Street, NW1. Telephone: 0171-267 4945

Back in the 40s, this late-Victorian pub was one of the first places in Camden to hold traditional Irish music sessions and it has been run by the same family, the Maloneys, since the late-60s.

The upstairs room was briefly used as a venue in the mid-80s, but the Etcetera Theatre took it over in 1987. One of the most famous plays to run here was *Bondage*, which was based on the late-night conversations that a Kentish Town taxi driver called David Hines had with the prostitutes who hailed his cab around King's Cross. Ken Russell came to Camden to see the play and used it as the basis for his Hollywood movie, *Whore*. The Oxford Arms was completely refurbished in 1990 but has maintained its traditional veneer, and a late-night licence has increased its popularity with the music business.

> *"Carnaby Street was so fascinating in the 60s that people used to sleep on the street in sleeping bags — honestly they did, they used to sleep there to try and catch a band. Now it's the same with Camden: everyone's fascinated by it; everyone wants to come here."*
> *– JESSE HECTOR*

17. THE VINTAGE MAGAZINE COMPANY
247 Camden High Street, NW1. Telephone: 0171-482 0587

This branch of the Vintage Magazine Company has a huge stock of postcards and posters and is frequently checked out by pop groups and movie stars — usually looking for pictures of themselves. As well as Jimi Hendrix and Beatles paraphernalia, among their bestsellers are anything to do with *Star Trek*, *The Avengers*, *Beavis & Butt-head*, *The Simpsons* and *The Magic Roundabout*. Famous customers have included Pamela Anderson, when she was guesting at the nearby MTV studio.

18. MUSIC & VIDEO EXCHANGE
229 Camden High Street, NW1. Telephone: 0171-267 1898

This is the shop where Quentin Tarantino picked up a secondhand copy of Urge Overkill's 1992 *Stull* EP, featuring their version of Neil Diamond's *Girl, You'll Be A Woman Soon*, which he later chose as the soundtrack for one of the pivotal scenes in *Pulp Fiction*.

Opened in the early-80s, this is one of seven London branches of the Music & Video Exchange and accepts all CDs, cassettes, secondhand vinyl and videos for cash or exchange. Like the other record shops in Camden, this one has had its fair share of musicians working behind its counter, including Mike Timmins from the Cowboy Junkies, Dave Cummings from Del Amitri and Epic Soundtracks. It also continues to attract musicians who are keen to turn unwanted records into cash.

"Nick Cave used to come in all the time," says Paddy James, who worked here in the mid-80s. "And so did Jeffrey Lee Pierce — he was great because he had brilliant taste in music and was always buying wonderful stuff. Nick Kent used to sell records to us all the time, and we always gave him more money than we should have, because we thought he was such a great writer and he had been a huge influence on us when we were adolescents."

19. CAMDEN PLAZA
211 Camden High Street, NW1.

This boarded-up site, which now provides a cardboard shack for a homeless old woman, used to be the Plaza Cinema.

Purpose-built as the Electric Cinema at the turn of the century, it was renamed the Plaza in the 1920s and became one of the best-loved flea-pits in the area. During the 40s and 50s, it was popular with gangs of local kids, who would try to get into the Saturday matinees for free, but it later became a haven for some of the residents of the nearby hostel for the homeless, Arlington House, who were forced to vacate their rooms during the daytime.

The old Plaza was killed off in the summer of 1977 and, when it reopened a couple of years later, it had been transformed into an art movie house showing the kind of European and American films that would normally be shown in London's repertory cinemas. "The only place you could see *Repo Man* when it came out was the Plaza Camden," says Barry Appleby. "I'd get all my mates knocking on my door, wanting to stay, all because of a film."

Repo Man was made by Artificial Eye, who were based above the Plaza. The film's director, Alex Cox, frequently hung out in the upstairs office, which is where he first met The Pogues' manager Frank Murray and agreed to direct a video for the band's 1985 single, *A Pair Of Brown Eyes*, which quite literally involved the use of a couple of artificial eyes. "We didn't want to replicate the images in the song, because that would be boring," Alex Cox said later. "So we took it a stage further and turned it into the adventures of this little girl who had been given a pair of brown eyes in a bag and who ended up going to watch The Pogues play at the Electric Ballroom." The video turned out to be an incisive comment on Thatcher's Britain, so much so that it was banned for showing one of the band spitting on Maggie's portrait.

The Plaza's new image did not, however, deter the old men from going to the cinema: they were soon back in their seats sleeping their way through consecutive screenings of films such as *Sid & Nancy*, which did its first run here in 1986. Like the Parkway cinema around the corner, the Plaza kept closing and reopening during the late-80s and early-90s, and it is currently awaiting further development. In the meantime, its front porch is a shelter at night and a market stall during the daytime.

"I know it sounds funny, but there used to be a much better class of alcoholic around Camden Town. Liverpool Lil and Casey were absolute characters. She came from Liverpool and he was Irish. She had children, one was a policeman, and he came down to take her back home but she wouldn't leave Casey. She died of cancer, in her 50s, and he died soon after — he died of a broken heart. They used to drink and they used to beg and he used to do the cheques, forged cheques, but they kept themselves very clean. Lil would say to him, 'Look at the state of you. Liven yourself up!' and she'd hit him with her handbag and he'd go, 'Lil, Lil behave yourself, I'm going off shopping now', but he was off to do his cheques. Liverpool Lil and Casey were very friendly with Mary and Davy. Mary has been here for years and then she met up with Davy — he died but, oh, they used to fight. Then there was another one called Paddy, she used to stand and whistle and do a tap dance. She lived in a squat and went home from the Tube Station one dinner time and fell in a fire — they had the fire outside the squat — and got burned to death. They were characters but, of course, there are rougher ones now." – MRS BELLAMY

NEWSREEL: THE 50s

Oh mother dear
I'm over here
And I'm never coming back
What keeps me here
Is a rake of beer
The women and the crack

'TEDDY BOY' BEATS
UP YOUTH AT DANCE HALL
The magistrate: "What do you mean by Teddy Boy?"
Mr C----: "They were wearing narrow trousers"

THREE PRIESTS FOLLOW EACH
OTHER TO CAMDEN TOWN

KICK INTENDED FOR WOMAN KILLED DOG

WOMAN SEES HUSBAND KILLED IN MIDNIGHT ATTACK

CROWDS AT
IRA MEETING
On Sunday, swarms of Irishmen invaded Arlington Road, for an IRA
meeting addressed by a carpenter

IN CAMDEN TOWN WE HEAR THE VOICE OF
'LITTLE DUBLIN'
Stocky, 21-year-old labourer, T---- M---, stood on a corner of London's
"Little Dublin" on Wednesday night and in a fervent Irish voice told
the North London Press: "We'll give Camden Town back to
the English if the English'll give us back our six counties"

NEW IRISH CENTRE
FOR CAMDEN TOWN
£25,000 DEBT TO CLEAR
Cardinal Griffen told a distinguished gathering at the opening of a new
Irish Centre in Camden Square, St Pancras, last week: "Like all good
Catholic ventures, the Irish Centre opens with a debt"

THE ROCK'N'ROLL GUIDE TO CAMDEN

COSMOPOLITAN CAMDEN HIGH
ITALIANS, CYPRIOTS, GREEKS & IRISH RUB SHOULDERS
The motley crowd, the smell of a spaghetti bolognaise, and the sight of
bright red peppers piled high in shop windows tell at once the
cosmopolitan nature of Camden High Street — a street with large
chunks of Italy, Greece, Cyprus and the West Indies

'GO BACK TO
IRELAND,'
SAYS MAGISTRATE

THREE HURT IN
IRISH TEDDY-BOY CLASH

'BE AS UN-IRISH AS YOU CAN,' SAYS MAGISTRATE IN
ASSAULT CASE

IRISHMAN JUMPED ON
A POLICEMAN'S HELMET
A disturbance in Camden High Street at 1am on Christmas Day
when a policeman was injured and his helmet jumped upon
had a sequel at Clerkenwell on Boxing Day, when two
Irishmen received prison sentences

WOMAN IN DRINK CASE SAYS:
I AM TEE-TOTAL
The only defence witness there was time to call at Clerkenwell last
week when adjourned summonses were before the court alleging the
supply of drink after hours at the Prince Of Wales public house, Carol
Street, NW1, said in evidence that she was tee-total and all she had
after the house closed was a cup of tea

In the pub they drank their sub
And up in Camden Town you'll find them
They sweated blood
And they washed down mud
With pints and quarts of beer
And now around the road again
With McAlpine's Fusiliers

CHALK FARM ROAD

"Sooner or later a new generation of teenagers will adopt some form of music with its accompanying lifestyle to symbolize and reflect their revolt. It may even be that at this moment, in a cellar or church hall in Runcorn or Middlesbrough, in the back room of a pub in Slough or Welwyn Garden City, a movement is gestating and will soon slouch towards the Roundhouse to be born."
— George Melly, 1970

1. CHALK FARM UNDERGROUND STATION

This is where Madness were photographed for the front cover of 1980's *Absolutely*, an album which was advertised as 'The Camden Cowboys Ride Again'. "We were going to do the photograph at Camden Town Tube Station, but it was too busy, with too many people going past," says Suggs. "So it was just much easier to do it at Chalk Farm." The station also featured in Madness's 1981 autobiographical movie, *Take It Or Leave It*.

CHALK FARM ROAD

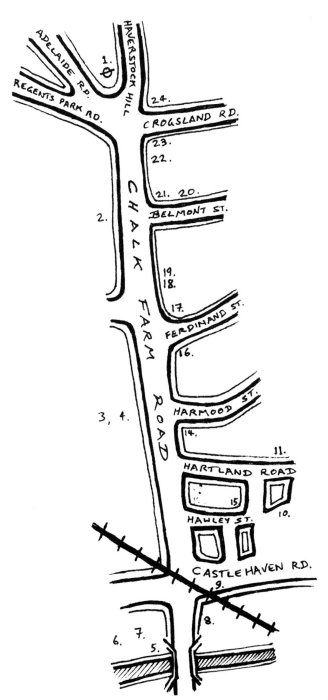

2. ROUNDHOUSE
99 Chalk Farm Road, NW1.

This former engine house has been described as 'the Albert Hall of North London' and is probably the most important building in Camden. During the late-60s and throughout the 70s, the Roundhouse was one of the most happening venues in the country, famous for its late-night raves, Sunday all-dayers and some of the earliest punk gigs, such as Patti Smith, the Ramones and the Clash, who all played here in 1976.

The Roundhouse was built as an engine shed in 1847 but, within 20 years, it was no longer practical to use it for that purpose. In 1869, it was leased to the distillers W&A Gilbey Ltd who turned it into a warehouse and added a wooden gallery. It continued to be used by Gilbey's for the next 100 years, when it was taken over by the playwright Arnold Wesker, whose longterm dream was to create a cultural palace for the people.

Wesker firmly believed in the idea of the arts being available to everyone, not just the intelligentsia, and fiercely attacked the unions for failing to support cultural activities. In September 1960, the Trades Union Congress responded by passing Resolution 42, which pledged greater support for the arts. Wesker, who was intent on staging arts festivals in various English towns and setting up a free arts complex in London, named his scheme Centre 42, after the TU Resolution, and started to look for a base in the capital. In July 1964, the millionaire and renowned patron of the arts, Louis Mintz, bought the 16-year lease of the Roundhouse and gave it to Centre 42.

However, although the Roundhouse had a huge performing area and good acoustics, Wesker wanted to rebuild it, at an estimated cost of £750,000, before actually staging an event here. Two years later, the underground newspaper, *International Times*, which was abbreviated to *IT*, asked Wesker if they could use the Roundhouse as the venue for their launch party. He agreed, and the first rock'n'roll event in Camden subsequently took place on October 15, 1966.

The *IT* party was London's first organised, all-night rave, featuring a screening of Kenneth Anger's *Scorpio Rising*, plus live sets from Pink Floyd and the Soft Machine, who were virtually unknown at the time. Although the Roundhouse was cold, wet and filthy with minimal lighting, a rickety balcony and just two toilets, the event was a big success. Around 2,000 people turned up and everyone was offered sugar cubes as they came through the door — the cubes were rumoured to be coated with LSD and, although this wasn't actually the case, some people managed to trip out on them regardless. Someone had made a giant jelly, moulded in a bath tub, but Pink Floyd's van ran into it while they were setting up their gear, so few people saw it in its original magnificence. Among the guests were Paul McCartney, Jane Asher, Marianne Faithfull, Monica Vitti and Antonioni, who was working on his latest movie, *Blow Up*. There was a psychedelic palm reading and

CHALK FARM ROAD

fortune telling tent and prizes were awarded for the shortest or barest fancy dress costumes — the winner was Marianne Faithfull, in a highly unconventional nun's habit, but Paul McCartney, who went as an Arab, dressed in white robes and headdress, left empty-handed.

The Soft Machine's performance included an amplified motor cycle, which had tiny microphones attached to it, and was revved up in accompaniment to the music. Later, its rider, who was wearing a long cape, gave girls rides around the venue while Pink Floyd played. Their set was enhanced by a tiny slide screen and a rudimentary light show — it was the first time that most of the audience had seen such a spectacle and, given that there was virtually no orthodox lighting in the Roundhouse, it looked brilliant. Pink Floyd also used a series of unconventional techniques, such as rolling ball-bearings down the guitar neck to produce Bo Diddley-style feedback, and made sure that everyone remembered them when they blew out the power during the closing *Interstellar Overdrive*.

As the night went on, the toilets inevitably overflowed, so many of the women took their dresses off to tiptoe through the mire, resulting in a queue of naked bodies surrounded by a most unerotic stench. The police eventually arrived outside, but the party carried on regardless. The *IT* and Roundhouse launch was much more than just another rock'n'roll show, it was the birth of a new way of life.

After the *IT* Party, the Roundhouse hosted three further all-night events in December. The first was Pink Floyd and the second was a double bill, over two nights, featuring Geno Washington and Cream, on December 30, followed by Pink Floyd, The Who and The Move, on New Year's Eve. The Who made the biggest initial impact by playing at deafening volume and letting off several smoke bombs, but someone quickly pulled the plugs on them. Two other songs were cut short in this way, so Pete Townshend responded by dragging on a pair of speakers and grinding them into the stage with his battered guitar. The Move went even further. During the climax of their set, they used iron bars to completely demolish a car in front of the stunned audience.

"I saw The Move at the Roundhouse when they smashed up the car," says Alan Jones, who was a music journalist at the time. "They had an effigy of Hitler, which they destroyed, and then they went for the car. At that time, the Roundhouse was very rough and ready, there were hardly any amenities, and it was basically just an open space. Bands came on and played — I don't think they worried about the sound quality, they just got up and got on with it."

On the same night that The Move were playing at the Roundhouse, the co-founder of *IT*, John Hopkins, had started a club called UFO as a way of helping to finance the newspaper. UFO, which stood for Unidentified Flying Object or Underground Freak Out, was basically a home for experimental pop groups and was also Britain's first psychedelic club. It was held every Friday at an Irish dance hall called the Blarney Club, on Tottenham Court Road, and the house bands were Pink Floyd and the Soft Machine, while John Lennon, Mick Jagger, Jimi Hendrix and Pete Townshend were among the regulars.

The UFO crowd also continued to attend occasional shows at the Roundhouse. For example, Paul McCartney did a short soundtrack for a late-night rave on January 28, 1967, and the Jimi Hendrix Experience played their first gig here just under a month later.

In June, John Hopkins was jailed for nine months on drug charges and, in August, the *News Of The World* ran a story about teenage sex and drugs at UFO and the police pressurised the Blarney Club's Irish owner into closing it down. Consequently, UFO's organisers were given four days notice to find a new venue. Brian Epstein apparently invited them to move into the champagne bar of the Saville Theatre, but this was deemed unsuitable.

In July, the Roundhouse was the venue for a fortnight-long seminar called The Dialectics Of Liberation, which aimed to bring together some of the most revolutionary thinkers in the western world, including William Burroughs, Allen Ginsberg, Emmett Grogan, Angela Davis, RD Laing and David Cooper, and also featured live music from the Social Deviants. Coincidentally, in the same month, the Prime Minister's wife, Mary Wilson, invited Arnold Wesker to an advisory tea party at 10 Downing Street to discuss raising funds for Centre 42 to buy

Jimi Hendrix at the Roundhouse, February 1967 [Graham Howe/Camera Press]

The Doors at the Roundhouse, September 1968 [Barry Wentzell/Repfoto]

the freehold of the Roundhouse. Mrs Wilson helped to raise £90,000, which was a start, but not enough, so it was decided that commercial events, such as pop concerts, should be allowed to continue.

This was good news for UFO, which moved up the road from the Blarney Club to the Roundhouse, officially opening on August 18, with the Crazy World Of Arthur Brown and the Incredible String Band. Over the next couple of months, Pink Floyd, the Soft Machine and The Move all played here, but the venue's high rent plus greater expenses from the increasingly successful bands forced UFO to close down on October 13.

The Roundhouse was, however, still associated with rock'n'roll and, in November, it was the location for the photo session which later wound up on the inside of the gatefold sleeve of *Electric Ladyland*. You can't tell from the picture, but the session involved building a big bonfire, with Hendrix standing very close to a 20-foot high wall of flames. That same month, the band headlined a seven-band package tour, which also included The Move and Pink Floyd.

"I saw Pink Floyd at the Roundhouse," says Lemmy, "but I also saw them twice a night on that Hendrix tour, with Syd Barrett, who was going through his first amazing breakdown with mirrors on his Telecaster. I came to London in 67 and immediately got to sleep on the floor of Noel Redding's flat and got a job as a roadie with Hendrix. Look at this for a bill, right: Hendrix, soon after his first album had come out; The Move, who had just got a big hit with *Flowers In The Rain*; the Pink Floyd with Syd Barrett; Amen Corner, who'd just had *Gin House*; the four-piece Nice; Outer Limits and Eire Apparent, for 7/6 a night — 7/6 to see all that. Nowadays you get two bands and one of them's crap. It's bullshit."

The void that was left by UFO was partly filled by Middle Earth, which took place in a Covent Garden basement and involved lots of light shows, incense, drugs, bands and DJs, such as John Peel and Jeff Dexter. On July 27, 1968, Middle Earth moved to the Roundhouse, with an opening performance from Traffic, who were followed over the next three weeks by Family, Tyrannosaurus Rex and the Crazy World Of Arthur Brown.

The first major Middle Earth event took place on September 6 and 7, when Jefferson Airplane and The Doors played two consecutive shows here. The latter had just hit the British Top 20 with *Hello, I Love You* and a quick visit to Carnaby Street had transformed Jim Morrison into a black-leathered lizard king for the first time. Not surprisingly, he wanted to headline but, following an argument, the toss of a coin went in Jefferson Airplane's favour. "I saw The Doors and Jefferson Airplane at the Roundhouse," says Lemmy. "Me and this bird, who was a barmaid at the Middle Earth club, were standing there looking at Morrison and he was so good looking, but he was just so pompous that we both turned to each other at the same time and said, 'What a wanker.' His records were all right but he turned out to be a complete tosser."

On the second night, however, Morrison was in a much better mood and played a blinding set. The show was filmed by Granada TV as part of a one-hour black and white documentary, *The Doors Are Open*. A couple of months later, Led Zeppelin made their London debut at the Roundhouse, topping a bill which also featured John Lee Hooker and the Deviants. Earlier that day, Robert Plant had married his girlfriend, Maureen — prompting him to later joke that his honeymoon had been playing a gig at the Roundhouse.

Over the next few months, The Who, The Pretty Things, the Jeff Beck Group, Fairport Convention and Moby Grape played here. The Beatles were rumoured to be doing a show at the Roundhouse in January 1969, but it never happened.

By March 1969, the Roundhouse seemed to be fulfilling Arnold Wesker's original dream of a cultural palace for the masses, when it staged Tony Richardson's production of *Hamlet*, which starred Marianne Faithfull as Ophelia. Wesker, however, did not really approve of letting the Roundhouse out for commercial ventures — particularly those which weren't necessarily in accordance with his original vision. The final straw came in July 1970 when the Roundhouse became the only theatre that dared to run the infamous nude revue *Oh Calcutta!* — starring Tony Booth, who would later become the father-in-law of future Prime Minister Tony Blair.

Wesker resigned in September, but the Roundhouse continued to be a cultural centre regardless. In October, it was the venue for a festival called *Cinema City*, which was an attempt to present 75 years of cinema history and showed 147 films in a month. It was attended by Gene Kelly, Shirley MacLaine and Richard Burton and Liz Taylor, then at the height of their fame but near the end of their first marriage.

The Roundhouse continued to be a rock venue and one of the most famous gigs to ever take place here was The Rolling Stones' farewell concert in March 1971, before they left England to temporarily live as tax exiles in France. The touts made the most of the occasion by selling faked £1 tickets for up to £10 apiece.

This was also the home of the annual Camden Rock Festival, which featured headliners such as Marty Wilde, Wishbone Ash, Fairport Convention, Dr John, Rory Gallagher and The Faces, before it evolved into more of a jazz event. However, the club which the Roundhouse became best known for was Implosion. First started during the summer of 1969, Implosion ran from 3.30pm till 11.30pm, usually featured five bands, had a great disco, was cheap to get into and quickly became the only place to hang out on a Sunday afternoon in London.

"We used to go to Implosion at the Roundhouse every Sunday," says Frank Murray, who worked with Thin Lizzy. "I saw The Who, Frank Zappa — so many great bands. People used to queue outside in the early afternoon, but you could turn up at any time you wanted. It was just this great loose atmosphere, with a really strong smell of patchouli

Marc Bolan in the Roundhouse at the height of TRextasy [Robert Ellis/Repfoto]

oil in the air. Everybody was a hippy, but it was very well organised and you could really empathise with whatever band was playing."

All the bands who played at Implosion were paid the same money, regardless of their pulling power, and the profits went into rebuilding the Roundhouse and helping underground organisations who were in financial trouble. Among the bands who played at Implosion were Deep Purple, The Deviants (who later evolved into The Pink Fairies), David Bowie, Tyrannosaurus Rex, Hawkwind, The Who, Elton John, Mott The Hoople, Thin Lizzy and Steve Marriott's All Stars.

"I first went to the Roundhouse as a customer when they had bands on all day on Sundays," says Lemmy. "I went to a lot of gigs, although I never saw any of the bands cos I was always chasing birds and, in them days, I was much better looking so I used to catch quite a lot of them. There were still bits of old railroad machinery lying about and I once made love to a girl in an old wagon in there. The thing was, nobody noticed, cos people don't look up — it's funny, there were legs sticking out over the top. It was great fun, yeah. They had curtains round the back of the seats, as well, so we'd sneak behind there with birds, too, and I met what turned out to be almost the love of my life there, only she died so she couldn't be... But that's too sad for this book."

Hawkwind were one of the bands who played at the Roundhouse on a regular basis and Lemmy became their bass player in August 1971. The first show he did here with them was on February 13, 1972, at the Greasy Truckers Party. The show was recorded and some of the highlights appeared on *The Greasy Truckers Party* and *Glastonbury Fayre*, two albums which were released a couple of months later. *Silver Machine*, one of the tracks which was recorded at the Roundhouse, was remixed as a single, with Bob Calvert's live vocals overdubbed by Lemmy's, and it reached Number Two in the charts.

"The Greasy Truckers Party was in the middle of all the mining strikes, and the electricity kept going on and off," says Lemmy. "We had an hour of electricity, so one side of the double album was called *Power Cut*, and there was nothing on it except people talking and laughing and shouting things, cos we were all sitting in the dark. Then the power

"We used to come up to Camden from Earl's Court and then just go straight back home on the bus, the 59. And I always used to get Jesus on the bus with me going home. Do you remember Jesus? He was the idiot dancer at the Roundhouse with long blond hair, he was really boring, cos he was a Born Again bloody Christian, and I always used to get caught with him. He'd sit and lecture me about the Second Coming all the way back to Earl's Court. Is that what I associate the 59 with? No, I associate it with scoring methedrine, actually." – LEMMY

came back on, and us and Brinsley Schwarz played. Another time, soon afterwards, at the Roundhouse, we spiked all the food and drink with acid and then we came onstage and threw acid out of bottle droppers on the audience, so that everyone was tripping. The first time I had seen Hawkwind was at the Roundhouse and all the audience was like this [*adopts wide-eyed glazed expression*], 600 of them all standing there doing the same thing. And I thought, 'Fucking hell, I'll have to join these guys, I can't watch 'em.' So I did."

Lemmy eventually proved too much even for Hawkwind and, during the band's fourth American tour in April 1974, he was sacked and sent back to England, after being arrested by Canadian customs for carrying speed. By May 1975, Lemmy had formed Motorhead.

"Motorhead's first show was at the Roundhouse with Greenslade," he says. "All I remember is that we used Nazi marching music, with the boots, to come in and go out, and we played very badly. I had a real human skull, which I had painted silver, on top of my speaker stack — that was in the days before I painted it black. We were in darkness anyway, cos you don't get to use the headline band's lights."

Some people regard Motorhead as one of the first punk bands and Implosion was definitely a breeding ground for the whole scene. The teenage Johnny Thunders had made a pilgrimage to London in 1969 just to check out various bands, and saw his heroes Tyrannosaurus Rex at Implosion. The young John Lydon and his mates spent virtually every Sunday afternoon at the Roundhouse, watching everyone from Hawkwind to Arthur Brown and Can, and listening to the Stooges and MC5 being played at deafening volume through the PA system. Lydon was probably the kind of revolutionary that George Melly was thinking of when he predicted that a new movement was gestating and would soon slouch towards the Roundhouse to be born.

Punk eventually arrived here on May 16 and 17, 1976, in the form of Patti Smith, who played two consecutive shows followed, seven weeks later, by a triple bill of the Flamin' Groovies, the Ramones and the Stranglers. The Ramones, who had released their self-titled debut album three months previously, were a revelation to most of the Sunday night crowd. By the time they returned to the Roundhouse, 12 months later, almost everyone who saw their debut show had formed punk bands of their own — including Shane MacGowan and Spider Stacy, who first bumped into each other in the Roundhouse urinal.

"The Roundhouse was a heavy place for scoring on a Sunday night," says Shane MacGowan. "You could get stoned and go and watch the band, and really get into them, or just hang around on the perimeter and wander about the venue, which is what lots of people used to do."

MacGowan, who formed the Nipple Erectors, is typical of the 70s teenagers who originally went to the Roundhouse to see bands like The Pink Fairies, but whose lives were changed by punk.

"I used to go to the Roundhouse to see Quicksilver Messenger

Service and The Pink Fairies, but I remember seeing The Troggs supported by the Damned," says Alie Allerton, who started working down the road at Rhythm Records in 1976. "I know that was pretty early on, because I'd never seen anyone wearing a dog collar before, and the audience was made up of all the people who were forming their own punk bands. There must have been about 30 punks there. A lot of the bands who were rehearsing in Camden were from Ladbroke Grove, like the Clash. I figured the Clash were one of the first bands to have enough money to be able to *rehearse* — most bands squatted in empty houses and just put mattresses over the walls."

The Clash, who rehearsed in an old warehouse on the Chalk Farm Road, played their fifth ever gig at the Roundhouse on September 5, 1976. They were bottom of the bill to the Kursaal Flyers and Crazy Cavan'N'The Rhythm Rockers. "The minute they walked in the building I knew it was all over," the Kursaal Flyers' drummer, Will Birch, recalled later. "To me, their sound mattered not one iota — they had the look. As a five-piece they made a right rotten racket."

Over the next couple of years, the Roundhouse continued to be one of the key places to see punk bands. Among those who played here were the Stranglers, the Jam, the Damned, 999, Wayne County, X Ray Spex, Elvis Costello & The Attractions, Adam & The Ants and Penetration. The Sex Pistols never played at the Roundhouse, but they did rehearse here for a brief period. By that time, John Lydon and Glen Matlock were arguing continually and Malcolm McLaren finally gave the pair of them 20 quid to go to the bar and sort out their differences. After several pints, they realised that they had a mutual love of The Doors, and they ended up using the riff from *Hello I Love You* as the starting point for their own *Submission*.

"The Roundhouse is probably the key place in Camden for me," says Suggs. "Because, although I had been to the Roxy, it was there that I first saw Ian Dury. I remember walking up the steps of the Roundhouse and seeing Lee Thompson in a pair of Oxford bags, blue brothel creepers and a Levi jacket with 'Kilburn & The High Roads' in bleach on the back — it was a very striking moment. I also saw Deaf School there, which was the first time I saw my prospective wife [she was a singer in the band and later had a solo career as Bette Bright]. Deaf School influenced Madness quite a lot, because they had that kind of theatricality lark and a lot of people in the band, which wasn't the thing at that time. In fact, I saw Deaf School playing at the Roundhouse with the Vibrators and Eater, or one of those dodgy old punk bands. Those are great memories, because they were the innocent days before I was in a band myself. The Roundhouse was just a great venue to go to."

Thelma Holt was appointed Theatre Director of the Roundhouse in 1977 and she decided to exploit its natural shape by turning it into a theatre-in-the round. This meant repositioning the stage and reducing the venue's capacity from 940 to 600. By November 1978, various significant factors, such as licensing restrictions, sound complaints from local residents and the reduced capacity, had forced the Roundhouse to stop putting on rock shows and devote itself to theatre.

"I worked at the Roundhouse during the period that Straight Music put all the great shows on," says Frank Murray. "Most of them were punk, people like Sham 69 and the Clash, but there was always a problem with noise. In order to sort out the problem you'd have to do something with the structure of the building, which you weren't allowed to do, because it's protected, so it was a real Catch 22 situation. During the week, the Roundhouse was a theatre, a great theatre, because Thelma Holt had real vision. I remember during one performance, a woman in the audience got so emotionally involved with the plight of the character that she ended up talking to the actor onstage. That happened a few times. The Roundhouse was Europe's Fillmore."

"I saw hundreds of people at the Roundhouse and it was mostly good," says Lemmy. "It was a great venue, but then they got in the Chinese wrestling and the flipping acrobats and the Feminist Of The Week meetings — it's no substitute for rock'n'roll is it, eh?"

In 1983, Thelma Holt announced that she was unable to run the Roundhouse on £120,000 a year and it was closed down. The stage was put back in its original position and the venue was given permission to host ten rock shows per year, although this failed to come into effect. There were long-running plans to turn the building into a black arts complex, but this was never properly realised, either.

Instead, the Roundhouse has been used by various TV, film and video crews. For example, The Mission teamed up with Slade to record a video for their charity single *Merry Christmas Everybody* and it was also the location for Richard Stanley's *Hardware*. A few bands and film companies have held launches here, including the Pet Shop Boys and the film *Tank Girl*. In July 1996, however, rock'n'roll returned to the Roundhouse for the first time in almost 18 years when Vince Power's Mean Fiddler organisation staged a series of concerts, opening with Elvis Costello and followed by other bands such as Suede.

"A friend of mine, Patrick O'Connor, and his brother, John, bought the Roundhouse and I rented it out to do some gigs," says Vince Power. "It had such a history of noise problems that it was very much a hot potato, but we managed to convince the authorities that it was going to be purely live gigs and some of them were very successful. There was a great feeling of warmth, people were really happy to be back there again. Elvis Costello was talking about playing 20 years ago, when it was just a shack, with the roof leaking, but it had this feeling about it. The Roundhouse is one of those places that is tied up with memories and history, and a lot of people wanted to relive the past, especially on Elvis nights. For me, it was like all the things I do in the Mean Fiddler, just doing something with a different angle. I did look into the possibility of running it permanently and I actually tried to buy it, but the whole place would have needed so much work to turn it into a proper venue, like The Forum or The Grand, that it just didn't stack up financially. And, at the end of the day, that's what I had to look at. Unfortunately."

There have been many different plans for the Roundhouse over the past 20 years. One of the most recent was to turn it into an architectural library, but many people still harbour Arnold Wesker's original dream to make it a lasting arts palace for the people.

3. STABLES MARKET
Chalk Farm Road, NW1.

Once a home for the horses who worked in Camden's large goods depot, this was originally called The Old Stables. When it opened as the Stables Market in the early-80s, this was nothing more than a rough car park with a few stalls selling bric-a-brac. However, when Camden Lock Market was redeveloped in 1991, the Stables expanded and it is now the best market in the area. It specialises in antiques, new pine furniture, carpets and rugs. There are also lots of clothes stalls — which range from Sparkle Moore's 50s clothing and accessories to goth gear and fetish wear — plus the usual range of arts, crafts, records and CDs.

"The Stables has that pioneering, treasure hunt feel to it," says Sylvia Keogh, one of the original stall holders at Camden Lock Market. "Those fantastic buildings have always been a goldmine sitting there waiting to be exploited."

Over the years, many musicians have run stalls at The Stables, including Boz Boorer, a former Polecat who is Morrissey's longterm guitarist; Chris Farlowe, who had a Number One hit with *Out Of Time* in 1966; Alan Williams, who was The Beatles' first manager; and Mary Byker, who rented out a stall to sell off Gaye Bykers On Acid T-shirts after the band split up. "I can remember selling a Bykers T-shirt to Kylie Minogue," he says. "I don't remember what the T-shirt had on it, I just remember it was when she was Kylie Minogue in the *I Should Be So Lucky* sense of Kylie Minogue — although it was when she was going out with Michael Hutchence, so she was getting a bit rock at that point."

Jarvis Cocker also ran a one-off stall here in the late-80s. "The reason that I ended up doing it," he says, "was that Russell [Senior, ex-Pulp guitarist] was an antiques dealer and he brought down all the rubbish that he couldn't sell and told us that, if we flogged any of it at Camden, he'd give us half the money. We took some stuff of our own as well and sold quite a lot of it. But then I spent all my money on walking round the other stalls and seeing things that I liked. Can I remember what I bought? I can actually, cos it was probably one of my worst ever items of clothing. It was this poncho, a short, hooded poncho, which was bright red and blue and yellow. It was when I was in my raving days and I used to wear it to raves — God knows how I did, cos it was really thick and terribly hot. I can't really believe that I ever wore it, but I thought it was really fantastic when I bought it."

4. REHEARSAL REHEARSALS
The Stables Market, Chalk Farm Road, NW1

Now part of the Stables Market, this was once the site of the Clash's live-in rehearsal space, Rehearsal Rehearsals — the beloved *Garageland* which they immortalised on their debut album.

It was the Clash's manager, Bernie Rhodes, who discovered this two-storey, British Rail warehouse shortly after Joe Strummer had joined the band in June 1976. He managed to get the lease for the disused building from British Rail, realising that it was the perfect place for the Clash to develop their sound. The building was christened Rehearsal Rehearsals and downstairs became the band practice area, while the two upstairs rooms were used as storage space, for pin-ball and fruit machines, and as an office and recreation zone.

Pride of place was given to Bernie's jukebox, which was stocked with everything from Elvis Presley classics to The Rulers' *Wrong 'Em Boyo* and Jonathan Richman's *Roadrunner* [the song that Mick Jones had asked Paul Simonon to sing when he auditioned for his previous band, London SS]. Before long, the Clash — who were originally Strummer, Jones, Simonon and Keith Levene on additional guitar — held auditions for a drummer and completed their line-up with Terry Chimes.

Paul Simonon subsequently came up with the name, the Clash, and, after just one month's preparation, they made their London debut here on Friday August 13, 1976 [their only previous show had been an unpublicised support slot to the Sex Pistols in Sheffield a few weeks earlier]. Bernie Rhodes decided that it should be a showcase gig in front of an invitation-only audience of music journalists and bookers. To make it look like a special event, the band painted the downstairs practice room shocking pink and hung matching drapes at the side of the stage area, while Paul Simonon painted a mural of London's Westway on the back wall. They also sprayed paint over their clothes and instruments, originating their famous Jackson Pollock look. The audience were given free drinks while they listened to records on Bernie's jukebox and then, at nine o'clock, the Clash walked onstage, plugged in their guitars and blasted out a 40-minute set.

Rehearsals was a popular place in the run up to the Punk Festival at the 100 Club that September — with the Clash, Subway Sect and Siouxsie & The Banshees, who featured Sid Vicious on drums, all practising here the day before. By this time, Paul Simonon and the Clash's roadie, Roadent, had moved into Rehearsals, even though it had no lighting and very little heating. There is an apocryphal story that they were so poor and hungry that, one night in October 1976, after the band had been flyposting for their upcoming gig at the ICA, Paul Simonon came back to Rehearsals, heated up the left over flour and paste on their one-bar electric fire and ate it.

Keith Levene was sacked from the Clash in September 1976 and Terry Chimes decided to quit a couple of months later, shortly before the

The Clash at Rehearsal Rehearsals, 1977 [Barry Plummer]

December 76 Anarchy Tour with the Pistols, the Heartbreakers and the Damned. The band advertised for a drummer in November and, after a series of auditions at Rehearsals, temporarily recruited Rob Harper.

When the Clash returned from the Anarchy Tour, Joe Strummer discovered that all his possessions had been thrown into a skip outside his West London squat and had no choice but to move into Rehearsals, sharing just a couch, the one-bar fire and a couple of blankets with Paul Simonon and Roadent. The rough, cold environs of Rehearsals, and a serious lack of food and money, helped to inspire the sound of the Clash's self-titled debut album during the early weeks of 1977. Terry Chimes agreed to play on *The Clash* since they still hadn't found a permanent drummer, which is why it was just Strummer, Jones and Simonon who posed in the alleyway opposite Rehearsals for the shot which subsequently appeared on the album cover. In April, Nick 'Topper' Headon, who had also once auditioned for Mick Jones's previous band, London SS, became the 206th person to try out on drums at Rehearsals. He got the job.

And it was Topper who was at the centre of the most infamous incident to take place here. On March 30, 1978, two of his old mates turned up — they were Steve and Pete Barnacle, and the latter had a powerful air rifle which he intended to sell to Topper. Impressed, the three of them, plus Paul Simonon and a friend of the band's called Robin Crocker, went up on the roof of Rehearsals to try out the rifle. They started shooting at pigeons on the other side of the sloped roof, firing off shots and watching the birds fly up in the air then splatter back down. However, their victims weren't regular Camden Town pigeons, they were expensive racing birds. The breeder had been tending to his birds at the time and came running over to grab the rifle off them.

The next thing they knew, a helicopter was circling above them and two uniformed police officers were clambering onto the roof with a loud-hailer: "Put your hands in the air. Armed police!" British Rail Transport Police had an office across the road from Rehearsals and, when someone saw the five of them on the roof with a rifle, assumed that they were taking shots at passing trains. They were immediately arrested and taken to Kentish Town Police Station, before being sent on to Brixton Prison, where they were held overnight.

Meanwhile, Joe Strummer and Mick Jones had been in the office downstairs, completely oblivious to what was going on, until they heard the helicopter overhead and several armed officers burst through the door and started searching the place for other weapons. They tried to get hold of Bernie Rhodes, but he wasn't at home, so Caroline Coon, Paul Simonon's girlfriend who was also a journalist and had co-founded the legal aid group, Release, in the late-60s, arranged for everyone [apart from the Barnacle brothers] to be released on bail of £1,500. They were picked up from Brixton the following morning, but had to check in with their bail officer every day until the charges were dropped, when the case was heard on May 10. The incident provided the inspiration for *Guns On The Roof*, on the Clash's second album, *Give 'Em Enough Rope*.

The episode was further immortalised by Paul Simonon, who painted a massive caricature of Bernie Rhodes on the wall of Rehearsals' office. It showed him surrounded by pigeons, all intent on shitting on his head. By this time, Bernie Rhodes was also managing Subway Sect, the Coventry Automatics [later renamed The Specials] and Dexy's Midnight Runners, who practised at Rehearsals. He had become increasingly involved with the Subways, organising gigs for them under the banner Club Left. By the time *Give 'Em Enough Rope* was released in November, the Clash had told Rhodes that his services were no longer required. He responded by kicking them out of Rehearsals and changing the locks.

The warehouse continued to be used by Rhodes's other bands, particularly Subway Sect, who converted it into an eight-track studio-cum-rehearsal room. Rhodes resumed his relationship with the Clash after a break of two years and they moved back into their old rehearsal room in 1983. It was renamed Atlanta Rehearsal Studios, and loads of bands, including Tenpole Tudor and The Sting-rays, used it in the mid-80s. The old rehearsal space was eventually pulled down during the expansion and development of the Stables Market.

5. CAMDEN MARKET
Camden Lock/Camden High Street/Chalk Farm Road, NW1.

Camden Market is not just the main focal point of Camden Town, but it is also one of the most popular tourist attractions in Britain, with 250,000 people passing though it every weekend. The market was founded by Eric Reynolds in 1972, when he bought a derelict site at Camden Lock. He redeveloped it in April 1973 and the market was opened the following March, gradually growing bigger until the stalls began to spread south down the High Street and north along Chalk Farm Road. "The day the market opened there were about 25 stall holders," says Sylvia Keogh, who was one of them. "It was great, because we were the pioneers, and we all used to buy from each other."

The original idea was to make Camden Lock a crafts market so, when it opened — at first, on Saturdays only — there were lots of potters, sculptors, people making jewellery, and others selling church furniture, old fruit machines, china, books and bric-a-brac. "In the beginning, it was quite hippyish," says Sylvia Keogh, "with people making leather belts and neck. There was a little old guy with a furry beard who used to sell stuff on this big narrow boat stall with all these huge painted kettles, right on the Lock. And there was another guy, a real East End joker-type, who used to sell things like flying horse eggs. He would also paint light bulbs and sell them saying, 'These are black-out bulbs — they're from the War.' There were loads of great characters at the market when it first started."

CHALK FARM ROAD

Sylvia Keogh's stall sold 30s and 40s dresses, which she would collect from rag merchants in the north of England. "In the early days we were really embarrassed about how much we charged," she says. "We'd buy something for 50p and then somebody would come along and offer £5 for it. In the beginning, I couldn't believe that people were buying my things — I used to blush as I took the money. But, after about two weeks, I thought it was OK."

By the beginning of 1975, Camden Lock had already expanded to 80 stalls and people were being drawn to it from all over the country. "I was living in Hull and my big dream was to get to London," says Dempsey, who got a stall here that year and now runs a candles and incense shop, at 1a, in the Market Hall. "My hobby was going to auctions and jumble sales and buying all this stuff which later got called art deco, but it was basically just the things that no one else wanted. Anyway, this friend came up from London and said, 'If you sold all this stuff on the market, you could buy a house', and that was how I heard about Camden Lock. So what started out as something involving 20-odd people got a good reputation fairly quickly."

1975 was also the year that the market was given permission to open on Sundays as well as Saturdays. There were already all-day gigs going on at the Roundhouse on Sunday afternoons, so the two places went hand in hand, with stalls being set up outside the venue to sell records and hippy paraphernalia, and later spreading along the Chalk Farm Road. "Camden Market became a very popular place to go," says Shane MacGowan. "We used to take speed and go around the market on a Sunday afternoon and then go to the Roundhouse."

When punk began to take off in the summer of 1976, with lots of the early gigs taking place at the Roundhouse, more and more people started going to the market on a Sunday afternoon. "Billy Idol and his girlfriend used to come down all the time," says Sylvia Keogh. "And when the first punk hairstyles began to appear, they used to parade themselves on the King's Road and at Camden Lock — there would be the most gorgeous hairstyles, loads of peacocks and huge mohicans."

Many of these hairstyles were maintained by regular trips to certain market stalls at Camden Lock. "I was the first person to sell Crazy Colour in this area," says Dempsey. "I used to dye my own hair in order to test the colours, then I'd wear a woolly hat when I was taking my kids to school."

In the late-70s, it was common to see musicians working on Camden Lock Market — Roland Gift, who would later form Fine Young Cannibals, worked on Dempsey's stall; Annie Lennox and Dave Stewart had a clothes stall when they were starting The Tourists; and even the Clash's Joe Strummer and Topper Headon were seen selling clothes on an open air stall the day after the press launch for *Give 'Em Enough Rope*, in November 1978. "We're broke, man. So you just have to do what you can do," Joe Strummer explained at the time.

"Most of the stalls were selling secondhand clothing, bric-a-brac and records," says Alan Jones, whose record shop, Out On The Floor, started off as a stall on Camden Market in 1978. "I can remember Madness coming to the stall, they were just starting out and they didn't have any money. It was the classic thing with groups, they've got a box of their own records but they haven't got any money, so they'd be selling copies of their own albums and singles. Marc Almond used to come round quite a lot, looking at records. In fact, I think it was on our stall that he first heard *Tainted Love*, which he later recorded. Adam Ant was around all the time and I remember Jamie Reid, who designed all the early Sex Pistols sleeves, selling me the original poster from the Pistols' first gig at the 100 Club. When he came to the stall, I didn't have much money, and I think he wanted £30 for it, so I turned it down. But he said he was going to the Electric Ballroom for a cup of tea — he was with Margi Clarke — and so I thought about it, and I found him in the Ballroom and bought the poster off him. I've still got it."

Camden Market began to get an international reputation and visiting film stars were soon mingling with struggling musicians. "I can remember Jack Palance coming to the market one day," says Sylvia Keogh. "When somebody famous turned up the word would go round the stall holders, but everyone tried to be cool. Julie Christie used to come down a lot and buy clothes, she was really nice. I also remember Raquel Welch coming to the stall one day, with this big entourage of people. She was pregnant and was looking for baby clothes on my stall — it was pretty obvious that I didn't have any."

By the early-80s, Camden Market had become a good starting point for many successful shops and designers. For instance, The Body Shop had its first outlet here and Red Or Dead, Body Map, Duffer Of St George and Nigel Hall all began as stalls in various parts of the market.

"Camden Market was really trendy in the early-80s," says Ben Jones, who started helping his father, Alan, sell records on his stall when he was just ten-years-old. "Paul Weller used to come to the stall quite often to buy soul records and Morrissey would come down on a regular basis. From my point of view, all the DJs would buy from us — Norman

> "One of our band members went to buy some narcotics off one of those dodgy characters that hang around the market area where it's dark. He spent £20, then got home and discovered that it literally was grass. He was drunk at the time, so he went straight back up to Camden and bought some more, which turned out to be exactly the same thing. Another friend actually ended up with a lump of broccoli. So I don't know how much in the way of drugs actually gets sold by Camden Market — although I suspect a lot of fruit and veg probably does." – ANDY ROSS

Jay, the boys from Soul II Soul, Dave Dorrell, Gilles Peterson — especially if they were after rare groove and funk stuff. Alan McGee, who now runs Creation, used to sell his records to my dad on the stall. Camden had such a buzz about it at that point in time. People used to come down and hang around for the weekend, real trendy London people. Now it's obviously become a lot more touristy."

Even so, it is still possible to see big fashion names, such as Kate Moss and Jean Paul Gaultier, trawling through the stalls. "John Paul Gaultier has always been very influenced by street fashion," says Dempsey. "In fact, when I was designing clothes, I realised that what I did was influenced by what I saw women round Camden wearing. One year, I noticed people were wearing really thick tights and ankle warmers, and that's when I started designing leggings, which have been worn by Tina Turner and Cher and lots of other people."

Although Camden Market now refers specifically to the open air stalls on the junction of Camden High Street and Buck Street, which specialise in secondhand clothes and contemporary fashion, Camden Lock is still the real heart of the market. In 1990/91, the Lock underwent a £4 million redevelopment, the outstanding feature of which was the new Market Hall, a three-storey, Victorian-style building which houses small shops and studios, selling clothes, jewellery, books, antiques, records, tapes, videos and New Age stuff. Most of the shops in the Market Hall are open seven days a week, a move that was pioneered by Abbey Books.

At weekends, the cobbled yards surrounding the Hall are filled with about 400 stalls selling arts, crafts, new and secondhand clothing, shoes, jewellery, handmade chocolates, hot snacks, CDs, videos and vinyl. Camden Market was for a long time the acknowledged centre of the bootleg trade — some musicians have bought tapes of their own concerts here (although most of them can easily persuade the stall holders to hand over whatever they fancy), others have just worked here, such as Liam Maher from Flowered Up.

In recent years, the British Phonographic Industry (BPI) and Trading Standards Officials have made several high-profile prosecutions of bootleg dealers here. In June 1990, 4,600 bootleg tapes were seized and, in October 1995, 1,600 bootleg CDs were taken away and a stall full of videos and other stock impounded.

The Market continues to be one of the most popular places to go on a Sunday afternoon. "Camden Market is as close as you can get to being at Glastonbury," says Mary Byker. "Whether you like crusties and dreadlocks and coloured-whatever or not, it has a magic in itself."

6. HQ CLUB
West Yard, Camden Lock, NW1. Telephone: 0171-485 6044
Opened in 1985 as a wine-bar restaurant, the HQ club was originally associated with Latin and jazz music but came into its own

when it introduced acid house nights in 1988. Since then it has hosted a variety of clubs, the best known of these is Paul 'Trouble' Anderson's long-running The Loft, which is a mixture of house, garage and guest slots on Wednesdays, but they also have live bands on other nights.

Back in 1993, the HQ ran a series of Tuesday night gigs, which went under the banner of Country Feedback and included appearances from Grant Lee Buffalo, who had just released their debut album, *Fuzzy*, and Liz Phair.

During 1996, this canalside club became the Thursday night venue for Club Skinny, which made it the official Camden home of Romo — the extremely short-lived New Romantic revival movement — which featured live sets from bands like Minty and Dexdexter. "When the 1995/96 football season came to a close," says Steve Lamacq, "I fell into going to HQ. I never went there when it was a proper Romo club, it was at the tail-end of Romo — as if there was a start — but all these new teen bands started springing up. The first time I went there, someone gave me a flyer for the Pin Ups, so I went down to see them. It was a hot night and the little terrace was open, so you could sit outside as well, and the Pin Ups were all about 16 and they were just great. They played five songs, one of which was a Ramones cover version, and it was like going back to the start again, seeing this young band of kids — the bass player looked a bit like Sid Vicious and the singer had wraparound specs and looked like a young John Lydon — and they did a song called *Robbie Left Take That*.

"All these bands were in their mid-teens and so more new bands kept forming and playing there. That's what Camden is good at: other people see a band and think, 'I could do that, I could be on *Top Of The Pops*.' HQ was full of misfit Romos, a load of young kids drinking Hooch, coming up from out of London — Kenickie used to hang out there and it's where Dweeb played their first big A&R gig. It really only lasted through the summer of 96, but it was a great place to go."

7. DINGWALLS
35 Camden Lock Place, NW1. Telephone: 0171-267 1577

Originally opened in June 1973, Dingwalls used to be one of the best places to see blues and R&B in the country, and it also played a major role in the early punk scene.

The venue took its name from the packing-case manufacturer TE Dingwall Ltd, who took over the site on which the club still stands in 1937. By the early-70s, this area had been singled out as a potential arts and craft centre and the old warehouse was replaced by Dingwalls, which played a big part in the eventual growth of Camden Market.

The original intention was that Dingwalls would be a six-nights-a-week, American-style music club, putting on rock and R&B bands, with a long bar, lots of tables, plenty of room to dance and a restaurant. Prior to this, the only places to go in London after midnight were the

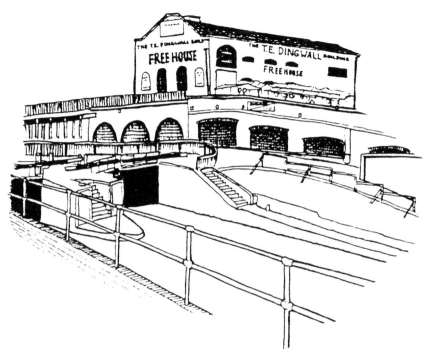

famous 60s nightclubs, such as the Whiskey-A-Go-Go and the Speakeasy, so it provided a good, late-night alternative to Soho. "Dingwalls was basically a late-night, alcoholics' watering hole or, more to the point, it was the *only* place where you could get a drink without being a member," says Barry Appleby, who became a regular soon after the venue opened. "We thought it was kind of swanky but, to Americans, it was heathen. They said, 'Can't we go anywhere else?' and we were like, 'No, this is all we've got.'"

Still, it was attractive to some visitors, such as the American country maverick Commander Cody, who played here several times in the early-70s, with His Lost Planet Airmen, and immediately declared, "Dingwalls is the best goddamn bar in town."

"One of the first times I ever went to Dingwalls was to see Commander Cody," says Ted Carroll, who was managing Thin Lizzy at the time. "They came and played for three nights, soon after it opened. It was bands like Commander Cody that drew in a crowd and made people aware of the place, so it got popular fairly quickly."

"Horslips were big fans of Dingwalls," says Roger Armstrong, who worked with them in 1973. "After they came offstage, we used to drive hell for leather from gigs, 100 miles out of town, just so we could make the last drink at Dingwalls."

Not surprisingly, the venue became a very comfortable setting for the thriving pub rock scene, which was the first 70s' backlash against a music scene that had taken itself too seriously for far too long. Spearheaded by bands like Bees Make Honey, Brinsley Schwarz and Ducks Deluxe, pub rock flourished in North London pubs like Kentish Town's Tally Ho, Holloway Road's Royal Nelson and Camden Road's Brecknock and, by the summer of 1973, the new Dingwalls.

At this time, the best pub rock band was Kilburn And The High Roads. They were fronted by childhood polio victim Ian Dury, who had a distinctive way of wrapping his small frame and leather-gloved hands around the microphone and spitting out his words in a venomous, Cockney accent, and whose many followers included the young John Lydon. However, the High Roads were soon overshadowed by Dr Feelgood, who wore sharp suits and shades and had a brilliant, chain-smoking frontman in Lee Brilleaux and a menacing Keith Richards-style guitarist in Wilko Johnson. "I saw the first gig that Dr Feelgood did at Dingwalls and I thought they were magical," says Lemmy. "Wilko was the dominant personality. He was demented — they'd have locked him up if he'd done what he was doing onstage in the street. He was brilliant, and so was Lee."

Dr Feelgood played at Dingwalls several times during 1974 and their psychotic sets helped to fuel a new breed of pub rock bands, such as Eddie And The Hot Rods, the Count Bishops and Joe Strummer's 101'ers. It was a gig at Dingwalls, in October 1975, that prompted Ted Carroll to offer the 101'ers a one-off single deal on his new label, Chiswick. However, Strummer had split the band to join the nascent Clash by the time the single, *Keys To Your Heart*, was actually released.

The Clash moved into a rehearsal space near Camden Lock in June 1976 and Dingwalls' late-licence made it an attractive hang-out for them, the Pistols and the Damned. When the Ramones made their UK debut at the Roundhouse on July 4, supported by the Flamin' Groovies and the Stranglers, they also played an extra show at Dingwalls the night afterwards. It was attended by many of the musicians who'd gone to the previous night's gig, including the Pistols and the Clash.

> *"Myself and Philip Lynott were up at Dingwalls one night when it first opened. We'd been drinking Southern Comfort and were definitely the worse for wear and Philip made some gesture towards a bouncer who came up behind us and whacked him one. A fight started and the bouncer was kicking us around the floor and it carried on into the courtyard, then out onto Camden High Street. One guy pulled a baseball bat out and started trying to smash up our cars, so I drove up the road trying to get away. Anyway, the guy turned out to be Callan, the mad mercenary who shot about six of his own men in Angola..." – FRANK MURRAY*

Muddy Waters onstage at Dingwalls, December 1978 [Paul Slattery]

THE ROCK'N'ROLL GUIDE TO CAMDEN

By December 1976, the Pistols had sworn at Bill Grundy on a tea-time news show and it became difficult for punk bands to get gigs. Many of the key bands continued to attend gigs at Dingwalls and use it as a late-night drinking joint. Just back from the Anarchy In The UK Tour, the Pistols, the Clash, the Heartbreakers and the Damned (who'd left the tour a little earlier than planned) plus Lee Brilleaux, Philip Lynott and Lemmy all turned up to see the Flamin' Groovies play at the *NME* Christmas Party here in December 1976.

"Dingwalls was where I met Rat Scabies," says Lemmy. "He came up to me and said, 'So, one of the old guard, hey?' And I said, 'Who the fuck are you, you snotty little fucker?' And he said, 'I'm Rat Scabies.' I said, 'Oh, I've read about you in the *NME*. They don't like you, do they?' He said, 'No' and I said, 'They don't like me, either, so that's all right.' He said, 'Come on then, I'll buy you a drink.' We got on very well after that, me and Rat."

By the summer of 1977, John Lydon was fair game for whatever late-night aggro was going. When he attended a Pirates' gig at Dingwalls, on June 23, 1977, he was hit by a glass and thrown to the floor. It probably wouldn't have been so bad if someone hadn't attacked him with a razor outside a North London pub four nights before that.

Yet it wasn't just the punk elite or those looking for a late-night brawl who were attracted to this place. Muddy Waters once insisted on being driven straight to Camden as soon as his plane had touched down in London, just so he could have a drink at Dingwalls before checking into his hotel in a completely different part of town. "I remember the legendary night Muddy Waters played at Dingwalls in 1978," says Barry Appleby. "We're in the queue for the guest list and my mate taps me on the shoulder and nods at these two guys in front of us. It's Eric Clapton — I mean, I'd already met him at a Buddy Holly night in Kilburn, I've had my time with Eric, thank you. So I say to my mate, 'What are you going on about? That's just Eric Clapton' and he goes, 'Didn't you see who he was with?' And it was only Bob Dylan, with his hood up. He was a tiny guy, whereas you expect someone Arnie Schwarzenegger's size — you know, Bob Dylan, big neon sign saying *Blonde On Blonde*, but Bob don't want none of that."

Van Morrison has also shown up at Dingwalls from time to time, such as on the night that Ben E King played in 1978. Among the other notable bands to appear here during the late-70s are AC/DC [featuring their 17-year-old guitarist Angus Young in his trademark shorts], Jet Harris, Elvis Costello, Blondie, The Cramps, Generation X and Madness. "The first time we played at Dingwalls, my mum and a load of her mates came down," says Suggs. "We were standing outside and they were getting a bit out of control. I mean, we had a reputation for being a bit rowdy but when our parents turned up, all hell was let loose. Anyway, the next thing was that my mum and her friends had fallen into the canal two minutes before we were due on stage. So it was

Debbie Harry at Dingwalls, January 1978 [Paul Slattery]

U2 on their first trip to London at Dingwalls, December 1979 [Paul Slattery]

pandemonium, fishing Madness's parents out of the canal, and then they just stood there, these bedraggled people, waving bottles of wine around at the front of the stage."

Dingwalls was one of the three London venues that U2 played at on their first visit to England in December 1979 — although they fared slightly better here than at one of the other gigs at Islington's Hope & Anchor, where only nine people bothered to show up. Still unsigned at the time, Bono was determined to emotionally connect with the audience. He shouted at them, sat among them, asked someone for a light and climbed on the amps in an attempt to communicate. However, the band couldn't help being disappointed by the crowd's indifference. "They were strange days when you're just off the boat in a foreign land," Adam Clayton recalled later. "I mean, England is a foreign land if you come from Dublin and it can make you feel very small."

In 1982, Dingwalls came under new management and they decided to open up a chain of provincial venues under the same name. Hence, Sheffield, Liverpool, Newcastle, Hull and Bristol all got their own Dingwalls, but some of them had closed down within six months. The main reason why Camden Dingwalls continued to be so successful was that it had an impeccable booker in Boss Goodman, one of the original London mods and former manager of the Social Deviants, who started booking bands here soon after the venue opened in 1974. Goodman firmly believed that music is best performed at club level and found that R&B legends like Muddy Waters, Queen Ida, Etta James and Bo Diddley were happy to play Dingwalls again and again. "In the States, artists like Dolly Parton still choose to play small clubs, like the Bottom Line, when they could easily fill Madison Square Gardens," Goodman once told journalist Roy Carr. "They do it because they're aware that they'll probably give better performances before a small and appreciative audience."

The fact that so many great R&B singers played here helped to attract a whole new crowd. "The great thing about Bo Diddley, back then anyway, was that it drew all kinds of people together," says Paul Cwynarski, who saw him at Dingwalls. "In those days, the poor old guys just didn't know what people wanted. They thought that to appeal to the kids, people of our age, in their late teens, they had to either do it like disco or do it like heavy rock. But we had the original 45s, we knew all the obscure B-sides, and we wanted it *exactly* like 1955, with the maracas. I was so indignant that Bo Diddley didn't have any that I actually went to the front and shouted, 'Where's the fuckin' maracas?'"

By 1982, Dingwalls had become the centre of a new trash scene — a scene which initially grew out of a small group of people coming to see Bo Diddley here. Bo had been supported by the Cannibals, who were fronted by Mike Spencer, the former singer of the Count Bishops, who had once auditioned for the Sex Pistols, and was a minor legend around Camden. It was Spencer who had the idea of founding a regular gig called Night Of Trash, which involved the Cannibals plus bands like The Milkshakes, The Sting-rays and The Barracudas.

"Mike Spencer's idea was to get that whole punk rock ethos going with all these bands who were playing a different type of music, which was called trash," says Bal Croce, former singer of The Sting-rays. "Boss Goodman really liked the Cannibals, cos they were playing no-nonsense R&B, so he'd give them support slots to Bo Diddley. Then when they headlined at Dingwalls, they let us support them, which was just the most exciting thing ever for us. I mean, I remember going to see The Stray Cats at Dingwalls, before they'd been signed, and it was one of the wildest and most amazing gigs I've ever been to in my life. It's not fashionable to say so now but, for sheer excitement and adrenalin, I've never seen anything like it."

The trash scene took off in the early-80s, attracting a variety of punks, mods and rockabillies who were all disenchanted with their own scenes. "The trash scene was all about everyone going, 'Agghhh!', drinking seven pints of snakebite and dancing down the front," says Ski, who was a regular at Night Of Trash. "The music was crap but the social scene was brilliant, because there would be at least a gig a week at Dingwalls or the Hope & Anchor. The psychobilly thing kind of got merged with it and then it got psychedelic, because people started taking acid. So there was a point where we'd go to those trash gigs at Dingwalls, but we'd be dressed in 60s gear, and all these psychobillies would go, 'Uh! What's that then, Crosby, Stills, Pie & Mash?'"

A big part of the new psychedelia were American bands like the Long Ryders, Green On Red and REM, who all played at Dingwalls in the mid-80s. "The first time that Camden ever registered with me was reading a review of REM in the *NME* by Max Bell," says Phill Savidge. "I remember noticing the place, Camden Dingwalls, and thinking, 'I wish I'd been there', because REM were the band that I loved more than anything. A bit later, I came down from Nottingham to see The Replacements at Dingwalls. They cancelled twice and I remember standing in the queue for the third time with all these people saying, 'Oh did you come last time, then?' And so Camden, and particularly Dingwalls, felt like a pilgrimage place, because we'd come there twice, and travelled such a long way, but had yet to see anything. When The Replacements did play, they were pissed out of their faces and couldn't stand up, but they were brilliant."

When Boss Goodman retired from booking bands at Dingwalls, after 12-and-a-half-years, in September 1986, his testimonial line-up was made up of Dr Feelgood, Nick Lowe and Graham Parker, while other old Camden Town faces, including Lemmy, Rat Scabies, Martin Belmont, Dire Straits' Terry Williams and The Pirates' Mick Green, got onstage to pay tribute to the man who had booked so many great gigs.

Even after Boss Goodman's departure, Dingwalls continued to book lots of blues, R&B and rockabilly bands — Buddy Guy, Junior

Wells, Johnnie Allan, Ted Hawkins and Hayden Thompson all played here in 1986. That same year, Dingwalls became the venue for a Saturday afternoon rockabilly club, which turned into something of a Camden institution and still runs today. It started almost by accident, one day in May 1986, when a rockabilly band called Red Hot & Blue played an afternoon gig here. The resident DJ failed to turn up, so the lead singer of Red Hot & Blue, who was called Mouse, offered to play records before and after their set. Enough people danced to make it look like he was doing a good job, so he was offered a four-week trial to see if he could turn Saturday afternoons into a rock'n'roll club.

"It was an instant success," says Mouse. "I don't know how these things happen, but at that time there wasn't much going down on the rocking scene. It was also the first and only rock'n'roll lunchtime club and, because everyone has a day off work, they all came along. There'd be 200 people in there at one o'clock in the afternoon and then they gave me a Bank Holiday Monday, so I did an all-dayer, and somehow it started the whole rocking thing in Camden Town."

Mouse, who also started successful rockabilly clubs at the Russell Arms and The Monarch, and at the Boston Arms in Tufnell Park, DJ'd at Dingwalls on Saturday afternoons until June 1996. "We had live bands every week for about six years," he says. "They would go on about 1.30pm and do a half-hour set. Ten years ago the scene was incorporating blues, rhythm & blues, rockabilly and rock'n'roll, and now there's more of the Link Wray influence, more trash and a lot of instrumental stuff, which was unheard of back then. The old breed never really wanted to investigate the 60s. They always wanted to stop at 1959 because, if it was past that, it wasn't rock'n'roll. I pushed it beyond those boundaries — I started off playing The Sonics in 1989 and got a bit of an ear-bashing cos the diehards couldn't understand why I was playing it, but it paid off in the end, cos it kicked the door open for lots of other stuff like that to come on the scene."

In May 1987, Dingwalls also started a new Monday night club called the Panic Station, which specialised in indie bands, like Gaye Bykers On Acid, The Shamen, Spacemen 3, The Wonder Stuff and My Bloody Valentine. The club was originally started in conjunction with the short-lived *Underground* magazine and, when that folded, sponsorship passed to the Camden-based music weekly, *Sounds*.

During the two-year period that *Sounds* was involved with the Panic Station, between July 1988 and May 1990, it put on some great gigs, including the Happy Mondays, Pulp, The Stone Roses, The Perfect Disaster, Crime & The City Solution and Primal Scream. The most legendary of these is probably The Stone Roses, who played here in May 1989, just before the release of their debut album. "Dingwalls was one of the early gigs that was packed," says Andrew Lauder, who signed the Roses to Silvertone. "That was when people first started to take notice of them in London."

Although the Roses already had a massive following in the North, their Dingwalls appearance inspired several people in the audience that night to form bands of their own. These included Liam Maher, who started one of the few genuine Camden bands, Flowered Up, and Mark Morriss and his brother Scott, who became the core of The Bluetones. "I went to see The Stone Roses at Dingwalls," Mark Morris said later. "I guess that was my spiritual awakening to music."

"I used to go to the Panic Station virtually every Monday regardless of who was on," says Steve Lamacq, who was then the Sports Editor of the *Harlow Gazette* but also running his own fanzine, *A Pack Of Lies*. "You could have a pint, get chips for a quid at the back, and it always had a really good atmosphere. I saw some of the best and worst gigs of the time there. The Shamen were terrible, absolutely awful, and I also remember seeing a lot of those C86 bands, like The Close Lobsters, who were really good. There were three bands usually with one quite big indie-pop headliner, so a few fanzine writers went down there. So if you didn't get in there, you were scuppered, cos most kids wouldn't buy two. Anyway, one night I got there quite late and my spirits dropped, cos I saw all these people flicking through this fanzine, and it turned out to be Simon Williams' *Jump Away*. That's how we met, we swapped fanzines, kept in touch and both of us eventually ended up on the *NME*."

Faith No More made their London debut at Dingwalls in January 1988 and other notable bands who played at the Panic Station include The Lemonheads, the Red Hot Chili Peppers and Blur, who did a gig here under their original name of Seymour in October 1989. They would have been offered a record deal a bit sooner if Food Records' Andy Ross, who had already heard their demo of *She's So High*, had been able to get past the Dingwalls bouncers.

"They were supporting The Young Gods and there was a queue of about 200 people," says Ross. "So I swanned up to the front and this big guy went, 'Where are you going?' And I said, 'I'm on the manager's list' and he goes, 'What makes you think you're so important?' I said, 'Excuse me? I'm on the manager of the club's list', but he wouldn't have it. So I went to the back of the queue, which was moving at a rate of one person every 30 seconds, and I missed their set. I saw them at the Powerhaus just under a month later and signed them shortly afterwards."

Blues and soul giants like Buddy Guy, Junior Wells and Curtis Mayfield continued to appear here but, by the summer of 1988, the rise of acid house had forced Dingwalls to widen its booking policy to include various club nights, plus Gilles Peterson's incredibly popular Sunday lunchtime jazz session. "My big memory of Dingwalls is Gilles Peterson's club," says Ben Jones, who was a regular. "It was so unbelievably trendy, with all this really fantastic dance-jazz music and great bands."

The atmosphere of these Sunday afternoons partly inspired Paul

Weller to choose Dingwalls as the venue for his low-key return to a London stage in November 1990. Six months later, Dingwalls ceased to be a regular venue when the Panic Station held its final night. Then, in the summer of 1991, Dingwalls' lease expired and it was forced to vacate Camden Lock, which was undergoing extensive redevelopment.

By the following year, Dingwalls had been given a complete face-lift, making it much bigger and completely revamping the stage and bar areas. Rather than returning to live music, the comedy club, Jongleurs, moved in, putting on stand-up comics four nights a week. In 1994, though, Dingwalls reintroduced live music and bands gradually started playing here again. These have included Spiritualized, Placebo, The Fall and My Life Story, who were signed to Parlophone on the strength of a month-long residency here in March 1996 — which was quite fitting given that lead singer Jake Shillingford used to book bands at the Monday night Panic Station in the late-80s.

8. FUSILIER & FIRKIN
7-8 Chalk Farm Road, NW1. Telephone: 0171-485 7858
Taken over by Fusilier & Firkin's brewed-ale chain in the early-90s, this was previously known as the Carnarvon Castle. It was the Clash's local when they lived and rehearsed across the road and they could regularly be found playing pool here.

The pub was also renowned for live music at lunchtimes, which generally involved a variety of R&B bands, such as the house regular, Wolfie Witcher. "There was always something on at lunchtime in the Carnarvon Castle," says Mike Hart, who started working in nearby Compendium in the early-80s. "There'd be these guys from Glasgow onstage doing a mixture of Hank Williams and Jerry Lee Lewis."

In the late-80s, the Carnarvon also put on a series of indie nights — although there was some dispute as to how noisy an indie band was supposed to be. "We played at the Carnarvon Castle and almost got bottled offstage," says Faith Healers' drummer, Joe Dilworth. "They were used to Wolfie Witcher and we went on doing this completely freeform Sonic Youth noise thing, which was great, because it was completely unacceptable. Everyone just stopped what they were doing and stared, and some of them were unsettled enough to take up the point with us later. The Dublin Castle and the Carnarvon were the only two places where we could possibly get gigs at that time and they both made it clear that they didn't want us back."

9. HAWLEY ARMS
2 Castlehaven Road, NW1. Telephone: 0171-485 2855
Now completely refurbished, this bar is barely recognisable from the old Hawley Arms, which was famous for a jukebox which had more or less stayed the same since the 60s and a table football machine which cost ten pence a go. During the 70s, the Hawley's close proximity to Camden

Lock made it incredibly popular with market traders. "We all used to go to the Hawley Arms straight after work," says Alan Jones, who started a record stall on the market in the late-70s. "It would be full of market traders and people in bands and it was really jumping in there every Saturday night. The jukebox was fantastic — you'd go in there and the records would be going full blast and everybody would be leaping around, it was just wild. It was a key feature, because it really sets the tone for a pub."

The jukebox — which was classic blues, R&B, rock'n'roll and reggae, included everyone from Elmore James and Etta James to Elvis, The Who and Bob Marley — also attracted musicians and music fans on their way to Dingwalls. "Basically, if you were going to Dingwalls, you went to the Hawley," says Mike Hart, who frequently went to both places during that period. "The people who worked in Dingwalls quite often drank there, too, so it was mostly people who were into music."

10. JUNGLE CLUB
20 Hawley Street, NW1.
Now band rehearsal rooms, the Jungle Club was once the best illegal drinking spot in Camden. Its peak period was 1992/93 when it was the home of the Booby Hatch, which ran on alternate Saturdays from pub closing time until 3am.

"Anyone who'd been in a pub in Camden that night would come along to the Jungle Club," says Ski, who was one of the two main DJs there. "You had to bring your own booze — although they sold beer downstairs — and everyone would be on E or skinning up at the bar. I would cover all the black sounds, from R&B into funky blues, funk and soul with a bit of heavy dub at the end of the night, and Tony Bailey would do all the white stuff, like 60s rock and pop and garage, and we'd mix it up doing 20 minute sets each throughout the night."

The Jungle Club was tiny, with a capacity of about 75, though the numbers were frequently double that. In order to get to the dance floor, you had to climb up a ladder, which was sometimes as hazardous for the drinkers at the downstairs bar as it was for the dancers. "My only lasting impression of the Jungle Club is of someone falling through the ceiling," says James Johnston. "I just remember seeing this body plummeting downwards, which was really funny. But then he was kicked out onto the street for having the audacity to ruin the ceiling, which wasn't quite so funny."

For some people, the Jungle Club summed up the essence of what Camden was once about. "There was a sound that you used to hear at the Jungle Club when all the rockabillies were dancing," says Mary Byker. "It sounded like somebody was doing a tap dance, but they were all dancing in unison and it was quite amazing. It was almost like they were involved in some dark rite, doing some masonic thing — all going down to the Jungle Club and dancing to rockabilly music."

11. ROYAL EXCHANGE
Hartland Road, NW1. Telephone: 0171-485 1547
This little bar tucked off the main road has a reputation for being one of the genuine rock'n'roll pubs in Camden and was temporarily taken over by squatters in 1991. It has also had live music from time to time, such as in 1980, when a new landlord made Juice On The Loose the house band, but the customers can generally be relied upon to make their own entertainment.

12. THE NEW POWER GENERATION
21 Chalk Farm Road, NW1.
This had a brief life span as The New Power Generation, a shop owned by The Artist Formerly Known As Prince and exclusively devoted to selling his own merchandise. The shop was spread over three floors, each one equipped with TV screens which provided a non-stop array of Prince videos and display cases showcasing some of his stage costumes. There were CDs in the basement and a snack bar on the top floor.

13. LONDON ROCK SHOP
26 Chalk Farm Road, NW1. Telephone: 0171-267 5381
Opened in 1980 by Dennis Waterman and the popular 70s dance troupe Legs & Co, this shop specialises in professional equipment, including guitars, keyboards, drum-kits, amps and tambourines.

14. THE LOCK TAVERN
35 Chalk Farm Road, NW1. Telephone:0171-485 0909
Once a Camden favourite of Noel Gallagher's, this candle-lit pub soared in popularity when the Good Mixer became too crowded during the peak Britpop-era of 1994/1995.

15. THE STAG'S HEAD
Hawley Road, NW1.
The last sacred pub in Camden, tucked away just off the Chalk Farm Road. The walls are dominated by photographs of Samuel Beckett, Patrick Kavanagh and Brendan Behan, and poetry by WB Yeats, and the place is renowned for its unadvertised, traditional Irish sessions. The Bad Livers, from Austin, Texas, specifically asked to include the Stag's Head on their 1992 UK tour, after seeing a video clip of The Pogues' Terry Woods and Ron Kavana doing a St Patrick's Day session here.

16. LUNA
48 Chalk Farm Road, NW1.
This roof-terraced diner was once a restaurant-cocktail bar called Ferdinand's. It was the first relatively upmarket late-night drinking spot in Camden and had a clientele that included Rod Stewart, Steve Harley and Dave Stewart. "Ferdinand's was quite classy," says Frank

Giromano, a former regular. "But it was one of those places where you could always grab a drink after hours."

17. THE MONARCH
49 Chalk Farm Road, NW1. Telephone: 0171-916 1049
Now completely refurbished, The Monarch first established itself as a venue with a five-week string of Tuesday night gigs in February 1993. Even though the bands played without a stage, in the corner of the pub, The Monarch was originally seen as a new Falcon, attracting a similar breed of indie hopefuls and a few out-of-towners, such as G Love & Special Sauce. Over the next couple of years, The Monarch also staged secret gigs by bands who had moved on to bigger venues, such as Drugstore, who made an unexpected appearance here in 1995.

That same year, Mouse, the DJ at Dingwalls Saturday afternoon rocking sessions, started a Sunday lunchtime club called Blues & Boogie. "As soon as Camden was granted all-day drinking on a Sunday, I was in there like a rocket," he says. "I basically started it to play great black rock'n'roll music. Sadly, many DJs on the rockin' scene seem to dismiss black rock'n'roll but people came down cos they love blues."

The Monarch was refurbished in 1996 and the venue was moved to a private room upstairs. The people who had previously run Club Spangle were the first to promote gigs in the new-look Monarch and it was hoped that it would take over from the Dublin Castle as the place to be on a Monday night. It didn't quite manage to do that — although Geneva and Imperial Teen are among the bands who have played. Whatever bands may play here in the future, this is now a decent rock'n'roll venue which has managed to bury the reputation that the pub had throughout the 70s and 80s. "The Monarch used to be the most horrible pub in the whole area," says Suggs. "There were always people coming out of there with bottles sticking out of their heads — although none of us were ever really interested in finding out exactly what went on in there."

18. MODERN AGE VINTAGE CLOTHING
65 Chalk Farm Road, NW1. Telephone: 0171-482 3787
This stocks a great selection of vintage clothing, from the 40s through to the 70s, and it also has a downstairs hire department where various bands, including U2 and the Manic Street Preachers, have kitted themselves out for video shoots. But the shop's most famous customer was probably Madonna, who hired several outfits from here when she played Eva Perón in *Evita*.

The women's section includes fake fur coats, dresses, original mini skirts, shoes, sequined tops, period swimwear and a wide range of accessories. For men, there are smoking jackets, silk tuxedos and a large selection of Hawaiian shirts. You can also rent ballgowns, cocktail dresses and wedding clothes although you won't be able to get hold of

Madonna's costumes because they went on exhibition and will not be coming back to the shop.

19. BELGO NOORD
72 Chalk Farm Road, NW1. Telephone: 0171-267 0718

This grey, bunker-like building houses one of the trendiest restaurants in Camden. A narrow drawbridge takes you directly above the steam and noise of the kitchen into a large dining area, which looks like a cross between a monastic refectory and a beer cellar. Much of this impression is down to the waiters, who dress as professional monks, in full-length burgundy habits offset by aprons. A favourite haunt of musicians, models, media types and comedians — Nick Cave, Shane MacGowan, Annie Lennox and Bob Geldof are all regulars.

20. CHALK FARM STUDIOS
Unit 2e, 10a Belmont Street, NW1.

Vic Keary's legendary little studio where loads of reggae stars, including Desmond Dekker, recorded in the 70s. It also attracted punk bands and this is where Joe Strummer's 101'ers mixed their debut single, *Keys To Your Heart*, in March 1976.

21. THE ENGINE ROOM
78-79 Chalk Farm Road, NW1. Telephone: 0171-916 0595

Before opening the Engine Room in 1991, Andrew James had grown up in, and later become the landlord of, the Devonshire Arms, which was the first rock'n'roll pub in Camden. The Engine Room's dark ambience, pool table, taped music and pop paraphernalia have given it a similar kind of atmosphere to the Devonshire in the mid-80s, but it has carved out a niche of its own by attracting musicians such as Morrissey, Jarvis Cocker and Tim Burgess to its Tuesday night Pop Quiz and by putting on live bands on Sunday afternoons.

When James and his wife, Jacqueline, moved into the pub it was still called the Belmont, which had already attracted its fair share of musicians in the late-60s and 70s, purely because it was directly across the road from the Roundhouse. "We used to drink in the Belmont, if we were going to a gig," says Lemmy. "It was just a normal boozer — although it wasn't if we were in there."

By 1991, however, it had been more than 10 years since a band had last played at the Roundhouse, and there wasn't a whole lot going on at this end of the Chalk Farm Road. The Belmont seemed like a particularly alien proposition to someone who had spent most of his life in the centre of Camden Town. "When we left the Devonshire," says Andrew James, "we were going to buy a bar in the States, and we were on the verge on signing a deal when we suddenly got cold feet and decided to come back. We looked around London and didn't see any pubs we liked, then the Belmont came on the market and, even though we knew it was pretty dead down this end of town, we decided to take it. At that time, there were just a few old boys drinking in here and some yobos in the back, who I ended up barring. So for the first three months, it was extremely quiet, I'm talking about half a dozen people on a Saturday night. Then we came up with the idea of putting the collage on the wall."

The Jameses covered the pub's walls and its ceiling in several decade's worth of cool pop culture: Hank Williams, Louis Armstrong, Little Richard, Jimi Hendrix, the Sex Pistols, The Stone Roses; film posters for *Angels With Dirty Faces*, *A Clockwork Orange*, the Adam West-era of *Batman*; plus gold discs and a commemorative mirror from The Pogues, which had once hung in a corner of the Devonshire Arms. The paraphernalia became the perfect backdrop to the Engine Room's Tuesday night Pop Quiz, which Andrew James introduced about a month after he had moved in.

"The quiz started as an attempt to drum up a bit of business," he says. "We had seven people down for the first one and we kept plugging away at it and word got round that it was good fun and more people started coming along. At some stages, it's been my busiest night of the week, even busier than the weekends. We've had phases where it's choc-a-block and loads of personalities started coming down. Liam Gallagher was sitting in the corner one night and I said, 'Look, who's over there' and Gordon, the compere, who hadn't even clocked him said, 'That's funny, I've got a question about an Oasis song here.' And when Gordon read out the lyrics, he turned around to him and said, 'Is that right?' and Liam goes, 'Hmm, maybe.' There were some people from *Melody Maker* down that night, so they had it in the paper the next week that Liam didn't recognise the lyrics to one of his own songs. It was quite funny. But the Pop Quiz does seem to have attracted a lot of bands, and certain bands that weren't really heard of when they first came, like Dodgy and Lush and Blur."

"I used to take Damon down to Pop Quiz all the time," says Andy Ross, MD of Food Records. "In fact, I take most of my musicians, cos it's good for hanging out with a band without looking like you're hanging out with one, because you've got a bona fide reason for being there. Chris Evans used to go when he worked at GLR, Ian Broudie used to go and Jarvis Cocker has also been down."

"I decided I should give the Engine Room Pop Quiz a go," says Jarvis Cocker, "when Mark, our guitarist, told me that the accumulator question was, 'What was the follow up to *Mouldy Old Dough*?', and apparently the person they asked didn't know the answer. There was £290 quid riding on that and I could have had it."

In addition to the weekly Pop Quiz, the Engine Room also started a Keep Britain Vinyl Campaign and, in May 96, got their representative, Lionel Vinyl, to record a seven-inch single called *My Love Is Vinyl* coupled with a cover of The Clash's *White Riot*, renamed

Vinyl Riot. "Basically, we were fed up of record companies and shops ripping people off with overpriced CDs," says James. "Real collectors don't want to buy CDs, they want vinyl."

The Engine Room started putting on Sunday afternoon live shows in 1997 and among the bands who have played are Edwyn Collins, Nikki Sudden and Beth Orton.

22. THE MARATHON
87 Chalk Farm Road, NW1. Telephone: 0171-485 3814
There used to be a faded sign above the door saying, 'Wine, Dine, Music', which is a rough approximation of what you can expect to find in this late-night Greek kebab house. It was named the Marathon, because its long opening hours present a bit of a challenge, and Shane MacGowan once did a complete 24-hour run. "Can I remember anything about it?" asks MacGowan. "Well, a lot of speed got taken and there was a lot of action in the toilet, which was a big, old outhouse with plenty of room to do anything you wanted. I don't remember there being a fight that night, although there must have been at least two over the course of 24 hours."

Steve Earle also came here during The Pogues' six-night stint at the Kentish Town Town & Country Club, in March 1988, with Spider Stacy and Cait O'Riordan, the former Pogues' bassist and wife of Elvis

Costello. Their all-night spree partly inspired the song *Johnny Come Lately*, which included a chorus line about drinking Camden Town dry in one night [Earle later invited The Pogues to play on the song when he recorded it for his 1988 *Copperhead Road* album].

"The Marathon is where I used to hang out in Camden Town with The Pogues," says Earle. "In the Devonshire and then in the Greeks. We'd end up in one of the two Greeks in the middle of the night, because they'd serve liquor until all hours. By the time I met The Pogues, Cait O'Riordan was out of the band and so I met her on that six-night stand at the Town & Country, and me, her and Spider went and closed down the Greeks. The old guy who runs the place said that he has known Spider and Shane since they were kids. He told me that they caught Shane stealing in there and made him work to pay for what he owed them — and he was only a teenager, I thought that was pretty funny."

Once a fairly low-key, late-night drinking joint, the massive rise in Camden's nocturnal population in recent years has made a 2.30am seat in the Marathon increasingly desirable. The take-away section at the front frequently resembles a scrum — with fights occasionally tumbling out onto the pavement — so the best place to sit is at one of the dining tables in the back. You have to order food, but can usually get away with stretching a Greek salad over a couple of bottles of wine. In the early-90s, Lush and Pulp were among the bands who regularly frequented the place after midnight.

"The Marathon used to be one of my favourite places to go for a drink in Camden," says Jarvis Cocker. "The main thing that it was good for was that you could still keep drinking after the pubs had closed, even though all you could buy were those small tins of Carlsberg for about £1.50, which was a right rip-off. The only reason people were there was to drink and you'd always see lots of people falling asleep at the table. It seemed to be like an endurance test to see who could be the last person standing, so it was a very appropriate name."

23. KYPRIANA HOTEL
89 Chalk Farm Road, NW1. Telephone: 0171-267 3912
The Kypriana has the distinction of being Camden Town's only rock'n'roll hotel — even though not many bands have actually stayed here. Originally opened in 1972 as a restaurant, four years later the Kypriana was developed into a 33-room hotel with a 3am kebab shop and a nightclub in the basement.

The nightclub was Frank's Funny Farm, which had started out above the old Marquee, on Wardour Street, and was run by Frankie Coe, a famous Irish rock'n'roll character who was a close friend of Keith Moon. Frank's Funny Farm was a semi-legal bar, with the Manhattan skyline painted on one wall, which opened after the pubs closed and ran until the early hours of the morning. "Frank's Funny Farm was the ultimate lock-in joint," says Shane MacGowan. "People went there just to drink and take drugs and pick up women. Also, it was very rock'n'roll. It wasn't like the Archway Tavern or something, it was quite elitist. Lemmy, Frank Murray, Phil Lynott, all those people went there — there were lots of Irish people at the mad end of the rock'n'roll business."

"Frank's Funny Farm was very much a muso and road crew's hang out," says Frank Murray. "You couldn't get a late-night drink anywhere in London, so you'd get all sorts of Americans, who'd come to town, do a show and then end up at the Funny Farm. It was full of heavy drinkers and nearly everyone used to drink cocktails, because Frank made such great ones. He was a dab hand at the cooking as well and, in order to keep his late-night licence, he'd give you a ticket to get some food when you came in. It was quite weird, though, because everybody was always drunk or had taken appetite suppressants, so nobody ever ate anything. At one end, he had this food bar which never really worked and, at the other end, was the drinks bar which everybody was always crowded around."

In order to join the Funny Farm, you had to knock on the door and then be personally approved by Frankie or one of his regulars — which generally wasn't too difficult. "Basically, most people who got kicked out of Dingwalls at 2am ended up going down the Funny Farm," says Andrew James, who was a frequent visitor. "It was probably more rock'n'roll than Dingwalls, though, because that was a venue with a big mix of people, whereas the Funny Farm was by word of mouth. I can remember meeting ZZ Top there — lots of rock stars used to go down, but everyone would be so shit-faced by the time they got there that nobody knew or cared who anyone else was. The only thing anyone was interested in was another drink."

Even though Motorhead were regulars, Frankie's place did not inspire their song, *Back At The Funny Farm* — "That's about being locked up in a lunatic asylum, but you never know, do you?" says Lemmy. Lots of people did, however, have surreal experiences at the Funny Farm, such as Joe Elliott, who bumped into his hero Phil Lynott in the toilets one night, just after Def Leppard had released their *Pyromania* album in 1983.

"Phil said, 'I just wanted to tell you, when I heard your album, it was one of the reasons I decided to split the group,'" Elliott told journalist Andy Strickland at Lynott's tenth anniversary commemorative gig in Dublin in January 1996. "I didn't know what to say. I didn't feel particularly flattered by it. It was weird, kinda *Twilight Zone*."

While the Funny Farm lasted, it made the Kypriana an attractive place to stay in — at least for 2-Tone bands, such as The Specials and The Selecter, who stayed here on early visits to London in 1979. "The 2-Tone tour started from London," says Rick Rogers, who managed The Specials. "We needed to find a hotel and we didn't have a big budget, so we started putting people up in the Kypriana, which was like £12 a night for a room or something. It was very, very basic, but it had one of the only late-night bars in London downstairs, which was Frank's Funny Farm. So you could go to Dingwalls, come back to the hotel, drink downstairs until 4 in the morning and then crash out — by that time no one knew what the rooms looked like anyway. It was a very useful little place at the time."

24. THE ENTERPRISE
2 Haverstock Hill, Hampstead, NW3. Telephone: 0171-485 2659
The Enterprise is not strictly a Camden pub, as it stands at the furthest end of the Chalk Farm Road and bears a Hampstead postcode. But it was an important point on the London folk circuit during the late-60s and early-70s, when Maddy Prior, Christy Moore, Terry Woods [who later joined The Pogues], Dick Gaughan and Sean Cannon all played at its Sunday folk club.

In the mid-80s, Joe Foster, who had been in Slaughter Joe and helped Alan McGee to start Creation Records, ran an indie night at The Enterprise. Among the bands who played here at that time were My Bloody Valentine, Miaow, The Go-Betweens and London garage scene stalwarts The Cannibals, The Wigs and The Sting-rays. "We played the Enterprise at one point," says ex-Sting-rays singer, Bal. "Our drummer Alec was very matey with Alan McGee and Joe Foster and he'd played on a Slaughter Joe single, so they gave us a gig there."

Later, the club was taken over by a promoter called Jon Beast [who went on to run The Time Bomb at the Bull & Gate in Kentish Town, but really made his mark as by encouraging people to shout, "You fat bastard!" at him at Carter The Unstoppable Sex Machine gigs]. It was at one of his Enterprise gigs, in August 1986, that Voice Of The Beehive were discovered by David Balfe and Andy Ross and subsequently signed to Food Records.

The Enterprise had a major facelift in 1994 and is now a modern Irish pub, dominated by a large square bar, with a coal fire in the corner, surrounded by shelves filled with old library books. The walls are lined with pictures of the great Irish writers — Patrick Kavanagh, WB Yeats, Brendan Behan, Sean O'Casey — and the faces of James Joyce and Samuel Beckett are etched into the swing doors, hanging side by side or clearing a path for the next customer.

Among the many who have stumbled through the doors over the years is Suggs, who has regarded The Enterprise as a favourite drinking spot since his days in Madness. "I keep seeing James Joyce in this pub," he told Roger Morton in 1995, "and he used to call it something like laser logic, where you could just record every fucking nanosecond of an instantaneous moment. That's what life's about! Because that's what you have to dwell in, you have to dwell there in the spark of when it really opens out and your life actually makes some sense, through the taste of a fag, and the taste of a pint of beer, when the sun's shining."

NEWSREEL: THE 60s

You used to ride on buses
Take a Tube to Camden Town
Now you go by aeroplane
But don't let nothin' bring you down

It's a shame, ain't natural for you
Baby, it's a sin
You know, you just can't win
When you are in

TEENAGE VIOLENCE FLARE-UP
Gangs of young thugs broke up a Greek-Cypriot café in Bayham
Street, Camden Town, and knifed a youth near St Pancras Station

THE 'LUSTY LIFE' OF CAMDEN TOWN
Gun battles and gang warfare among Greek cafés and nightclubs,
Greek Orthodox church services at "peculiar times" and the foreign
atmosphere which the Greek and Cypriot community brought to the
streets of central Camden Town, were advanced by representatives of
St Pancras Borough Council at a lands tribunal on Tuesday as reasons
why property there should not be highly valued

CAMDEN TOWN GOES ONE-WAY

CAMDEN'S 'REBEL' MAYOR
Cllr Paddy O'Connor, the Irishman who once led a hunger strike
through the streets of Dublin and later imprisoned the entire urban
district council, became Camden's new mayor on Monday.
Cllr O'Connor stepped on to the dais in the council chamber in his red
robes, fingering his new chain of office, and told the guests at the official
ceremony: "This will not be the first time an Irishman has been put in
chains. These are, however, more pleasant chains than is usual"

'LITTLE SOHO' IN CAMDEN? —
CLLR ATTACKS CLUB PLAN

TV FILM ON ARTISTS OF CAMDEN

GREENWICH VILLAGE IN CAMDEN TOWN

THE ROCK'N'ROLL GUIDE TO CAMDEN

DOWNING ST PARTY FOR CENTRE 42
Arnold Wesker, head of "Centre 42" — the Roundhouse at Chalk Farm — went to an advisory tea party at No 10 Downing Street, to talk about £600,000, money that needs to be raised to convert the former engine shed into a cultural centre. He was invited to the tea and talk party by Mrs Harold Wilson, wife of the Prime Minister

ROAD THROUGH CAMDEN TOWN MAY GO IN A CUTTING

GIRL ROBBED IN PARKWAY AT MID-DAY
— AND NO ONE TOOK ANY NOTICE

'WE BUILD THE HOUSES YET WE ARE
FORCED TO LIVE IN SLUM GHETTOES'
The Irish in Camden are still having to live "in slums and ghettoes", a political forum at Camden Town Hall, Euston Road, was told last week

MAN 'SOLD DRUGS FOR A LIVING'

Ways of helping the Borough's 'winos' — unwanted alcoholic vagrants who roam the streets looking for the next drink and a quiet corner to sleep — are being urgently considered by Camden Council

LOCAL PROTESTS HALT
ALL-NIGHT POP SHOWS
AT ROUND HOUSE

IT'S SEND SHAMROCK TO ENOCH WEEK
Irishmen in North London are reacting with mixed feelings to Mr Enoch Powell's recent statement that they should be classed as aliens. They have made September 7 to 14, 'Send shamrock to Enoch week'

Now the road is dark and lonely
But you gotta bear that load
You're up in Park Lane now
And I'm somewhere round the Tottenham Court Road

It's a shame, ain't natural for you
Baby, it's a sin
You know, you just can't win
When you are in
No, you just can't win
When you are in

KENTISH TOWN ROAD
&
CAMDEN ROAD

THE ROCK'N'ROLL GUIDE TO CAMDEN

"The dark end of the street is where the good bars are; it's where the hookers are; it's where you fix up; it's where people always meet... The dark end of the street is where the answers are."
— Shane MacGowan, 1991

1. ROCK ON
3 Kentish Town Road, NW1.
"Rock On closing? That's the end, isn't it? Full stop," said Suggs when he heard that Camden Town's most famous record store was closing down. Recently converted into a specialist dance record shop, it was Rock On that basically kickstarted the whole idea of pop stars hanging out in Camden.

The shop grew out of a popular record stall of the same name, which was at 93 Golborne Road, as part of Portobello's weekend market. The Rock On stall was set up in August 1972, by Ted Carroll, a genial Dubliner who had started importing records from America and specialised in soul, R&B, doo wop, rock'n'roll, rockabilly, country and New Orleans gems. The stall was one of the few places selling rock'n'roll rarities at the time and one of Carroll's best customers was Malcolm McLaren, who bought records for the shop that he and Vivienne Westwood had opened in November 1971 at 430 King's Road.

KENTISH TOWN ROAD

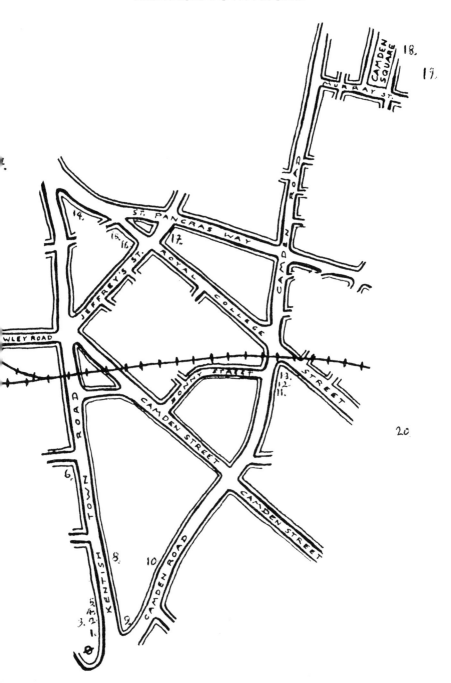

THE ROCK'N'ROLL GUIDE TO CAMDEN

"Malcolm used to send some rocker guy to the stall to buy all these records from me," says Carroll. "He'd buy five copies of this and six copies of something else and pull out a great big wad of notes. I eventually asked him who he was buying for and started dealing with Malcolm directly. I'd import a thousand 45s from the States and, each time I did, I would give him the list and he'd take a whole bunch. In fact, it was Malcolm's money paying for the import."

After a while, the adjoining stall was taken over by John and Molly Dove, who designed their own clothes, such as screen printed T-shirts in unusual fabrics. They decorated their stall with Elvis Presley wallpaper, which complimented the music that was being played at Rock On, and it became one of the hippest parts of the Portobello Market. When the Doves moved out, Rock On expanded into their stall as well, mainly because Carroll loved the wallpaper. "I was always getting requests for it from customers," he says. "People kept asking me to get a run of it, but it never happened."

In addition to running the Rock On stall, Carroll co-managed Thin Lizzy with Chris Morrison [whose charges now include Blur and Elastica] and, before long, Philip Lynott had immortalised both "*Teddy boy*" and his record stall on Thin Lizzy's 1973 single, *The Rocker*. Lynott wasn't the only rock star who could regularly be found hanging out at the Rock On stall. It quickly became a Mecca for anyone who was seriously interested in music.

"Loads of people used to come to Golborne Road," says Carroll. "We got used to attracting people like Jimmy Page, who bought a load of Sun records once, and Joe Strummer, who was always looking for a record called *Junco Partner* by some old blues singer. Then Malcolm McLaren started bringing down the Sex Pistols, who would buy Yardbirds records and stuff like that."

Carroll soon came to realise exactly what kind of records his customers were interested in. "A lot of French kids were coming to the stall," he says. "They'd come to buy mainly 60s stuff. I discovered that all The Rolling Stones and The Beatles EPs were still available from EMI and Decca, plus a lot of records that people were always looking for, such as anything by Them and Procol Harum's *A Whiter Shade Of Pale*. At that time, the wholesale price for 45s was about 38p, so we had all that stuff, and these French kids used to come over, record dealers, who were going round all the flea markets in Paris picking up all these great French EPs, of people like The Yardbirds, so we'd trade stuff."

By the summer of 1974, Carroll had decided to stop managing Thin Lizzy and concentrate on Rock On. "I was looking forward to having a fairly laidback lifestyle," he says. "I was going to run the stall in Golborne on Fridays and Saturdays and maybe do a little mail order and just drive round the country looking for records."

However, a diversion came when he got a phone call from another Irish friend, Sylvia Keogh, who asked him if he was interested in sharing a stall at the recently opened Soho Market in Newport Court. "I was already doing a stall at the markets at Portobello, Camden and Camden Passage," says Keogh, "so I asked Ted if he wanted somewhere to expand to at weekends. I was selling really good Victorian lace and all these wonderful theatrical kind of things and I thought we were going to make a mint because of all the theatres in the West End. Instead, Ted made a fortune and I went bust."

For a while, though, the arrangement worked very well — Keogh sold clothes in the early part of the week and then Carroll transformed it into a record stall at weekends. "We used to abracadabra the stall every Thursday night," says Keogh. "We had these heavy, gold brocade curtains and we used to draw them across and stick all our stuff into the back. Then Rock On would come and disguise that by pinning albums on the curtains. Ted managed to get other people to do Soho, because Portobello was his pride and joy in those days."

The Rock On stall was initially run by Frank Murray, who had also worked at Golborne Road. However, Murray was also Thin Lizzy's tour manager and serving behind a record stall didn't quite match the excitement of being on the road. So, after a couple of weeks, the Soho stall was taken over by Roger Armstrong, who had met Carroll when he was Social Secretary at Queen's University in Belfast in 1969. "I'd been shuffling around out of work for a while, so when Ted asked me if I wanted to run the stall while I was sorting myself out, I said, yes," he says. "It was great — just standing around and playing records all day, loads of which you'd never heard before but which turned out to be brilliant. Actually, it was all right when I joined in the summer, but then winter came and standing behind a stall was hell."

Armstrong would go 'junking' for records with Ted Carroll, trawling through boxes of old 45s at Petticoat Lane Market in the early hours of most Sunday mornings, while trying to ignore their hangovers from the night before. Word spread about this great new record stall in Soho and they were soon attracting a regular crowd. "The reason that Rock On took off was because record collecting was a middle class occupation," says Armstrong. "To a certain extent, you had to have money — you certainly had to have a job, to buy these secondhand rarities. We used to get these guys in their business suits, who I would later see at record fairs at the weekends in their jeans and sweatshirts. Rock On was like heaven to these business men who suddenly realised that their hobby was collecting records and at lunchtime they could go and indulge their perversion. These were the days when spending a tenner on records was quite heavy and I remember a couple of them asking me to give them a receipt for £2.50 to show the wife. Literally [*laughs*]. Mind you, it was the ones who used to come in wearing pinstriped suits to buy Iggy & The Stooges albums that I used to worry about — y'know, go home and change into leather and get into Iggy. In fact, one of the people in pinstriped suits who did turn up quite early on to buy Iggy & The Stooges records was Shane MacGowan. When I first met him he had hair down to his shoulders and wore this giant Oxfam pinstriped suit that was several sizes too big for him. Without a doubt, he was working in an office job and had to have a suit — I doubt if it fits the legend."

Other proto-punks who turned up at the Rock On stall were Joe Strummer, Mick Jones and various members of the Sex Pistols. "Most of the early punk bands used to come and buy records from us," says Armstrong. "Even though punk's roots were in the New York Dolls and the Stooges, most of them liked to buy a lot of different things, such as rock'n'roll and soul. That was the secret of Rock On — we were selling Northern Soul records when the other shops wouldn't have known what it sounded like if it had hit them on the head. We also found out that you could still order the two Stooges albums from Spain and that the MC5's *Back In The USA* was on catalogue in France so, through an importer, we brought truckloads of them in. At that point, you could buy Flamin' Groovies records by the thousand if you wanted to, but nobody did and we did. We had punks, Teddy Boys, old guys who collect blues, Jamaicans who bought a certain class of R&B — they all came to us. That was the great thing about Rock On."

Meanwhile, Ted Carroll had got together with one of his regular customers, Barry Appleby, and decided to open a shop in order to cater for his clientele all week round. "We wanted to sell reggae, surf, 60s garage, punk, country. That was the whole idea — sell the lot," says Barry Appleby. "Me and Ted were vinyl junkies as well. I'm not saying that the main plot of the shop was that we would increase our record collection, but we knew that people would bring in good stuff that we both wanted. "

Carroll looked at a couple of properties in Camden but eventually decided upon 3 Kentish Town Road, which had previously been a card shop. "The cheapest part of London was the Holloway Road or Camden," says Barry Appleby. "The Holloway Road was a bit of a trek for record punters but Camden was on the Northern Line and so our first advertising said something like, 'Only three stops from the West End', it's five actually, but we didn't mention that it was the Warren Street end of Tottenham Court Road."

Rock On opened for business in August 1975 and there was a

> "I first came to Camden in 1979 on a record-hunting, beer-drinking, rock'n'roll trip. I bought records in Rock On and had a drink in the Devonshire and hoped that I would bump into somebody famous, like Joe Strummer or Shane MacGowan, which I did. I remember leaving Rock On and thinking, 'I'm going to live here one day, I just know it.' I had to live in Camden. I couldn't live anywhere else." – PHILIPPE KORPAR-MIGRENNE

launch party in the shop, attended by the Flamin' Groovies, a few journalists, such as Nick Kent, plus record dealers and some regulars from Golborne Road and Soho. It was a free and easy atmosphere that would characterise the shop for the next 20-odd years. "We always had great evenings in Rock On," says Frank Murray who initially worked there a couple of days a week. "When the shop closed, one or two of the serious collectors would come in — such as someone from the original French record labels or Bleeker Bob from New York — and we'd sit there for hours. Anybody we knew who saw us sitting there would just knock on the window and come in. They were like spontaneous little parties that would go on from 6pm till about 9pm."

At first, Carroll continued to run the Rock On stalls in Golborne Road and Soho as well as the shop in Camden. The Soho stall secured its place in rock'n'roll history when the Jam's transit van pulled into Newport Court one Saturday lunchtime in October 1976, set up their gear on the pavement and played for almost an hour. They were watched by some journalists from the music press and the Clash, who happened to be eating their breakfast in a nearby café.

"When the Jam did the famous gig in Soho," says Roger Armstrong, "our market stall provided the electricity. I heard them, but I didn't actually see them because I couldn't close up the stall. They set up on the pavement outside the gate, plugged into our stall and played. People seem to forget that the Jam were in before anybody, they were a real early band, and Paul used to come down to the market stall all the time to buy Motown records."

In 1978, Ted Carroll sold the Soho stall to Stan Brennan and Phil Gaston, who later owned Rocks Off, another cool record shop in Hanway Street, and who employed Shane MacGowan to work there [Brennan was instrumental in the early days of The Pogues and produced their debut album]. Carroll also sold the Golborne Road stall. " I sold it to a guy called Rockin' Rex for three hundred 45s," he says.

By this time, Carroll was fully immersed in Chiswick Records, the label that he had set up with Roger Armstrong in December 1975, in a small room above the Rock On shop. [See separate entry on Chiswick: The First Record Label]. The presence of Chiswick Records and Rock On's close proximity to Camden Town Tube Station made the shop a natural hangout for musicians. Among the regulars were early Chiswick signings, the Count Bishops, the Gorillas and the 101'ers. By the summer of 1976, Joe Strummer had split the latter and joined the Clash, who rehearsed in a dilapidated warehouse on the Chalk Farm Road.

"Camden really became an in place in 1976 when Ted opened the shop and started his record label upstairs," says Jesse Hector, the frontman of the Gorillas. "The Clash were always there and so were the Damned — it was all young, flash-looking, short-haired guys who were hanging around in those days. It was a really fresh time, a bit like the mods all over again."

THE ROCK'N'ROLL GUIDE TO CAMDEN

"The Clash used to come in to the shop for a warm up," says Barry Appleby. "And Madness came in and bought *Prince Buster's Greatest Hits*, each of them, a week on the trot. They'd come in and then chip in together to buy it. They were nice boys, you never felt threatened or that they were going to nick anything. The Clash were a bit strung out some of the time, when they'd been up all night, but they were generally good lads. They were into music — when I first met Mick Jones he used to go round people's houses just to play their guitar."

Ted Carroll had become aware of the demand for records with picture sleeves, so he would import them from an innovative French record label called Skydog. "At one time, our speciality was picture bags," says Barry Appleby. "You already had the same record ten times over, on single, albums, compilations, but you still wanted that picture bag. We'd ring some guy that Roger knew in Sweden and ask for 25 Costello picture discs and give him 25 pub rock singles the next time he came over in exchange. So we'd have everyone from Van Morrison to Neil Diamond coming into the shop, checking out the mechanicals, to see if they were getting paid royalties on all their records. The famous people who came in always wanted to be anonymous. The Crickets came up on the Tube — I'm expecting a limo and there they were on the fucking Tube! Led Zeppelin were rehearsing next door in the Ballroom and came in and bought a load of blues stuff. They all had credit cards, but Rock On didn't take credit cards, so Planty was going, 'Here I am again, you bastards, the only one with cash.' Of course, the others were laughing because he had to pay for their vinyl fix. They bought an album each, but the guy who was working in the shop at the time had the nerve to say, 'Oh, I see you're from Led Zeppelin, do you want to buy any bootlegs?' So they got three of their own bootlegs and one of them was such bad quality that they were all laughing at the Jimmy Page solo — but they still bought it."

Elvis Costello was a regular customer at Rock On — but his most publicised visit to the shop was in October 1979 when he bought £50 worth of singles and albums on the Stax and Atlantic labels. The story made its way into the *NME* gossip column and was seen as the inspiration behind his soul album, *Get Happy*, which was released the following year. Among the musicians who have worked in Rock On over the years are Ron Kavana and Philip Chevron, whose band, the Radiators, had been signed to Chiswick and who worked here from shortly after the band split up in 1981 right up until he joined The Pogues in 1985.

"Working at Rock On was a really good job," says Chevron. "It introduced me to a lot of music that I only knew something about up to that point — R&B, soul, country, western swing, cajun — and so it was very educational. While I was working there, I had this idea of doing a single of *The Captains And The Kings* [a song from Brendan Behan's *The Hostage*] and, having heard *Pills And Soap*, I knew that I wanted

KENTISH TOWN ROAD

Elvis Costello to produce it. Everyone said, 'Forget it, you'll never get to him' but, because he was a customer at Rock On, I was able to talk to him when he came in the shop. He was interested, liked the demo and ended up putting it out on Imp, which he kept on as a record label."

Other people to work here include Bob Dunham, who became something of a minor legend when he served Bob Dylan — who bought records here in 1986 — and told him that he would have to queue up just like everyone else. The longest serving member of staff at Rock On was Paul Cwynarski, who started working here in 1985. "The thing about Rock On is that it attracted all the characters of Camden," says Cwynarski, who originally came to the shop to buy rock'n'roll records in the mid-70s. "Music is like a pied piper to them – and some of them are on drugs that musicians can only dream about."

Most of the regulars automatically assume that Rock On is the North London record store on which Nick Hornby based his best selling novel, *High Fidelity*. Even though Hornby says that the book was not based on any one place in particular, there are huge parallels between Rock On and his fictitious Championship Vinyl. "Hornby's book could easily be about Rock On," says Ted Carroll. "He managed to suss out the perviness of record collectors and just how far they will go to obtain certain singles or albums."

In recent years, Bobby Gillespie could regularly be found hanging out in the shop and Noel Gallagher made occasional visits when he lived locally. However, Rock On remained largely untouched by the arrival of Britpop in Camden. "The only thing that we noticed," says Cwynarski, "was that we suddenly started getting teenage girls coming in which, up until then, was totally unheard of. They'd come in and buy records that their favourite groups had recommended. They're into these groups who've mentioned Big Star in interviews and they'd come in and say, 'Have you got any Alex Chilton?' We'd laugh because we're so cynical and later on they started asking for Georgie Fame and The Small Faces."

In the 12 years he worked at Rock On, Cwynarski served everyone from Robert Plant to Matt Dillon, though only one of his customers managed to leave a really vivid impression on him. "The thing about Britpop," he says, "is that I don't consider any of those bands to be stars. They don't exude any charisma or magnetism, they're just like blokes you'd be next to in the pub. As soon as a real star makes an entrance, you're immediately aware of their presence, and that's what it was like when Barry White's missus, Glodean James, came in. She was the lead singer of Love Unlimited and she had the accent and the whole look to go with her fantastic name. She just swept into the shop, wearing this fantastic, figure-hugging, cream outfit with a high collar and a trail — it was like a stage costume, not the sort of thing that you wear in the street, much less the Kentish Town Road — and it was trailing behind her, and her fingernails were these gold, four-inch talons.

KENTISH TOWN ROAD

She came up to the counter and said that she had to have Johnny Ace's *Memorial Album* because it was Barry's favourite record ever, he'd got it when he was a teenager and he'd lost it over the years. Of course, I had a copy of it because Ted and Roger had reissued it on Ace and she was absolutely over the moon and said, 'I'm taking this straight back to Barry.' She was marvellous."

It is ironic that Rock On, which did so much to attract musicians to Camden, eventually became a victim of the area's popularity. In 1996, the rent of the building increased from £17,000 to £40,000 [it was £1,250 when Carroll moved here in 1975]. This prompted Carroll and Cwynarski to call it a day and Rock On officially closed its doors on the last day of 1996, although it carried on opening at weekends only until the following summer. It has now become a completely different kind of record shop.

2. AH HOLT
5 Kentish Town Road, NW1. Telephone: 0171- 485 8505

Originally opened in the late 19th Century to provide Irish labourers with work boots, Holt's was the first place in England to sell Doc Martens and is still one of the oldest and best shoe shops in London.

The original owner was Alfred Holt but, in 1916, he sold the shop to the Blackman's, a wholesale company who supplied him with work boots. Holt's is still owned by Victor Blackman, but it was his partner, Alan Romaine, who gave the shop its character. Born in London's East End to a Russian father and French mother, Alan Romaine started working here in 1962 and continued to do so until he died in July 1994, at the age of 71. He was a musician who had played in both the Johnny Miller and Billy Cotton band — the latter was a favourite of the young Marc Bolan, who once said, "When I was a kid I used to listen to all the Billy Cotton Band Show programmes."

Holt's specialised in Dr Marten boots, which were worn by skinheads and then adopted by almost every youth cult since. These days, you can get DMs all over the place but, during the punk era, Holt's was one of the very few shops in London which stocked them. Consequently, Alan Romaine was nicknamed 'Papa Doc' or just Alan Holt, which he used as his working name.

When the Rock On record shop opened next door to Holt's in 1975, it gradually attracted more bands to Camden, and some of them — like the Clash, the Damned and the Nips — would buy their shoes here. As a musician himself, Alan Romaine was predisposed towards these young bands and, in 1977, he was happy to let Chiswick Records expand from Rock On into a room above Holt's.

The Chiswick office also became the home of Trigger Publicity, a PR company set up by Rick Rogers. Trigger quickly expanded into management as well as PR, and their charges included the Damned [at the time of their chart success with *Love Song* and *Smash It Up*], The

THE ROCK'N'ROLL GUIDE TO CAMDEN

Specials and The Selecter. By 1979, Trigger had moved to 9 Kentish Town Road and Madness took over the upstairs office. The band spent so much time hanging round in Holt's that they included footage of the shop in various videos and got Alan Romaine to introduce their *Divine Madness* collection.

"Alan used to have a few stock stories about Madness," says Suggs. "The famous one was that we were upstairs in the office waiting to see if we were going to be on *Top Of The Pops*. But we were really late and, in the meantime, Secret Affair, or whoever it was we were competing for a place with, had hired a helicopter and flown down there. Alan had an affinity for musicians and every now and again a Japanese film crew would come over to do something on Camden Town and they'd always go straight into Holt's, where there'd be posters of Madness all over the wall and he would reel off a load of stories."

The videos and worldwide press inspired hundreds of Madness fans to buy their footwear at Holt's, too, or just come here to meet Alan Romaine and hope they might bump into at least one of his famous customers. "I was always very keen to tell my friends that my granddad knew Madness," says Nick Roumana, who has managed Holt's since Alan's death. "I had a Madness watch that I used to wear to school and my Dr Marten brogues. He also got me and my sister a copy of The Specials single, *Ghost Town*, which he'd got Jerry Dammers to sign for us, so that was our favourite record for about three months. He had great stories about all the famous people he'd met, like Shakin' Stevens and Boy George — the Damned didn't really mean much to me, cos I was only a nipper then."

The first time Nick Roumana came to his granddad's shop was in 1982, after his father had taken him to a Tottenham Hotspur match. "It was about 5.30pm, but the shop was absolutely packed with all these skinhead guys," he says. "My granddad gave me a cold drink and an ice-lolly, from the fridge that he had, and sat me down in his chair, while this whole melee of boots were being thrown everywhere. In those days, you couldn't get the boots out of the shop fast enough. There was none of this trying on 15 pairs and then walking out with nothing — the choice was much smaller then and everyone knew what they wanted. Basically, it was a choice between black or cherry red."

Nick Roumana took a part-time job in the shop in his early teens and seems to have inherited his grandfather's ability to remember faces

"When Bernie Rhodes was managing the Clash, he used to go into Holt's and buy seven pairs of exactly the same brothel creepers — one for each day of the week, so that his shoes always looked brand new. He'd come back about once every six months and pick a different colour." — RICK ROGERS

and shoe sizes, in much the same way that a good publican knows what their regulars drink. "If someone had been into the shop more than two or three times, my granddad would recognise them," he says. "I used to run the shop as manager when he was on holiday, a couple of times a year, and he trusted me. I could never replace him, but I think his spirit's still here in the shop looking after it."

Since 1989, lots of other shops selling Doc Martens have sprung up on Camden High Street, but Holt's continues to attract a loyal clientele — and the faded, graffitied posters of Madness and The Specials that line the shop's back wall bear testament to its rock'n'roll history. "Morrissey used to come in all the time when he lived in Camden," says Nick Roumana. "Liam Gallagher came in once, but he didn't buy anything. Dave Vanian still comes in and Madness do, obviously. Even Tony Benn, the MP, has been in. Camden's full of famous people — if you walk out of the door you'll bump into five of them."

Although Holt's stock some of the fancy Doc Marten footwear, they still specialise in the classic eight-hole DM boot in black, cherry red and green. "We cut our teeth on hobnail boots and we used to sell socks as well," says Nick Roumana. "Working men would come in and ask for a pair of hobnail boots, size ten, a pair of socks and a pair of leather tongs — which were basically laces — and they'd give you the money, go out the door, be picked up on the lorry and go off to work. My granddad had a very fond place in his heart for the Irish navvies. He always remembered who they were, no matter how little they spent, because they'd be back every year for a new pair of boots, rather than someone who'd spend £100 and not come in again for years. He never forgot the fact that selling so many work boots round here was directly linked to us stocking DMs, because we first started selling them as a basic work shoe. The first few years they didn't sell at all, and the rest is history."

3. CAMDEN TOWN RECORDS
5 Kentish Town Road, NW1.
The upstairs of Holt's shoe shop is also the home of Camden Town Records, a label started by Nick Garrard in 1989 which was exclusively devoted to releasing seven-inch singles. The label was launched with the help of a loan from Roger Armstrong, who co-founded Chiswick Records in 1975, and the name Camden Town Records was a nod to the older label. "I always wanted to do this," says Nick Garrard. "But it was only when the record industry started to phase out the single that I knew I had to make it a seven-inch label."

Camden Town Records focussed on local bands, and its first three releases were The Johnson Family's *(I Don't Wanna Boyfriend, I Just Wanna) Motorcycle*, followed by the Earls Of Suave's *A Cheat/Who Will The Next Fool Be?* and Dave Vanian's Phantom Chords' *Town Without Pity.*

THE ROCK'N'ROLL GUIDE TO CAMDEN

4. THE FRIENDLY DINER
7-9 Kentish Town Road, NW1. Telephone: 0171-482 0901

The two buildings that this Chinese restaurant now occupies have a fairly significant rock'n'roll history. Number 7 was once a restaurant, run by a Greek-Cypriot family called the Evangelis, whose son, Barry, started Proto Records in a room upstairs. His first signing was Hazell Dean, whose success enabled Evangeli to do a licensing and distribution deal with Divine. He shared the office with the record producer Pete Waterman, who wrote *I'm So Beautiful* for Divine and also produced Hazell Dean. While Stock Aitken Waterman became extremely successful, Evangeli ran into serious financial difficulties and ended up doing an overnight runner to Cyprus, leaving Proto Records to go into liquidation. Meanwhile, downstairs had been turned into a French restaurant, with extremely generous licensing hours. It was another of Shane MacGowan's favourite haunts and this is where The Pogues conducted most of their interviews between 1985 and 1989.

Trigger Management, who were responsible for The Specials and The Selecter, moved into an office above 9 Kentish Town Road in 1979, which was then an electric shop. So this building— like Holt's shoe shop — was heavily associated with 2-Tone. In 1986, the office was taken over by Frank Murray's management company, Hill 16, which looked after The Pogues and Kirsty MacColl.

5. TSUKUSHI
11 Kentish Town Road, NW1. Telephone: 0171-267 1086

Tsukushi is one of the smallest Japanese restaurants in London but, before it opened in the early-90s, this building was the home of the Giromano family, who ran a legendary Italian café. It was originally called the Favourite and later renamed Pascal's and served the biggest, best and cheapest dinners in Camden Town and inevitably attracted lots of musicians and local characters.

Joe Giromano was a farmer who came to the area in 1966 after his sister, who had a place on Camden Road, assured him that, "Café society is what London is all about." The Giromanos took over the Favourite, which had been an English caff and — without changing the name — turned it into an Italian fry-up joint. Maria Giromano was a brilliant cook and served such enormous portions that her husband was soon renamed 'Pork Chop Joe' by the Irish workers who ate big, greasy breakfasts before they went to work at 5.30am and returned for their dinner 12 hours later.

"It was predominantly an Irish working men's café," says Frank Giromano, who was four-years-old when his family moved to Camden and spent the next 22 years of his life here. "It had sawdust on the floor and loads of watches on the shelves — if anyone wanted credit, my father would take their watch off them and hang it on the shelf until they got their wages and could pay their bills. My father used to open the place up at 5 o'clock in the morning and I could hear the Irish workers from my room upstairs, shouting, 'Come on, Joe, get the fuckin' boiler on, it's freezing.'

"What made it for me, when I was young, was it had a scary appeal. It would be dark at that time in the morning and the characters had hard-set faces. I used to wait for this guy to turn up. He never spoke to me, he'd just stand there with a suitcase, open it up, take a flask out and give it to me. I never took my eyes off him — I'd hand the flask to my father, who'd fill it up, then he'd give me a sixpence, put the flask of tea in his case, take a concertina out and play me a tune. I'd be standing there hypnotised listening to this music, then he'd put it back in his suitcase and walk away. Every morning, the same thing. There were magicians as well — there were loads of magicians about in those days — and they'd show me the tricks they could do while I was eating my breakfast before school. I'd have bread and coffee and they'd go, 'Whatcha got there, boy?' in these strange accents. It was fascinating, but those characters all disappeared over the years."

As well as being popular with Irish labourers, the Favourite was an early morning haunt of the original punks who would stay up all night and then come here for a 7am dish of spaghetti bolognaise and chips. "The Clash came in, Phil Lynott came in — they all did," says Frank Giromano.

"I had spaghetti bolognaise and chips in the Favourite with Vince Taylor," says Barry Appleby, who was working in Rock On when Taylor's *Brand New Cadillac* was released on Chiswick. "All I'd been told was, 'Vince Taylor's turning up, look after him', which meant take him for a cup of tea and give him a ten minute chat about London's history. There was me thinking he was American — his baby driving up in a Cadillac and all that — but he wasn't, he was English, he used to hang out with Bowie. But, yeah, I think he had spaghetti bolognaise and sausages, and it was beautiful."

By the early-80s, the building trade had started to decline and there was less demand for fry-ups. It was at this point that the Favourite was revamped into an Italian café and renamed Pascal's, after the Giromanos' eldest son. A take-away service was installed at the front, selling sandwiches and pastries, and there were just four, much-coveted tables in the tiny room at the back. Despite being a fairly well-guarded secret, Pascal's was always packed, with a queue waiting, at lunchtimes. At Christmas, Maria would produce a huge bottle of whiskey and insist that her regulars had a 'little' shot, before pouring out a glass that was almost as huge as her platefuls.

"The Giromanos were a great family who really enriched the whole area," says Frank Murray, who ate here all the time. "We used to call Joe's wife Mama, because she had a very motherly approach and would slag you off if you didn't clear your plate and would give you an extra piece of chop if you were lucky enough to be one of her favourites.

Later on, when I had an office next door, she would send up my dinner to me on a plate."

Unfortunately, after a lengthy legal dispute with one of their neighbours, the Giromanos were forced to leave their home. Hundreds of local people signed a petition to try to stop them from being evicted, but the café closed in October 1988. A little community was destroyed overnight and only George & Niki's, on Parkway, has ever come close to capturing the spirit of the old Favourite or Pascal's.

6. THE DEVONSHIRE ARMS
33 Kentish Town Road, NW1. Telephone: 0171-284 0562

The Devonshire Arms has the distinction of not only being the first rock'n'roll pub in Camden but also being the first pub in London to hold a regular weekly music session. The latter had been established by 1948 when six musicians from the West Coast of Ireland gathered here with fiddles and flutes on a weekly basis, before relocating to the Black Cap on Camden High Street a couple of years later.

However, it is for its rock'n'roll years, which lasted from the late-70s until the late-80s, that the Devonshire is best remembered. At that time, the pub was run by Ned and Ailish James, an Irish couple from Sligo and Dublin, who had previously run the Lamb Tavern on the Caledonian Road, before moving here in 1966. "My parents were offered several pubs in different parts of London, but they liked the location of Camden Town," says Andrew James, who grew up here and now runs the Engine Room on Chalk Farm Road. "When my parents first moved in, it was very much a working men's pub, so there was no ladies toilet downstairs. The way things were in the 60s, very few ladies went into a pub on their own, from what I've been told anyway [*laughs*]. But, if any did come in, they had to use the toilet upstairs. In those days, there were three bars and an off-licence. It stayed the same until the early-70s, when keg beer came in and all the breweries started changing the pubs around — that's when we took the snug and off-licence out."

It was the arrival of Ted Carroll, in August 1975, at the nearby Rock On Records, followed by the birth of Chiswick Records, in a room above the shop that December, which transformed the Devonshire into a rock'n'roll pub. Initially, though, Roger Armstrong, who co-founded Chiswick Records with Carroll, and Rick Rogers, whose PR company, Trigger Publicity, was based in the same office, drank in the Halfway House, most evenings after work.

"One night, just coming up to Christmas in 1977," says Roger Armstrong, "Rick and I went across to the Halfway House and asked for the usual order of a couple of pints and two toasted cheese sandwiches, and the woman behind the bar turned round and said the classic phrase, 'The new guvnor doesn't believe in sandwiches.' It became a standing joke for years — you know, the idea of *believing* in sandwiches! But, since sandwiches were pretty much what we were living on at the time,

we just turned round and walked out and the first pub we came to was the Devonshire. We went in and said, 'Do you do sandwiches?' And Ned said, 'What do you want? We can do them fresh for you.' He rang Ailish upstairs and two toasted cheese sandwiches arrived, and he got our two pints of Guinness and set them down on the counter, and behind them were two free measures of whiskey, and behind that were two Devonshire Arms pens, and we thought, 'This is just the ticket.'"

The pub also happened to be quiet, which definitely added to its appeal. "After Rock On closed, we'd pop down to the Devonshire Arms," says Frank Murray, who worked in the shop a couple of days a week. "There was a lounge and then a back bar which had a pool table. There was a little door that was about three and a half feet high, so you'd have to push that open and duck underneath to go through. There was never more than two men and a dog in the lounge, but there was never *anybody* in the back bar, so you could play pool to your heart's content. Also Ned and Ailish, the landlords, were really great people, who always looked after us, and you just can't reject hospitality like that."

As Chiswick began to expand, the bands on the label also started drinking in the Devonshire — including the Damned, Motorhead, the Radiators (From Space) and Jesse Hector. For Andrew James, who was in his early teens at the time, the new customers were fascinating. "Dave Vanian would come down to the pub on a Saturday afternoon fairly regularly," he says. "I remember him bringing this little kid into the pub with him — he'd parked his hearse outside and the two of them were dressed up the same, with the Dracula cloak on and the hair slicked back. The poor kid! Ted and Roger used to bring new faces into the pub every day of the week. It didn't mean anything to anybody because they were nobodies at the time, it was only years later that I went on to realise who they all were."

Shane MacGowan, whose band the Nips released their third single on Chiswick, was one of the regular faces in the Devonshire. "I knew Andrew from the time he was about ten-years-old, serving behind the bar before his voice broke," says MacGowan. "He was convinced that I was in the Damned, when he was a kid, so I used to tell him I was Captain Sensible. I mean, if I had to be someone in the Damned, I'm definitely more of a Captain Sensible-type character."

By 1979, Rick Rogers had moved his Trigger office to 9 Kentish Town Road and started to manage The Specials. Coincidentally, Madness had an office above Holt's shoe shop, at 5 Kentish Town Road, so the embryonic 2-Tone movement also gravitated towards the pub at the end of the road. "When I started managing The Specials," says Rick Rogers, "they came to the Devonshire Arms with me, so Madness would come there, too. Then, as the 2-Tone thing grew, we started doing interviews there. The pub got mentioned in features a few times and the place started filling up, but not horrendously."

Despite the Chiswick and 2-Tone connections, the Devonshire

continued to be a quiet, old men's pub until the early-80s. "I remember the first time I took a girlfriend into the back bar of the Devonshire," says Nick Garrard, who started doing art work for Chiswick in 1979 and became a regular. "I got the first round of drinks for free. I said, 'Why?' and the landlord said, 'Because I've never had a girl in this bar before.' That's what it was like. If anyone brought their wife in they'd sit in the saloon — the back room was spit and sawdust with lino on the floor. There were about 30 or 40 of us, who would take over the back room; we actually forced the old boys out. There was Bob Dunham from Rock On, Nigel Lewis and Mark Robertson from The Meteors and Dave Preston, who was a drummer from the 60s who played with The Creation and Nirvana and bands like that."

Garrard and his crew soon made themselves more at home by bringing in their own records for the jukebox. "We had a jukebox in the late-70s," says Andrew James, "and then Nick put a load of his records in there and that's what we used to listen to all the time. There was a gang of them who used to come in every weekend, so it was like their jukebox, because nobody else really played it. It wasn't a music pub or anything then, it was just your average local boozer."

The real change to the pub came in 1982 when the new breakfast television company, TV-am, moved into an expensive new building across the road. Around the same time, the Devonshire itself underwent a major refurbishment and was converted into one big lounge bar and decked out in red velvet. The TV-am crowd subsequently started drinking here, bringing the guests who had appeared on the early morning show with them, and ordering bottles of champagne more frequently than pints of Guinness. This came to an abrupt halt one day when someone ordered another bottle of champagne and Ned James told them that he'd run out. "When will you be getting some more in?" they asked. "We won't," he said.

It was moments like this that stopped the Devonshire from ever becoming another media pub. By this time, Andrew James had finished school and was working in the pub on a full-time basis and he decided to get rid of the jukebox and either play records or put on compilation tapes of the records that he was buying in Rock On or Rhythm Records. "People in Camden latched on to the fact that we were playing good music and then lots of young bands started drinking in the pub," he says.

"They used to have a record player in there," says Alie Allerton, who worked at Rhythm. "I mean, you could bring your records in and actually play an album in the pub, which nowadays sounds like a really strange idea, but we used to play Charlie Parker albums and punk records and all kinds of stuff. By then, most of the people who went to the Devonshire knew each other on nodding terms. There was this disparate group of people, not big enough to actually be any sort of scene but big enough so that you needed somewhere for everybody to go and listen to something different."

THE ROCK'N'ROLL GUIDE TO CAMDEN

"For me, the early to mid-80s were really good times because we'd go to the Devonshire most nights of the week," says Nick Garrard who moved into a flat on the Kentish Town Road in 1982. "Dee Dee Ramone hung out there for a while and you'd have Jeffrey Lee Pierce sitting at the bar or Tav Falco in the corner. To see these weird Americans, whose music I really admired, in my pub, was great. "

The most important band to start drinking here on a daily basis, however, were The Pogues. "I'd been hanging out in the Devonshire since the late-70s," says Shane MacGowan. "It was a pretty quiet Irish pub which swelled out at the weekends with rock'n'roll kids. By the early-80s, I was hanging out in Camden all the time — The Pogues used to drink in all the pubs round there but the Dev was the coolest."

The Pogues' relationship with the pub was sealed when Frank Murray became their manager in December 1984 — Murray had been a regular for almost ten years and the Devonshire became The Pogues' official HQ. "The great thing about the Dev was that I could use it as an office," says Murray. "I was initially working from home and everybody knew that if they didn't get me on that number they could get me at the Dev. They didn't have a public phone, but there was a phone behind the bar. It was constantly, 'Frank, phone!', 'Frank, phone!' and they'd pass it over to me — I even had phone calls from the States. The Pogues would meet me there and then their friends started coming down and, within eight months, it started getting packed out. Everybody used to make up tapes to play behind the bar and I nearly always played the first tape of a new Pogues track in there. As soon as I got it from the studio, I'd go down the Devonshire, put it on the stereo and have a listen. You could tell everyone in the bar, 'This is our new single' and they'd all tell you what they thought of it, right there and then [*laughs*]. Everyone took an interest in The Pogues down there, they all wanted to know about where we'd been and hear our tales, so it was a really nice place to come back to when you came off tour."

When The Pogues made their first trip to the United States in February 1986, Andrew James and his future wife, Jacqueline, went with them. "Other groups take their drug dealers on tour," quipped Pogues' guitarist Philip Chevron. "We take our barman!"

"Those were exciting times," says Andrew James. "The whole vibe around The Pogues was electric. It was great to be around a band that was really happening and played great music, because you can stick most of the 80s down a toilet and flush it."

On a similar note, one band who actually formed in the Devonshire was Shit — which was a kind of Pogues spin-off group featuring Shane MacGowan plus three of his drinking mates. "Their press photograph was taken in the gents toilet in the Devonshire," says Andrew James. "It was quite funny because they did a gig up at the Mean Fiddler and there was a band called Head supporting them, so the posters read: SHIT HEAD."

KENTISH TOWN ROAD

A more significant event in the Devonshire was the Sunday morning Irish music session, which was instigated by Ron Kavana in the mid-80s. "Sometimes you'd have 15 or 20 musicians playing on a Sunday afternoon," says James. "Of course, in those days you had to close at 2 o'clock, so it wasn't like it is now when you can stay open all day. The band would be just getting into full swing when you had to call a halt to it, which ruined it, especially with live traditional music. We used to get a lot of really talented musicians coming down, like bluegrass artists from the States, who'd come over to do a couple of gigs in London, and would just turn up. Ron Kavana was very diverse and, in some of the sessions, the sound was fantastic. You'd get various members of The Pogues coming down and other Irish musicians living in the area. There used to be this unknown actor who came down every Sunday morning, with Ron Kavana and all his mates. Everyone called him Ben, but his real name was Patrick Bergin, then he moved out to the States and the next thing I knew he was in a big blockbuster movie [*Sleeping With The Enemy*] with Julia Roberts. He was another one that made it from that scene. It's pretty amazing when you look at the people who have made it out of Camden."

One of the enduring stars of the pub was the James's Alsation, Duke [or, to give him his full title, the Duke Of Devonshire], who barked at 10.55pm every night to signal last orders and then went round the bar selectively growling at various people until they had finished their drinks. "That was a great dog," says Alie Allerton. "It barked at anyone it didn't like, which was brilliant – I actually stood on it once, but it never bit me."

By the late-80s, the Devonshire had become a favourite haunt of *Sounds* journalists, who worked down the road in Mornington Crescent. "A lot went on at the Dev," says Andy Ross, who first started drinking here in 1985. "It was my first real local — it wasn't actually my local in terms of geography, but it was my spiritual local. The Dev was one of those classic places where, if you stay there long enough, the world comes to you."

The Devonshire was the first place that Mary Byker ever came to in Camden. At the time, he had just formed Gaye Bykers On Acid, but was working as a roadie for his girlfriend's band, The Bomb Party. "I drove them down from Leicester to do an interview with Andy Ross in the Devonshire," he says. "The Dev was the music pub then and it was like, 'Madness come in here, all the *Sounds* journalists come in.' The fact that all these people went in this pub gave me a consciousness of the area and made me think, 'Yeah, I like the idea of this place.' So when I moved to London, I ended up hanging out with the Irish crowd in the Dev, they were drinkers and they were into music and it was just a great place to be. I can still remember the exact moment I heard *Everything's Groovy* on one of the tapes that they played in the bar and it was like, 'Yes, I've made it!'"

THE ROCK'N'ROLL GUIDE TO CAMDEN

By 1988, the Pogues had become so popular that it was no longer possible for Shane MacGowan to drink in the Devonshire. However, there were new bands coming through, such as Gallon Drunk. "The Devonshire was a good place to meet people, especially if you were starting a band," says Gallon Drunk frontman James Johnston. "We didn't even have a record label then, so I'd sort of force myself to go in there, just in order to get gigs or whatever, and that's where I met Nick Brown, who signed us to his record label, Clawfist. After a while, though, the cycle of the Devonshire Arms followed by the Falcon and then just collapsing on our maraca player's floor became a bit much."

At the end of 1988, Ned and Ailish James retired. Andrew and Jacqui James took over, but later moved to Ireland for a while, leaving a relief manager in charge. The taped music was immediately replaced by a CD jukebox and the regulars started drifting up the road to the Duck Inn, down the High Street to the newly-opened Liberties Bar and eventually round the corner to the Good Mixer.

"The Gallon Drunk lot were drinking in the Dev by the end of the 80s and when they started going to the Mixer I followed," says Nick Garrard. "By that time the star spotters had moved out, because all the stars had gone and the new manager put a CD jukebox in, which played U2 at full blast."

The pub has recently undergone a complete refurbishment and is barely recognisable as the Devonshire of old. However, some of its old spirit lives on at the Engine Room, the pub which Andrew James opened on the Chalk Farm Road in 1991.

7. HONKY TONK RECORDS
235 Kentish Town Road, NW1.

This isn't quite on the Camden Town map, but it's worth an honorary mention because it was once the home of Honky Tonk Records, which was a shop, a rehearsal room and a general hangout for young musicians. In 1980, the shop also spawned its own record label, which was formed by Dave Henderson and Nigel Wilkinson, and whose bands included the Mysterons, 23 Skidoo, the Insex, Table 12 and Henderson's own Disco Zombies [Andy Ross, the future MD of Food Records, was also in the band and they had one great single in *Drums Over London*].

"The Honky Tonk scene was a crossover between older people who had the organisational nouse to actually get records out and younger people who wanted to play music," says Joe Dilworth, who was a schoolboy Mysteron at the time. "Plus it was a place where you knew you could go to smoke dope. I remember going to school one day and someone said, 'Did you hear that Honky Tonk burnt down last night?' And I was like, '*What*? My drums are in there!' So I ran down and saw the fire brigade carrying all the records out. The woman who lived upstairs had apparently left her gas on, but they did reopen Honky Tonk in the same place."

KENTISH TOWN ROAD

8. WKD CAFE
18 Kentish Town Road, NW1. Telephone: 0171- 267 1869
This futuristic café-bar looked completely at odds with the traditional terraced shops on the opposite side of the Kentish Town Road when it sprang up in 1990, but perfectly in line with the metallic Sainsbury's further along. Beth Orton played here as part of the annual Camden Crawl in 1996, but WKD is best known as a dance club.

9. HALFWAY HOUSE
2 Kentish Town Road, NW1. Telephone: 0171-267 2622
This is the nearest pub to Camden Town Tube Station and its main claim to rock'n'roll fame is that the Clash, and various other punk bands, drank here in the late-70s. "The Halfway House was brilliant," says Roger Armstrong. "It was a really Irish pub and sometimes they'd have this duo playing: it was this woman, a huge woman — I mean, an *enormous* woman — who would be sitting there as you went in the door, with this big old bass drum, with a snare and a cymbal, and she'd play the drums while her husband attempted to play the accordion, although he was usually so plastered that he'd just be lying beside her, with the accordion on top of him. It was a bizarre scene."

At the end of 1977, a barmaid uttered the immortal phrase, "The new guvnor doesn't believe in sandwiches" and the Chiswick crew decamped to the Devonshire Arms further down the Kentish Town Road. However, the Halfway House did have one great moment of rock'n'roll glory on the night of the Vicious White Kids show at the Electric Ballroom in August 1978.

"Before the gig, you had Sid Vicious, Rat Scabies and Glen Matlock all sitting in the Halfway House," says Roger Armstrong. "This was after the famous No Sandwiches incident, but obviously those guys didn't want to know about sandwiches anyway. On the Damned's *Machine Gun Etiquette* album, there's a track called Melody Lee, which is about a female character in a comic that girls used to buy called *Bunty*. Captain Sensible was a big *Bunty* reader, so he wrote a song about Melody Lee. Anyway, round about the time of the White Kids gig, *Bunty* dropped Melody Lee and so the Captain had spent the day of the gig picketing its publishing office. So he turns up in the middle of this *grand guignol* of punks — all the big punks are there, apart from Rotten, and they're all being very moody, welling back lagers and snorting speed — and the Captain walks in with a sign saying, '*Bunty* unfair to readers: Bring back Melody Lee!' I'll never forget walking into the Halfway House and seeing the Captain sitting there with his pint and his sign."

10. SAINSBURY'S
17-21 Camden Road, NW1. Telephone: 0171-482 3828
This large branch of Sainsbury's is housed in Nicholas Grimshaw's hi-tech building, which was hailed as an architectural landmark when it

was unveiled in 1988, but continues to be loathed by many of the locals. It was previously the site of the ABC Bakery, which was one of the most beautiful buildings in Camden but was demolished to make way for Sainsbury's. The ABC Bakery was open 24 hours a day, so it was common to see punks on cheap speed stumbling into it at 4am. "Sometimes we'd come back from a gig and go over to the bakers and have a fresh pasty," says Barry Appleby. "You could just go in and say, 'All right, mate, here's two bob, can I have some buns?' It was that kind of deal. You weren't going to graffiti the place, you weren't going to steal anything. They just knew you wanted buns."

These days, Sainsbury's has become the North London equivalent of Rockin' Ralph's, the infamous Los Angeles supermarket which doubles as a modern-day singles bar. It is also a good place to see local celebs doing their shopping. Noel Gallagher came here to fill up his empty fridge on the Saturday afternoon that he moved into his flat in Albert Street in January 1995 and was promptly followed back to his new home by a crowd of Oasis fans who sat outside singing one of his songs. He got used to the attention, although he quickly decided that trips to Sainsbury's were the worst thing about living in Camden Town. "You get people looking in your shopping basket going, 'Oh he eats them, does he?'" he told Stuart Maconie in June 1995.

Jarvis Cocker also shopped here when he lived in Camden. "Sainsbury's kept me alive during that period," he says. "I was still at college and I had no money, but they had this thing where you could pay for your groceries with Switch and also ask for up to £50 cashback, so I just built up an overdraft of about £1,000 getting cashback. I used to like going in there in the summer, cos you could take your sandals off and walk around with no shoes on, and it was also a good place to look for girls. I once saw Little Nell, who was in *Jubilee*, pushing her trolley round — she's getting on a bit now but I was quite impressed. I toyed with the idea of talking to her, but I didn't dare."

11. VINYL JAPAN (UK) LIMITED
98 Camden Road, NW1.

Vinyl Japan is a Japanese-owned record company associated with hardcore punk, garage, psychobilly and rockabilly, and has released records by The Flaming Stars, Snuff, the Revillos, the Television Personalities, The Stargazers, the Monochrome Set, BMX Bandits, Thee Headcoats, Thee Headcoatees and the Earls Of Suave. It was set up in 1990 by a Japanese record collector called Tetsu Nakatani, with the help of Dave Rhino, who owns Rhythm Records.

"I first came into contact with Tetsu in about 1984," says Paddy James, who now runs the label. "He used to come into Record & Tape Exchange and I used to call him Mr Cramps, because he had a leather jacket with 'The Cramps' written on the back and, of course, that band were the gods to so many scenes. Tetsu was interested in that whole

KENTISH TOWN ROAD

punk-rockabilly crossover, so he put out a record by The Polecats and a Snuff record. They also had a really good band on the label called SKAW (Some Kind Of Wonderful), who were a kind of Stonesy version of the indie dance thing that was happening in 89/90, with a fantastic blues harp." [SKAW later evolved into Pusherman].

Originally located on Camden High Street behind Rhythm Records, Vinyl Japan moved to its current location in 1996, Tetsu's only stipulation being that the word 'Camden' had to appear in the address. "The rocking scene and the 60s garage scene is still very much alive and kicking in Japan, so we do lots of garagey stuff and even noisy speedcore, like Extreme Noise Terror," says Paddy James. "We've also done other things, such as BMX Bandits who did an album for us before they signed to Creation."

12. ROSIE O'GRADY'S
102-104 Camden Road, NW1. Telephone: 0171-267 8806
Now a new-style Irish pub, this used to be The Eagle and was Suggs' local in the peak Madness era. "I spent a lot of time in there," he says. "I remember quite a few of us going in there once and dropping acid. We were all wearing those green bomber jackets and we turned them inside out so we were like the dayglo skinheads, the cosmic skinheads. Then we went off and had a very peculiar time down at Dingwalls."

13. SWANKY MODES
106 Camden Road, NW1.
This is the site of a famous women's clothes shop called Swanky Modes, which opened in 1974 and survived until the early-90s. It is worth mentioning because it was once the home of various musicians, including Clive Langer and Bette Bright [who had both been in Deaf School, the art-rock band that kickstarted the Liverpool new wave scene of the late-70s]. "One of the real milestones of being in Madness," says Suggs, "was meeting our producer Clive Langer who was living in Swanky Modes. Consequently, I met Bette Bright, who became my wife, so I started living above the shop as well. That was in the very early-80s and it was an extraordinary time — there was me and Clive, and six or seven girls, living a very bohemian lifestyle."

14. THE BLACK HORSE
313 Royal College Street, NW1. Telephone: 0171-916 1612
Back in the late-50s, the Black Horse became the first pub in Camden Town to have a jukebox installed. It was famous for its Cellar Folk Club, which was actually held in an upstairs room and attracted some big names during the mid-80s, including Ewan MacColl and Peggy Seeger.

The Black Horse also put on younger, noisier bands, such as The Wigs. Then, in 1987, Jeff Barrett — a promoter and press officer, who later set up Heavenly Records — chose this as the setting for a Saturday night indie club called The Back Door To Babylon. Among the first bands that he put on were the Happy Mondays, who played in March and returned again a couple of months later, dragging two crates of beer onstage with them to aid their performance. At the time, Barrett was doing press for the Mondays and other Factory bands and his PR assistant was Emma Anderson, who later formed Lush with her school mate Miki Berenyi. But back in 1987, she was the bassist in a ramshackle band called The Rover Girls, who also played at the Black Horse.

15. ULTIMATE
271 Royal College Street, NW1. Telephone: 0171-482 0115
Launched in 1990 by Maurice Bacon and Andy Winters [a former *Sounds* journalist who also manages Dodgy], Ultimate has released records by Terry Bickers, The Werefrogs and Submarine and they are also responsible for Club Megadog's Planet Dog label.

16. OLD EAGLE
251 Royal College Street, NW1. Telephone: 0171-485 3134
Another of the classic old Camden pubs, which has enjoyed an upsurge in popularity since The Falcon started putting bands on again.

17. THE FALCON
234 Royal College Street, NW1. Telephone: 0171-485 3834
The Falcon might be Camden's most famous indie venue — Happy Mondays, Blur, PJ Harvey, Pulp, Verve, Suede and Liam Gallagher have all been on stage here — but it was once a strip joint with a reputation for schoolgirl strippers.

The strip show plus disco, which ran four nights a week and also on Friday and Sunday lunchtimes, started in 1973 and — despite frequent complaints from the local neighbourhood association — continued until the late-70s. "The Falcon was always a drifters' pub," says Joe Dilworth, who grew up in nearby Camden Road. "There was a story about girls stripping in their school lunch break and, although I'm not sure how true that was, the Falcon definitely had an edge to it."

In the summer of 1982, a new landlord attempted to take the Falcon upmarket by introducing jazz music, seafood and Monday night theatre, which kicked off with a play about Oscar Wilde called *Work Is The Curse Of The Drinking Classes*. The theatre faded out but the pub continued to attract a bohemian crowd. "I drank in the Falcon from when I was at school," says Joe Dilworth, "because you could always get a drink there and the piano wouldn't stop when you walked in the door. It was pretty grim but it had a couple of pool tables, so we used to take mushrooms and go and play pool in there for hours. My friend Tom Cullinan, who had always been in bands, including the X-Men, put on one or two gigs in the back room but he only charged 20 pence entrance so no one bothered to go in."

KENTISH TOWN ROAD

In September 1987, Jeff Barrett, who had been putting bands on at the nearby Black Horse, switched venues to the Falcon. His club, which was named Babylon Revisited At The Falcon, really began to take off in February 1988 when Pulp played, followed by Lush, who did their first ever gig here in March. It was closed for a couple of months soon afterwards and then, having installed a fire escape, Barrett reopened it in July 1988 as the Phil Kaufman Club. It was named in honour of Gram Parsons' hard-living tour manager, who famously stole Parson's body and cremated his ashes at the Joshua Tree. One of the first gigs at the new club was the House Of Love, who had released their self-titled debut album a couple of months previously and were so popular at the time that as many people were locked out of the venue as those who had managed to get in [the official capacity was just 150].

"I remember Jeff Barrett saying, 'You've got to come up to Camden', when he started his club at the Falcon," says Mary Byker, who went there when the Phil Kaufman opened. "And it was this groovy little pub, full of the kind of people that you wanted to hang around with. But that was back when indie was indie."

Possibly the most famous gig to ever take place at the Falcon was The Sundays, who played here in August 1988, as a supposedly low-key support to Caretaker Race and instantly became the most talked about new band in London. "I'd actually gone to the Falcon to see the Caretaker Race," says Steve Lamacq, who was in the crowd that night. "But I got there early and I was sitting in the bar, reading the latest issue of Daredevil, when Jeff Barrett came out and said, 'I think you might be interested in this group, The Sundays, who are just about to go on.' So I wandered in and they were brilliant, just astonishing — it was one of those nights where it made perfect sense. At the time, the Falcon had one orange light bulb, no shade, that was the lighting, so the atmosphere was like you'd just walked into their rehearsal room. There was only a smattering of people, but it just so happened that those people included Robin Gibson from *Sounds*, Chris Roberts from *Melody Maker* and me and Danny Kelly from the *NME*, and we all thought it was great. The Sundays were quite different to anything else that was around at the time and it was so refreshing to hear this music that wasn't just an assault on the senses or something with a late-80s dance feel to it. The songs sounded chilling that night, really icy, but they sparkled, and it was all off-set by the fact that there was just this one orange light which sort of bounced off Harriet's face in the middle of the stage. Of course, the Caretaker Race didn't stand a chance after that, because everyone was in the bar talking about The Sundays and how amazing they were."

Like the Black Horse before it, Jeff Barrett made the Phil Kaufman a London focus point for the burgeoning Manchester scene, staging early gigs by Happy Mondays, who he was also doing press for, and the Inspiral Carpets. "Jeff Barrett was a catalyst," says Joe Dilworth, who continued to drink at the Falcon throughout that period.

THE ROCK'N'ROLL GUIDE TO CAMDEN

"He brought the outside world into Camden — he brought the Happy Mondays to the Black Horse and the House Of Love to the Falcon. But the main emphasis was on your jangly bands, like East Village and that kind of thing, and he would sometimes let me and my mates go in and have a look at whoever was playing and we'd go, 'Not really doing it for us.' But it did inspire us, because we'd all been in bands before and we just thought that whatever we could do would be more entertaining than most of what we were watching."

When his friends, Tom Cullinan and Ben Hopkin, formed a noisy band called th'Faith Healers, Dilworth muscled his way in on drums. After playing at the Carnarvon Castle and the Dublin Castle and being immediately banned from both venues, th'Faith Healers asked for a gig at the Falcon, but were turned down on the grounds that they hadn't done any recording. They solved the problem by asking the girl behind the bar, who was called Roxanne, to be their singer.

"Roxanne added some kind of focus to the whole enterprise," says Dilworth, "and it also meant that people would give us a gig. We had one rehearsal before we did our first gig with her and it really was just like free-form noise with shouting over the top, which was fine as far as we were concerned. I mean, the whole point was to be as loud and as obnoxious as possible, in a Mary Chain kind of a way. There was much more of a squat gig circuit around Camden then — My Bloody Valentine lived in Lady Margaret Road, in this big house with a very transient population — but the Falcon was the centre of the squat scene. At that time, the Falcon was completely underground, simply because no one else was interested in it and it didn't occur to us that anyone ever would be."

However, the Falcon wasn't destined to remain underground for much longer. By the summer of 1989, the Phil Kaufman Club had been taken over by Roger Cowell and renamed the Vertigo Club, which charged a 50p membership fee plus £3 for admission. It was during the Vertigo period — particularly on the night that Thin White Rope played here in July 1989 — that the Falcon fully established itself as the smallest, sweatiest and darkest venue in London.

"I've never been to a gig as hot as that Thin White Rope one," says Philippe Korpar-Migrenne, who lived locally. "The band's drummer almost passed out at the end of the set, in fact, he actually had to be carried out and laid on the pool table. You couldn't even light a cigarette in there because there was no oxygen. It was great. Talk about pub rock being hot and sweaty, that beat everything."

Thin White Rope's gig passed into minor legend and made the venue even more attractive to the upcoming bands of the time. "The Falcon's classic period was late-89 going into 1990," says Steve Lamacq, "because it was just as the whole underground/alternative thing was beginning to build. I saw Ride supporting the Popguns there, which again was a case of the support band doing better than the headline act

— I think a few A&R people already knew about them but from thereon in it went Creation's way. And Teenage Fanclub was one of the best gigs I ever saw there, it was absolutely fantastic. They started drinking as soon as they got in the van in Glasgow, so they were pissed when they arrived at the Falcon — they soundchecked and then they went back to the bar and by the time they got onstage they could barely stand. They started this one song, got it wrong, and stopped, so they started it again, got it wrong and stopped halfway through. They started for a third time, got it wrong, and then Norman went, 'No, no, *no*! Hands up who wants us to have another go at this one? Hands up who thinks we should just go on to the next one?' I think it was a few weeks before *Everything Flows* came out, so there was quite a bit of expectation around the band, but even though it was an absolute shambles and they knew it was falling apart, they were great. But if you played the Falcon at that time, that was it — that was the gig that set you up. Some nights, if you'd put a bomb in the corridor, you'd have blown half the music industry away."

Blur, Lush, Ride, Chapterhouse, Swervedriver and Slowdive all played at the Vertigo Club several times during this period which sowed the seeds for the much-derided 'shoegazing' movement. "I remember the first time that Chapterhouse played at the Falcon," says Joe

Dilworth. "They were really nervous and we didn't know why. At one point, somebody shouted out, 'Lemon Squeezer' and they got even more nervous so, after every song, someone else would shout, 'Lemon Squeezer' and, by the end, virtually the whole audience was shouting, 'Lemon Squeezer', because it was so palpably making them nervous."

By 1990, th'Faith Healers and Silverfish were spearheading a very different scene of their own. The two bands frequently played at the Falcon and also at the Sausage Machine, at the White Horse pub in Hampstead, and suddenly found that several other bands, such as Sun Carriage, Milk and Headcleaner, were playing a similar type of music. "A lot of bands who hung out in the Falcon had either started out as being very noisy or reinvented themselves," says Dilworth. "It was almost like being a teenager for the second time, cos it was like punk rock again. And it showed you just how far things had gone during the mid-80s that, all of a sudden, you could make an awful racket and be completely socially unacceptable — which was great."

This noisy North London scene was given extra focus when *Now That's Disgusting Music!* — an album recorded live at the Sausage Machine — was released towards the end of 1990. Even though some of the bands on the album didn't really have anything in common with th'Faith Healers or Silverfish, it was enough to constitute a scene, which was christened 'the Camden Lurch'. "I reviewed *Now That's Disgusting Music!* for the *NME*," says Steve Lamacq, "and it was then that it dawned on me that there might be a little bit of a scene going on. Th'Faith Healers' first single, *Pop Song*, had just come out and I thought it was brilliant, cos it was a really great, ramshackle punk record. Anyway, I went to this gig at the Falcon — I think it was a Silverfish gig but the girl from th'Faith Healers was in the audience — and there were all these people down the front who were throwing themselves backwards and forwards, doing this strange kind of lunging motion. There were loads of them doing it — when I say loads, I mean loads for the Falcon, which was probably about 20 people — and I was standing there with Duncan from Milk and I said to him, 'It's not so much the

> *"There's a great story about one of the other landlords in Camden. He was serving afters one night, till about 2 o'clock in the morning and the place was absolutely rammed. Someone called the police and they came in and said, 'Your licence ran out at midnight, it's now 2am, what's going on?' So he goes, 'Private party, darlin', private party'. So the copper turned round and said, 'If it's a private party, you'll know the names and addresses of everyone in here' and he goes, 'It's 2 o'clock in the morning, I can't even remember my own name and address, never mind anyone else's.'"*
> *– ANDREW JAMES*

KENTISH TOWN ROAD

Lambeth Walk, more the Camden Lurch.' And that was it, the Camden Lurch was born. The thing was, me and Simon Williams wanted to do features on Silverfish and th'Faith Healers in the *NME*, but no one would give us the space cos they were still laughing at our little Camden bands. They'd be having discussions about putting Prefab Sprout or someone on the cover and they'd be like, 'Are they big on the Camden scene at the moment, Steve?' So the Camden Lurch was basically just a tool to get th'Faith Healers and Silverfish into the *NME*."

Another band who didn't get roped into the Camden Lurch scene, but were also making a noise that was quite distinct from everything else that was going on in 1990/91 was Gallon Drunk. "One of the very few places where we could get a gig at that time was the Falcon," says their frontman James Johnston. "What we were doing was quite an anachronism at the time and no one we knew was directly involved in anything to do with indie music. We didn't feel part of all that, which was what was so good about it."

The Falcon continued to be an important venue for new bands throughout 1991/92, when Therapy?, Suede, Verve and PJ Harvey all played here. "I can remember seeing PJ Harvey at the Falcon," says Mary Byker. "and it was phenomenal. She looked like Nick Cave and she had also taken all these things from Gallon Drunk and polished it down into something of her own."

In October 1993, Oasis signed a six-album deal with Creation and celebrated at various nightspots in London. Most of the band wound up at the Falcon, where Liam, Bonehead and drummer Tony McCarroll got on stage with the Scottish band Whiteout and shambled their way through a couple of numbers.

Elastica also played at the Falcon in 1993 and were signed to Deceptive on the strength of their performance. "I'd never known a band to create such a buzz of chitchat among the Camden people and all the journalists," says Steve Lamacq. "It was a nightmare, because you could barely get into the back room, but it was a great gig. I never went to the Roxy but it was how you would like to imagine those early punk gigs might have been — it was jam-packed and sweaty, and then they came on and were this brilliant, contemporary post-punk band."

By April 1994, local residents had started to complain so bitterly about the Falcon's noise levels that Roger Cowell decided to close the venue down. In 1996, however, the back room of the Falcon underwent a major renovation and reestablished itself as the place to see upcoming bands in Camden. It was turned into a six-nights-a-week club called Barfly, which is promoted by the people who had previously run the Splash Club, at the Water Rats pub in King's Cross, which put on early London shows by Oasis and Beck.

"The Falcon is back in business," says Steve Lamacq, "although it's going to take a couple of bands to have really amazing gigs down there to fully establish it. Embrace played one of their earliest London

THE ROCK'N'ROLL GUIDE TO CAMDEN

The Pogues in the shadow of JFK at Camden Irish Centre, March 1984 [Paul Slattery]

gigs there but I only saw about three songs by the time I actually managed to get inside. I think the problem with Camden, since the Britpop thing, is that everyone's yearning to be part of something when it's small rather than just letting things evolve naturally. There's no gestation period anymore."

Barfly is one of the places where you are at least in with a chance of seeing some of the big names of the future at a very early stage. However, much of the Falcon's reputation continues to rest on the major names that came through here in the early-90s. "Everyone aspired to Camden at that point," says Steve Lamacq, "and I'm sure a lot of bands who travelled a long way down to London to play the Falcon must have been *so* disenchanted and *so* disappointed by the fact that this thing that they'd read about was just the back room of a pub with mad barmen and stuff. They'd been made to think, 'This is where it all happens' but, of course, it wasn't happening there every night of the week. They'd be like, 'Are there any journalists in here?' Well, no, there's four drunken Irish men over there, and a couple of people who've come with the support band in there.

"One of the best descriptions ever of the Falcon came from this guy called Johnny Thatcher, who lived in Sheffield, but did a review there for the *NME*. He said something like, 'Having been to the Falcon in Camden, I now know what it would be like to climb inside a fridge, shut the door and see the light go out.' [*laughs*] And, of course, to some bands, the Falcon would have been *exactly* that — this freezing cold, dark, backroom with rotting vegetables in the bottom compartment. It must have been just a killer for some of them, poor sods."

18. CAMDEN IRISH CENTRE
50-52 Camden Square, NW1. Telephone: 0171-916 2222

Opened in 1955, the Camden Irish Centre has long served as both a social and welfare centre for the area's large Irish population. In the late-60s, it introduced a traditional Irish music session after Sunday morning Mass and, over the years, it has played host to a variety of illustrious names, including Margaret Barry, who was billed as 'The Irish Ballad Singing Gypsy Queen' when she sang here in 1966. Barry frequently busked her way around the pubs of Camden, passing round a church offertory bag rather than a hat, and her big boast was that she could "out drink Brendan Behan".

One band who might have been equipped to share Barry's claim are The Pogues, who played some of their early gigs at the Irish Centre in 1983/84, under their original Gaelic name of Pogue Mahone. This was also the place where they posed for the cover of their 1984 debut album, *Red Roses For Me* — and the sleeve featured five out of six members of the band sitting beneath a portrait of that enduring Irish Catholic icon, John F Kennedy. That same portrait stared down at Spider Stacy as he bashed his forehead with a beer tray a total of 288 times when The Pogues recorded a video for *Waxies Dargle* at the Irish Centre.

In recent years, the Irish Centre has played a major role in helping to undo various miscarriages of justice, running campaigns to release the Birmingham 6, the Guildford 4 and the Bridgewater 3.

19. PLAYGROUND STUDIOS
Unit J, 44 St Paul's Crescent, NW1. Telephone: 0171-485 7412
Large rehearsal space which has been used by most of the indie bands who hang round Camden, including Lush, Flowered Up, Chapterhouse, Swervedriver, The Bluetones and Kenickie.

20. ARTHUR RIMBAUD
8 Royal College Street, NW1.
The French poet Arthur Rimbaud lived here with his lover Paul Verlaine for a couple of months in 1873, and his best known book, *A Season In Hell*, was at least partly inspired by the time he spent in Camden Town.

Rimbaud's mystical vision and ability to express teenage angst has made him a lasting rock'n'roll figure — revered by everyone from Jim Morrison to Kurt Cobain, whose favourite book was Rimbaud's *Illuminations*, extracts of which were read by his wife, Courtney Love, at his funeral in Seattle in April 1994.

"When I first read Rimbaud I felt like my feet were on fire," Marc Bolan once said, a feeling that was echoed by many of those on the New York punk scene in the early-70s. It was a photograph of Rimbaud that prompted Richard Hell to crop his hair and cultivate wasted features — a look the young John Lydon also arrived at and which was subsequently copied by thousands of punks. "I got Rimbaud in my blood," said Patti Smith, who came to be regarded as a visionary artist in his tradition. Rimbaud was certainly a central figure in the creation of Smith's 1975 debut album, *Horses*, the recording of which she later described as being "like A Season In Hell" for both herself and producer John Cale.

During Rimbaud and Verlaine's own season in hell in Camden, their frequent quarrels became worse and, after one particularly stormy row, Verlaine abandoned Rimbaud and went to Antwerp. Alone in Camden, without any money, Rimbaud wrote a famous letter to Verlaine, begging him to come back and saying, "For two whole days I have done nothing but weep!" In between crying bouts, Rimbaud wrote the prose poem *Night In Hell*, which became the third chapter of *A Season In Hell*. On receiving Rimbaud's letter, Verlaine wrote back, asking for forgiveness. Rimbaud joined him in Brussels but they had a vicious row which led to Verlaine being charged with attempted murder and sentenced to two years hard labour. Rimbaud returned to France alone, where he completed *A Season In Hell* in August. However, bitterly disappointed by the critical reaction to it, he turned his back on the literary world for good. He hadn't yet reached the age of 20.

KENTISH TOWN ROAD

NEWSREEL: THE 70s

Back in the garage with my bullshit detector
Carbon monoxide makes sure it's effective
There's people ringing up making offers for my life
I just wanna stay in the garage all night

We're a garage band, we come from garageland

The controversial nude revue "Oh, Calcutta!", which opened at the Round House, Chalk Farm, last Friday, has hit trouble. Complaints from spectators have been passed to Scotland Yard's Obscene Publications Squad by Kentish Town police

NO MORE SKY FLATS — COUNCIL
Camden Council have decided not to build any more blocks of sky flats in the borough because people living high off the ground often suffer from depression illnesses

Go-go girls will carry on dancing and the music will play on at the Landsdown pub in Gloucester Avenue, Chalk Farm — despite opposition from local residents

HOT PANTS WILL BOOST ROAD SAFETY

FREE MILK FOR ALL

200 FLEE FROM IRISH CENTRE IN SECOND BOMB SCARE

£50,00 SCHEME FOR CAMDEN TOWN
CANAL-SIDE MARKET

Carrying banners and shouting "No school uniforms" and "No caning", about 1,000 children at schools all over Camden walked out of their lessons on Tuesday morning and joined in a "strike" for pupils rights

TOWN HALL MAKE IT HARDER FOR SQUATTERS

'HARD PORN' FOUND IN HIGH STREET SHOP RAID

THE ROCK'N'ROLL GUIDE TO CAMDEN

With 'winos' and meths drinkers,
vandalism and pilfering among young people
loneliness among elderly residents and many
other problems, Camden Town may be described as
PROBLEM TOWN

HIGH STREET SHOPS STAFF FEAR DRUNKS

Albert Street, Camden Town, is a mixture of the good, the bad and the
ugly as far as housing goes but it took more than a fistful of dollars to
persuade the tenants to move

RESIDENTS PETITION TO KEEP 'WINOS' OUT
Winos, vagrant alcoholics, live "in a state of almost pure Communism"
in many parts of Camden

SPECTRE OF THE DOLE IS HAUNTING CAMDEN

BULLDOZING THE CHARACTER OUT OF OLD CAMDEN

POOR, JOBLESS, SQUALID
SLUMDEN
1977

Dossers and Town Hall dignitaries, homeless people and MPs,
hundreds of ordinary local residents and politicians from Camden Council
and the Greater London Council, all came together on Friday afternoon
to pay homage to Paddy O'Connor, who had become known both
in the borough and throughout London as a "Man Of The People"

NAZI-LED VIOLENCE FLARES IN CAMDEN

PUNKS IN STREET BATTLES
Gangs of punks, skinheads and "soulboys" clashed on the streets of
Camden over the weekend

MURDER CHARGE FOR MUSIC MACHINE BOUNCER

I don't want to know about what the rich are doing
I don't want to go to where the rich are going
They think they're so clever, they think they're so right
But the truth is only known by gutter snipes...

We're a garage band and we come from garageland.

CAMDEN HIGH STREET SOUTH SIDE

"We did Camden Live on Radio 1 in 95, so the studio was in a truck which was parked outside the World's End pub. When I got there, one of the engineers said, 'Three hours we were here. Just three hours before the first tramp pissed on the side of the BBC truck."
— *Steve Lamacq, 1997*

1. THE BLACK CAP
171 Camden High Street, NW1. Telephone: 0171- 428 2721

A popular gay bar famous for transvestite cabaret and a late-night licence at weekends. Originally built as a prison, it was previously known as the Mother Black Cap and, during the 60s, it was one of Camden Town's traditional trouble spots — one landlord barred more than 400 men during his tenure and the pub frequently had a police van stationed outside it. Indeed, this was the rough Irish pub on which Bruce Robinson based the scene in his semi-autobiographical cult film, *Withnail & I*, where Richard E Grant and Paul McGann encounter a particularly fearsome navvie.

However, in 1968, a new landlord called Harry McCafferty introduced nightly drag acts and the Mother Black Cap then became more famous for its onstage entertainment than its offstage fights. Danny La Rue was among those who performed here and the pub was a favourite of George Melly, who lived around the corner on Gloucester Crescent. "The Mother Black Cap was a great drag pub," he says. "Although it became much more aggressive once the clones moved in."

That said, the Black Cap continued to be one of the best pubs to see drag near central London — a reputation which it still holds today.

CAMDEN HIGH STREET - SOUTH SIDE

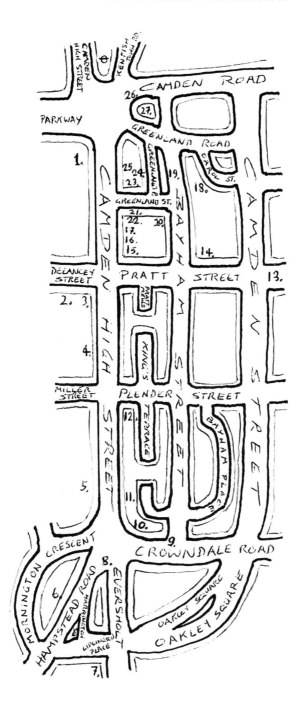

2. CAFE DELANCEY
3 Delancey Street, NW1. Telephone: 0171-387 1985
Opened in 1984, this was the first Continental-style brasserie in Camden Town, but it took its name from the original Café Delancey, which sold bacon sandwiches and strong tea, in the same spot.

It was here that Noel Gallagher arranged to meet Alan White for the first time in August 1995. Gallagher had no idea what the potential new member of Oasis would look like, and had started to worry that he might be ugly and weigh 20-odd stone, when White came over and offered to buy him a Stella lager. It was a good start — Gallagher drank the beer and told White he was officially in the band. And, within a few days of the meeting, the new drummer was playing on Oasis's first Number One single, *Whatever*, on *Top Of The Pops*.

Café Delancey has a fairly laidback jazz vibe and continues to be popular with the Albert Street literati, although it was a sign of the changing face of Camden when they started to include the weekly music press in the paper rack.

3. THE SPORTS DOME BAR & GRILL
111-113 Camden High Street, NW1. Telephone: 0171-911 0667
An American-style sports bar, which opened in 1996, and features a multi-screen video wall showing a variety of events, including football, boxing, athletics and motor racing. It also serves food and cocktails.

Until 1991, however, this beautiful old building was the home of the Brighton, one of the most famous Irish bars in the area. "I still miss the Brighton because you used to get a lot of elderly people in there," says Alo Conlon, landlord of the Dublin Castle on Parkway. "But that's all gone now."

The Brighton was renowned for traditional Irish music in the 50s and 60s, and for country & western in the 70s and 80s. Johnny McCauley was a regular here during the 60s — he made his name writing songs such as *Four Country Roads*, which was a big hit for the kings of the Irish showband scene, Big Tom And The Mainliners. McCauley could later be heard on Irish jukeboxes all over the land singing his own songs, such as *Destination Donegal*, and Burt Bacharach/Hal David's *The Story Of My Life*.

Throughout this period, the Brighton was a central meeting point for Irish people in London and, because big-name contractors like John Murphy and Frank Chambers drank here, it was also a good place for people to find work. "The Brighton was like a labour exchange," says John Fitzgerald, who took over the pub's tenancy in 1957 and ran it for the next 12 years. "People used to come here from all over and, if they wanted work, they'd meet up with the contractors and be sent out on a job. In those days, the pub was very busy — it was packed every day of the week. When I first came here, you could get 17 pints for a pound, it was one and tuppence a pint, and when you had ten or 12 blokes in a round, wanting stout & mild, and brown & mild, and pints of mild, by the time you had one dozen served, the next chap would say, 'Give us the same again.' So you had to just serve away and keep going with the crowd. There were no spirits in those days, there was a scarcity of them, so it was nearly all beer. And it was mostly a men's trade, you didn't have a lot of women in pubs, and especially not Irish girls — they didn't drink at all, except for a bottle of orange. It was the men who did the drinking then," he says, laughing.

When John Fitzgerald moved to the St John's Tavern in Archway, the Brighton was taken over by Bat Broslan, who established himself as the longest-serving landlord in Camden Town by running the pub until it closed down in 1991 and then taking over the Albert on Royal College Street. Meanwhile, the Brighton was given a £2 million facelift and turned into Bar Royal, a glitzy cocktail bar, before becoming the Sports Dome four years later.

4. SCOPE
73 Camden High Street, NW1. Telephone: 0171-380 1455
Jarvis Cocker was a regular at this charity store when it was still called the Spastics Society Shop. "I used to cycle over from Camberwell to Camden quite regularly in the early-90s," he says. "From the Tube to Mornington Crescent was quite a good strip for charity shops, so I used to do that tour up and down. Because lots of trendy people live in Camden, I'd always thought that you wouldn't be able to pick up anything good, but they actually get some very good items.

"I once got this kind of pin-striped gangster suit, which I wore in the video for *Razzmatazz*, from the Spastics Society Shop, which has now changed to Scope, of course, as they all have. If I know there's a charity shop nearby I can't bear not to go and have a look — well, I used to, I feel a bit stupid doing it now. If somebody spots me they'll think, 'God, what a tight get. He can obviously afford to buy some decent clothes and yet he's still sniffing round Sue Ryder.' The other day, I was in a Relate shop round Fulham and somebody came in and asked for my autograph — signing autographs in charity shops just doesn't seem right, really."

5. GOOD FELLAS DINER
29 Camden High Street, NW1.
Once a downmarket daytime caff, this place came into its own in the early-90s when it started staying open until 3am in order to serve burgers and chips to the post-Camden Palace crowd. It subsequently became one of the most crowded places around.

6. SOUNDS
Greater London House, NW1
This former cigarette factory, whose exterior design was modelled on an

Egyptian temple, was once the home of the music weekly, *Sounds*, plus various other titles, such as *Kerrang!* and *Record Mirror*.

Sounds moved here in the summer of 1985 and this was its base for the next four years, before it moved to Blackfriars where it was sold to EMAP Metro and immediately folded in April 1991. "*Sounds* was the only music paper worth reading, because it seemed to me like it was written by people who actually liked music," said Kurt Cobain on the morning Nirvana played the 1991 Reading Festival — at the time he was wearing a *Sounds* T-shirt which had been given to him by journalist Keith Cameron and which he wore in many of the early Nirvana shots.

Among the other journalists who worked on *Sounds* during its Camden Town period were Andy Ross, who became the MD of Food Records; James Brown, the founding Editor of *Loaded*; Radio 1 DJ Mary Anne Hobbs; Robin Gibson, who co-launched the CD magazine, *Volume*; John Robb, who was also the singer of The Membranes; Hugh Fielder, who edits the Tower Records magazine; and various other music writers, such as David Cavanagh, Paul Elliott, Neil Perry, Shaun Phillips, Ron Rom, Mr Spencer, Cathi Unsworth, Jon Wilde, Roy Wilkinson and Damon Wise.

Metallica regularly called in at the *Sounds* office when it was based here, but the most memorable visit was a slightly less welcome one from Axl Rose, who tried to have a personal meeting with the freelancer who had compared him to a six-foot hamster who'd had his balls electrocuted, in a review of Guns N'Roses' first London show at the Marquee in June 1987.

"I just thought Guns N'Roses were laughable even though everyone else was really into them," says Andy Ross, who worked under his pen name, Andy Hurt. "So I wrote this fairly damning review and they decided to come to the *Sounds* office and exact their revenge on me. It was only later that I found out they'd actually brought their press officer along with them — I mean, it's not exactly spontaneous, is it? So they turned up at Greater London House and the first thing they did was go into reception and say, 'Right, we want Andy Hurt.' Of course, the receptionist didn't have a clue who I was because I didn't actually work in the office. So instead of beating me up and pissing all over my desk, which they were apparently going to do, they said, 'Er, is Malcolm in?' and went for a pint with Malcolm Dome and Krusher [two *Kerrang!* journalists] instead.

"They did leave me a post-it note, though, which had a rather crude drawing of male genitalia, with a knife cutting through it and little drops of what was presumably blood dripping from it, with the words: 'Andy Hurt, next time we catch up with you, this is what we're going to do, signed, Axl Rose'. The whole thing was exceedingly funny — I got instant notoriety from it and they went on to sell billions of records. But, no, I haven't seen them since."

Kurt Cobain in that *Sounds* shirt, August 1991 [Ed Sirrs]

7. THE RUSSELL ARMS
Lidlington Place, NW1.

This used to be the Russell Arms, which was built in 1973 as a local for the residents of the nearby Ampthill Estate, but it has also featured live bands and a variety of club nights.

The most famous of these was the Wednesday rockabilly night, which ran for six years and was started in 1988 by Mouse, who also DJ'd at Dingwalls' Saturday lunchtime rocking sessions. Morrissey sometimes came down here on Wednesdays and was among those who crowded into the Russell on a hot summer night in 1992 to see Gallon Drunk play. Seymour Stein [the man who discovered the Ramones and Madonna] signed the band to his Sire label on the strength of that gig, while Morrissey promptly took them on a two-month tour of the United States. "That gig was principally set up for Seymour Stein to watch us play live," says Gallon Drunk frontman James Johnston. "There wasn't a real stage or anything, so we just played in the corner of the room and all I remember is that it was disgustingly hot. We were very much an English band at that point, and I think that was probably why someone from Warners in America would be there to see us. We seemed like a real London band, and that wasn't something that people were trumpeting at the time. At all."

Sometime after the Gallon Drunk gig, the back room of the Russell became the Thursday night home of the Sausage Machine, which had been forced to move out of the White Horse pub in Hampstead. During their time here, the Sausage Machine put on bands such as Stereolab and local legend Jessie Hector.

However, the greatest musician to ever grace the Russell's stage was Dan Penn, who wrote such classics as *The Dark End Of The Street* and *Do Right Woman*, and played here in the summer of 1994. "That was a legendary gig, people still talk about it," says Philippe Korpar-Migrenne, who was in the crowd that night. "This guy called Tim Tour had been to Memphis with Primal Scream and met Dan Penn, and managed to get him over to do a secret gig at the Russell. He started with *Dark End Of The Street* and did it again later in the set — it was the best gig I've ever seen. I was a bit ashamed, to be honest, because the place seemed like too much of a dump for a bloke like that to play in. But he loved it."

"Dan Penn at the Russell Arms was a real buzz," says Paul Cwynarski who DJ'd that night. "I stand up when I say Dan Penn. He is a god in my Pantheon, he really is. Bobby G and all the Primals fraternity were there, it was a real coming together of the clans, and it was just so atmospheric. He did all his songs, obviously, like *It Tears Me Up*, and all the great stuff that he's written for other people. He's not a brilliant singer, but he's got so much soul in his voice. Tim [Tour] came up to me and I was crying and he was crying — the whole night was really emotional."

8. MORNINGTON CRESCENT UNDERGROUND STATION

This notoriously leaky old Tube Station closed in 1992, briefly reopened and was then shut down again, but that didn't deter My Life Story from featuring it on the front of their 1994 debut album, *Mornington Crescent*. The station's pop fame was short-lived, however, because the photograph of the Tube sign breached London Underground's logo copyright and the band were ordered to withdraw all copies of the album and were forced to repackage it with a new cover.

That wasn't the first time that Mornington Crescent Underground Station had attracted the attention of pop stars. In 1986, ex-Beatle Ringo Starr pledged his support for a Camden-based pressure group dedicated to saving certain Tube stations from modernisation — and Mornington Crescent was top of their list. Currently still closed, the station looks safe enough from modernisation just yet, although there are definite plans to open it by the beginning of 1998.

9. HOPE & ANCHOR
74 Crowndale Road, NW1. Telephone: 0171-387 9506

Conveniently close to the Camden Palace with live music and comedy nights. However, this pub should not be confused with the much more famous Hope & Anchor in Islington, where Madness first met The Specials, played riotous gigs and even recorded in Dave Robinson's upstairs studio, which was called Pathway.

10. CAMDEN PALACE
1a Camden High Street, NW1. Telephone: 0171-387 0428

Of all the venues around here, this one has probably taken on the most guises: theatre, BBC Studio, nightclub, punk venue, the Camden Palace. As the latter, it has had a wide variety of youth scenes passing through its doors — from punks, skinheads, New Romantics, goths and ravers to the ever-changing legions of indie kids who switched from Ned's Atomic Dustbin to grunge to Britpop in the space of just five years.

Built at the turn of this century as an Edwardian playhouse, the Camden Theatre, as it was originally known, was opened in December 1900 by the actress Ellen Terry. She had lived just down the road from here as a girl and there is still a plaque in the foyer to commemorate her visit. With a capacity of 3,000, it was one of the largest theatres in the London suburbs, and its marble staircase and deep red upholstery also made it one of the most beautiful.

After the First World War, the Camden Theatre was turned into a cinema and has probably only survived because it was taken over by the BBC in 1945, who used it as a radio and recording studio. It was the home of *The Goons* for several years and, although the studio was mainly used by classical bands, The Rolling Stones recorded here in March 1964. They had already played 40 gigs and recorded their debut album, *The Rolling Stones*, in the first couple of months of 1964, so they were well rehearsed to say the least when they knocked out four tracks in the Camden Theatre, including a version of Arthur Alexander's *You Better Move On*.

The BBC vacated the premises in 1972 and the building briefly became Nero's nightclub and restaurant, which opened with a live set from The Drifters in December 1975. However, punk spared the old theatre from becoming just another tacky nightclub, by providing the impetus to turn it into the Music Machine in April 1977.

With an elevated stage, large dance floor, balconies, various bars and a foyer with pin-ball machines and a pool table, the Music Machine was an ideal venue and the fact that it was open till 2am six nights a week made it a good alternative to the West End. One of the first big gigs to take place here was the Heartbreakers, supported by Siouxsie & The Banshees, in May, which was attended by most of the premier punk faces, including John Lydon and Debbie Harry.

By June, the summer of punk had turned violent and, a week after John Lydon had been viciously attacked outside Dingwalls, Bob Geldof was assaulted onstage at a Boomtown Rats' show at the Music Machine, supported by 999 and the skinhead band Skrewdriver. Before the Rats came onstage, someone took over the DJ booth and started haranguing the punks into going down the King's Road to beat up teds the following Saturday afternoon. Other people passed the time by throwing glasses off the upper balconies and watching them shatter on the dance floor below. A few songs into The Boomtown Rats' set, one of the crowd walked onstage and hit Geldof, knocking him to the ground, before casually strolling off again. Although the right side of Geldof's face was swollen and his lip was bleeding, he carried on singing and, when the police arrived, refused to press charges.

One other victim of that night's violence was Leee Black Childers, the Heartbreakers' manager and a forerunner on the New York punk scene, who had gone to the gig with Mick Jones of the Clash. Childers, who had his hair slicked back and was wearing 50s gear as usual, was attacked as he left the Music Machine, and beaten and kicked until his assistant, Gail, pulled up outside the club in a taxi. A few weeks after Childers had been beaten up, the new wave ted band, Darts, played at the Music Machine, watched by John Lydon.

Lydon was in the crowd again in November to see Richard Hell & The Voidoids do a one-off show at the Music Machine. The band had just toured the UK supporting the Clash, so were fired up to be playing to their own crowd at last. At the end of their set, Lydon came onstage to cajole the crowd into shouting for more — they obliged, and the Voidoids returned to do *I Wanna Be Your Dog*. Its creator, Iggy Pop, also sang that song during his two-night stint at the Music Machine, the following June.

"The Music Machine was great," says Lemmy, "because they had all these bands that you wanted to see more than the ones they had

in Dingwalls — I mean, you got sick of Brinsley Schwarz after a while, so you started going down there, where they had all the punks on. At that time, the stage stuck out from the wall like a shelf, and it was really high with nothing underneath it. The second time Motorhead played there, this kid appeared over the front of the stage. Some of the crowd had done a human pyramid and he was on top of it, and he climbed up and jumped on us. I think he should have got the George Cross for bravery. Was he ceremoniously booted off? We couldn't boot him off something like that — he'd have broken his fucking back. And then another time in the Music Machine, we had this new smoke machine that was going to be wonderful and would really knock people out and shit. But we started it off and the entire venue went hoarse, you couldn't even see your hand, you were stumbling around coughing; it was a terrible failure. But they were good days, them."

    The Clash did a four-night stint here in July 1978, supported by The Specials and Suicide, and among those who joined them onstage were Sex Pistol Steve Jones, to play guitar on *London's Burning*, and Sham 69's Jimmy Pursey, who shared vocals with Joe Strummer on *White Riot*. The Clash's backdrop was pulled down every night by a good looking fan with red, gold and green-coloured dreadlocks; his name was Roland Gift, who reappeared seven years later as the singer in the Fine Young Cannibals.

Sid Vicious and Nancy Spungen hung out at a benefit gig for the National Council For One Parent Families, headlined by the Steve Gibbons Band and the Slits in August. Sid wasn't to know that within two months he would be in need of benefit gigs himself, after Nancy was found dead from a single knife wound in New York's Chelsea Hotel and he was charged with second-degree murder. The Clash played for the Sid Vicious Defence Fund at the Music Machine on December 19, playing the whole of their new *Give 'Em Enough Rope* album and doing a truly great gig.

Two nights later, the Jam held their Christmas Party here, supported by the Nips, whose line-up featured Shane MacGowan, James Fearnley, Shanne Hasler and Jon Moss [who would respectively reappear in The Pogues, The Men They Couldn't Hang and Culture Club]. "We were all wearing women's nightdresses," recalls James Fearnley, "and Jon Moss had a pair of frilly pants on, so he wouldn't come to the front of the stage to do backing vocals when the Jam played *The Holly And The Ivy*."

Throughout this period, the Music Machine was widely recognised as a great place to see bands and to score drugs. "It was always free to get in if you had a ticket, which people used to pass round at school," says Joe Dilworth. "I remember seeing The Fall there, supporting Chelsea with the Snivelling Shits [producer Steve Lillywhite's punk band], and that was insane. We all used to do this stuff called Zoff, which was some kind of solvent that you'd soak your sleeves in, and we'd all be drinking pints of snakebite. By the end of the night, the place was just full of piles of sick, it was totally out of hand. There was this guy who used to sell blues in the Dublin Castle and I remember him being down at the Music Machine — three blues for a pound, and that would be your evening's entertainment. In those days it was more about cheap speed and solvents than alcohol."

By the late-70s, some local residents had definitely had enough of the Music Machine and complained to the local papers about people urinating on their walls, smashing windows and having sex in their lifts. Their complaints were given credence in January 1979 when a 20-year-old man was stabbed to death in the venue, as he stood chatting to a friend on the stairway. A similar incident occurred the following September, when a 28-year-old man was also killed there.

"I knew someone who was stabbed to death in the Music Machine," says Suggs. "It could be a horrible place, because you'd get a lot of kids coming down from Kings Cross, stragglers, who'd just got off the train. We used to go there before the band came on or just after they'd finished. You used to be able to climb up the back and jump in through the green dome — you took your life into your own hands, just so you'd get in without paying — and you'd pop up in what was known as the VIP bar, although there was never anyone in it, not in those days, anyway. But I do remember that when *The Prince* first came out, we

Lemmy with Rat Scabies & Gaye Advert at the Music Machine, 1978 [Paul Slattery]

used to go down to the Music Machine and make the DJ put it on. There'd be no one else in there and we'd just dance to it ourselves. Those were the days... simple pleasures, simple pleasures."

Like Madness, many other musicians would turn up at the Music Machine after the bands had finished playing just to hang out or get another drink. And it was here that AC/DC singer Bon Scott drank his last drink, before collapsing in the back of his car in the early hours of February 20, 1980.

The Dead Kennedys livened the Music Machine up when they played here in October 1980, by almost causing a riot. The Californian band had just released their *Fresh Fruit For Rotting Vegetables* LP and, with songs like *Kill The Poor*, *California Uber Alles* and *Holiday In Cambodia*, they attracted a new generation of punks. As frontman Jello Biafra leapt around the stage — now somewhat lower than its original 20 feet — a couple of dozen kids climbed up to join him, and he invited more of them to do the same. As a result, two microphones disappeared, bringing the gig to an early close. A couple of weeks later, The Birthday Party, who had arrived in England from Australia earlier in the year, played one of their first London gigs here.

During 1981, the dying embers of punk had been put out by the burgeoning New Romantic scene, and the Music Machine ceased to be a live venue. However, in June 1982, it reopened as the Camden Palace and its gaudy splendour, multi-tiers and upper level cocktail bar became the perfect setting for Steve Strange and Rusty Egan's Club For Heroes, which had been born in a gay disco in Soho four years previously but was now ready for mass consumption. The opening night was attended by bands such as The Human League, Spandau Ballet and Siouxsie & The Banshees plus Lemmy, and the new management were keen to stress that the Camden Palace would not be overrun with punks and skinheads as the Music Machine had been. "I went to the opening of the Camden Palace," says John Best who frequently travelled up from Kent for a night out in London. "I remember it being impossibly glamorous and very exciting. But quite quickly it became like the Trocadero, a really shit place to go. I remember an off-duty paratrooper doing a citizen's arrest on Steve Strange for snorting coke in a toilet cubicle — I can't imagine that happening now."

Over the next three years, the Camden Palace fully established

"I went to this one party somewhere round Camden where they kept playing The Farm and I remember it cos my mate was kissing this girl and she threw up in his mouth. It served him right because she only really agreed to kiss him because she was so drunk she just wouldn't know who she was snogging. I laughed my head off, but I realised that it wasn't too good for him." – JARVIS COCKER

itself as a Mecca for all-night people and started to fill up with the schoolkids and tourists who'd read about it. "I grew up in Camden Town and Wednesday was the night that you tried really hard to get your parents to let you out," says Ben Jones. "That was the 60s night at the Camden Palace, with Adey Croasdell DJ'ing, and it was just a really brilliant, fun night. Everyone sang along and *Shout* always brought everyone on to the dance floor — the Isley Brothers' version, although I swear Lulu's became big on the back of the Camden Palace."

In addition to a variety of successful dance nights, the Camden Palace also continued to put on live bands, such as Hüsker Dü, who played here in May 1985, a gig which was released as a live video three years later. "Going to see Hüsker Dü for free at the Camden Palace was one of my best ever nights in Camden," says Alie Allerton. "It was a one-off, but not everybody knew about it. The mid-80s was a great period for American rock and that was a powerful gig. It was that reinvention of punk rock in a musical way, which Americans are so good at — just taking something and, in some ways, making it better or even more listenable."

Suicide also played here the following year, in one of their first London appearances in quite some time. "I saw Suicide at the Camden Palace and it left a massive impression on me," says James Johnston who was in the process of forming his own band, Gallon Drunk. "I'd always thought Suicide were a band you would never get to see, cos they were from the 70s, although, with hindsight, it wasn't really that long after their heyday. I just remember that they were so astonishingly loud and I was totally blown away. It's very hard to describe exactly what it was — it was just the very nature of the band, with their hats and sunglasses, and this pudgy Elvis bloke screaming his soul out. They were absolutely superb."

Prince also did a 'secret' gig at the Camden Palace at the height of his fame, a visit to the area which might have prompted him to later open his own merchandising shop on the Chalk Farm Road.

The tradition of the old Music Machine, with a touch of Club For Heroes, is being carried on at the Camden Palace's Tuesday night slot, Feet First, which started in February 1988 and is now one of London's longest-running clubs. Jonathan and Eko were the first London DJs to play bands like Happy Mondays, The Stone Roses, Mudhoney and Nirvana. In between the music, they also stick on a live band at 12.30am, and many of the big indie names of the past decade have done a live set here, including Blur and Pulp.

"Can I remember anything about playing at the Camden Palace?" asks Jarvis Cocker. "Well, it's hard, because if they put you on at midnight, then you just get really drunk before you go on. I suppose I just think of the Camden Palace as being a big tourist place. You always meet students from Israel who say, 'Why did you not come and play in our country?' and all that. I don't know if they've still got them now, but they used to have all these black and white pictures of Steve Strange from when it was a big disco during the New Romantic days, and I remember being quite impressed by those as we went in. It was a long time before the attempt at the New Romantic revival, and they were just really funny to see."

Feet First continues to put on a diverse range of bands, from indie to hip hop, and an array of temporarily unfashionable pop stars can usually be seen hanging around at the bar.

11. ALFRED KEMP
20 Camden High Street, NW1

Now a solicitor's office, this was once the site of Alfred Kemp's, the best secondhand clothes shop in Camden, which sold quality menswear for more than 60 years. 'Alfred Kemp Fit Anyone', said the neon sign outside, and the entire window was filled with racks of suits, coats, jackets, trousers, shirts and shoes, which cost from as little as a couple of pounds.

"Alfred Kemp's was a fantastic shop," says Suggs, who was a regular customer in the late-70s. "I got a brilliant green tonic suit in there and loads of other great stuff. It really was wall-to-wall clothes, in all sizes, plus loads of old shoes, like brogues, proper shoes, not like a load of old junk. At that time, you could still get clothes from the 60s, but when you started getting stuff from the 70s, in the mid-80s, it was hopeless, there was no point in having a shop like that. But they really did have the most amazing stuff in there at that time. It was pretty cheap, but not that cheap because it was one-up from an Oxfam shop in that they had these old salesmen in there, who treated you really well. It was like you'd gone into an old-fashioned tailor's and you were a gentleman, even though you were buying secondhand clothes. I sometimes wonder what happened to all the old blokes who worked in there, but I guess they were getting on a bit even then."

12. CHARLIE'S GENTS HAIRDRESSER
93 Plender Street, NW1.

Charlie is a real old-style barber who made his name cutting the original teds' hair in Elephant & Castle in the 50s before moving up to Camden 20-odd years ago. "When Charlie cuts a quiff," says one satisfied customer, "he washes your hair, then he gets a blow dryer, lays this little brown net across the top of it, sculpts it into a James Dean-style and hairsprays it. He takes about an hour but he always says, 'I like my customer to go away happy.'"

"You can tell he's cool," says another, "because he says, 'How do you want your DA? Do you want it Boston?' And that's crucial, cos that's the square-off cut at the back. These young hairdressers, you say, 'Boston DA' and they haven't got a clue. Charlie, no problem. Plus he's got a Little Richard moustache."

13. PRATT STREET

Pratt Street, which is also known as Greek Town, can seriously lay claim to being one of the most rock'n'roll streets in Camden, even though many of the restaurants which gave it that status are no longer here. "Pratt Street was a Greek area, ruled by the Greeks, where the coppers never went," says Shane MacGowan, who spent a great deal of his time down here. "There used to be this brilliant little place, which looked like a real Greek taverna, where they'd look at you as though you were mad if you ordered something to eat, because it was really just a drinking joint. But if they did get in the mood to cook something, it would be great — they'd give you these big fish, with their heads and tails still on, and that would sate your appetite so then you'd go on to the ouzo. Every now and again one of the Greek guys in there would just get up and start dancing or singing a song while another would tap the beat, or they'd tell fisherman's stories."

Some of these restaurants, which also doubled as drinking and gambling dens, occasionally hired out their upstairs rooms or basements as private clubs. "One of my mates got in with all the Greek guys round Pratt Street and that's how he got his own illegal drinking club," says Ben Jones. "Normally, the room would be a Greek gambling den but he'd ask them to let him have it on a Saturday night and tell them that he could generate more people and more money for them. You'd only get 40 or 50 people in there, but it would be packed and it was always great fun. Those places don't exist any more, but most of the best restaurants in Camden are still around Pratt Street."

14. QUEEN OF SHEBA
23 Pratt Street, NW1. Telephone: 0171-267 5445

This tiny Ethiopian restaurant was once one of the best of the Pratt Street drinking joints. It was officially called the Marathasa, but generally referred to as 'The Greeks'.

Opened in 1983, it quickly became a favourite haunt of Shane MacGowan, who immortalised it in one of the Pogues' best songs, *The Broad Majestic Shannon*. Its main asset was that it was one of the very few places in Camden Town where you could drink until morning, the only prerequisites being the purchase of something as cheap as a Greek salad and the ability to stomach Soave, ouzo or a variety of their limited range of spirits. "It was the flashest Greek joint on Pratt Street," says MacGowan. "The restaurant was a front for a gambling club upstairs, where loads of rich Greek men used to go. They'd arrive in expensive cars with silly-money coats on, and they'd go upstairs and drink and gamble and take coke, while the wives stayed downstairs. We used to act respectfully, because you knew you didn't fuck around in there, whereas at the Marathon [another late-night Greek restaurant on Chalk Farm Road] they didn't care what you did as long as you were drinking."

The restaurant became a regular venue for Pogues' post-aftershow parties and the starting point for some of MacGowan's songs. These include *I'll Be Your Handbag* — whose original lyrics were scrawled onto a serviette, during the acid house summer of 1988, and emerged six years later on the Popes' debut album, with the chorus still intact — and *Hell's Ditch*, the title track of the Pogues 1990 album. "I had already written the music for *Hell's Ditch* and I wrote the lyrics in 20 minutes in The Greeks one night," says MacGowan. "It was three times as long as the finished song, and was far more obscene and far more explicit. It's inspired by Genet and it was as graphic as Genet, but it was sort of censored by Jem [Finer, fellow Pogue]."

One occasion when things did get out of hand in The Greeks was when Mary Byker rounded off his stag night here, amid the company of MacGowan and Green On Red's Dan Stuart. The celebrations came to an abrupt end when Stuart, who was a big Pogues fan and had specifically requested to meet his songwriting hero, inadvertently insulted MacGowan. Stuart carried on pushing forkfuls of food into his mouth, while MacGowan just stared at him in stunned silence. He then picked up a dish of taramasalata and screwed it into Stuart's forehead, threw an ashtray at him, and then tipped the rest of the taramasalata onto his own head.

"Mary was getting married and I didn't like the guy who he was with," remembers MacGowan. "So it turned into this mad night, where we ended up throwing plates and knives and forks at each other. But the waiters didn't give a shit, they just thought, 'Crazy English', you know."

"That was one of my fantastic nights out," says Mary Byker. "Sometimes I say to people, 'Look, you don't know how rock'n'roll I am but, when I got married, my stag night was with Shane MacGowan and this American guy people have no longer heard of called Dan Stuart.' Dan was such a massive fan of Shane's that he kept going, 'Yeah, man, he's like Hank Williams, man' and all the time I'm going, 'Dan, don't say that to Shane. Don't be this dumbstruck person', but he did start fawning over him. I clearly remember the first order of cigarettes in the restaurant and then plates started flying round. I ended up having to take Dan away, and he fell over and broke his arm on the way home. The thing is, it was my stag night and instead of someone saying to me, 'Mary, behave yourself', I spent all night telling someone else to behave. But that was one of the nights where I really felt like I belonged in Camden Town and, every time I go by Pratt Street, I always think about it."

15. LIBERTIES BAR
100 Camden High Street, NW1. Telephone: 0171-485 4019
When the old Camden Head was converted into Liberties in 1990, it was one of the first new-style Irish bars to open in North London. Among its initial regulars were Shane MacGowan, Gerry Conlon, Paul Hill and

George Best, who launched his autobiography, *The Good, The Bad & The Bubbly*, here in October 1991.

Liberties has an open fire and a big, central bar and attracts a wide range of customers, from old men who stare over the top of their pints out onto the changing face of Camden High Street to young Irish couples. There's a private function room upstairs which, like many such places in Camden, has been the scene of various popstar-studded parties over the past few years.

16. RUBY IN THE DUST
102 Camden High Street, NW1. Telephone: 0171-485 2744
Now an established chain, Ruby In The Dust was christened in Neil Young's honour, taking its name from a line in the song, *Cowgirl In The Sand*. The Camden Town branch opened in the summer of 1986 and quickly became the favoured lunchtime drinking spot of *Kerrang!* journalists who were attracted by the frozen vodka shots. It also serves great cocktails and tends to get extremely crowded.

17. WATERSTONES
128 Camden High Street, NW1. Telephone: 0171-284 4948
This large, two-storey branch of Waterstones books is good for contemporary fiction and biographies, and it also has an extensive rock'n'roll section plus New Age and local interest books. It has regular signings and literary events in the basement and the guests have included Ray Davies and Greil Marcus.

18. CAROL STREET
This street was largely made up of squats throughout the 70s and early-80s. The squatters actually saved one side of the street from demolition and, in 1983, they were given permission to turn those 23 houses into a Housing Co-Op for single people.

The most famous squat was 1 Carol Street, which was Scritti Politti's house. "Loads of people moved in and out of the house and there were always people staying over," says Paddy James, who lived there in the early-80s. "They used to rehearse in a room on the first floor. They had to practise quietly, so that they didn't annoy everyone else in the street, which is one of the reasons why their live sound was a bit weird."

Scritti singer Green Gartside wrote about Camden Town in *Rock A Boy Blue* on the band's debut album, *Songs To Remember*. And, in 1986, Madness had a hit with Scritti's early single, *The Sweetest Girl*.

19. STIFF RECORDS
Bayham Street, NW1.
This building next to the hospital was once the home of Stiff Records, who were originally based in a small shop in Notting Hill, but moved to

Camden during the peak Madness years of the early-80s. The label was started in July 1976, by Jake Riviera and Dave Robinson. The latter managed Graham Parker and the former was a one-time tour manager of Dr Feelgood, which was lucky, because it was the Feelgoods' singer, Lee Brilleaux, who lent them £400 to start the label. Like Chiswick, Stiff was one of the pioneering labels of the late-70s, releasing records by Nick Lowe, the Damned, the Adverts and Elvis Costello. Stiff suffered a temporary hitch when Riviera took Costello and Lowe with him to found the Radar label, but Robinson discovered new stars in Madness, who he signed after inviting them to play at his wedding [he was apparently impressed that they had managed to provoke Elvis Costello into getting up and dancing].

During the time that Stiff were based in Bayham Street, the label released records by various acts who were based in or associated with Camden, such as The Belle Stars, Kirsty MacColl, Dave Stewart and, obviously, Madness. "The Stiff office on Bayham Street was a fantastic place," says Suggs. "We used to do all the videos there — Dave Robinson directed them himself and the people who worked there used to make the sets. When we did *Cardiac Arrest*, we made the inside of a brain in the office, with little red sheets and polystyrene."

"One of my best Camden memories," says Nick Garrard, "is of being an extra for one of The Belle Stars' videos in Bayham Street in the summer of 1982. They weren't paying anyone any money but it was floor-to-ceiling crates of wine, The Belle Stars were doing the conga, and we were pissed-up all afternoon. It was when Madness had their first Number One with *House Of Fun* and they were having a private party at the Bull & Gate so we all left The Belle Stars' video and carried on drinking there. Then Etta James just happened to be playing at Dingwalls, so we all went to see her. It was a great day out."

20. THE LAUREL TREE
113 Bayham Street, NW1. Telephone: 0171-485 1383
This quiet gay pub was briefly transformed into the centre of the Britpop universe by the nouveau mod club, Blow Up, which was opened by Paul Tunkin in October 1993. Tunkin had previously DJ'd at the Pink Toothbrush in Raleigh and then started a monthly club in Southend called Periphery. "Paul used to play Northern Soul, 60s stuff, The Small Faces — basically, uplifting music that you could dance to," says Todd Parmenter, who lived in Southend and went to Tunkin's club most weeks. "Then he got the Laurel Tree in Camden Town, so a lot of people from Southend used to come up to London at the weekends. It was at a time when the whole grunge thing was still going on. I was really into Sonic Youth, but I was just so sick of seeing people in baggy T-shirts and army greens and Doc Marten boots, so I just went back to my roots and dressed smart, which was totally against what was happening at the time."

Blow Up was originally called Londinium and Tunkin, who also had his own band The Weekenders, played a mixture of classic British bands like The Small Faces, The Kinks, The Who and the Jam, plus soundtracks and dance music. "It was primarily a mod affair," says Andy Ross, who hung out there in the early days. "But I suppose the defining thing about Blow Up is *The Italian Job*. It was *the* film and inspiration behind it."

The Buzzcocks, Blur, Elastica, Suede and Pulp were among the club's regular Saturday night faces. "Blow Up was quite exciting because it was new," says Jarvis Cocker. "It's like anything, if you catch it early enough, then it's good. The thing that impressed me about it was the fact that people would talk to each other. My previous thing had been raving, where you'd just dance all night. I mean, you would talk, but you wouldn't say a whole lot. Obviously, that had become a bit tarnished for me, so it was quite nice to go to a club where you could dance if you wanted to but you could also have a decent conversation, rather than just one that went, 'Yeah, man, buzzing, yeah, right, brilliant, yeah, sorted, yeah.' I DJ'd at Blow Up once, in the upstairs bit."

If Blow Up was exciting to people like Jarvis Cocker, then it was doubly so to a group of out-of-towners in their early 20s. "From a Southender's point of view," says Todd Parmenter, "it was like, our friend has gone to Camden Town and is doing this club, and it was a bit like seeing Hollywood written in massive letters, and realising there's something really big going on here. The people who were turning up at the club were Elastica, Pulp, the Jesus & Mary Chain, Suede — all these famous bands turning up at what was basically a Southend club, but it just happened to be in Camden Town. And for us it was just like, 'Wow, this is amazing.' It was a bit like if you'd been let loose in a sweetie shop when you were young: you get to steal everything and do as much as you can in the time that you've got. So it was, 'Right, let's just start a band, fuck it, let's do something, let's get somewhere. We're out of Southend now, we haven't got to walk around talking about how shit the area is, we're in Camden. It's the world of opportunity.'"

Meanwhile, Blow Up continued to grow in popularity, so much so that *Select* magazine devoted four pages to Blow Up in its September 1994 issue. Parmenter — plus fellow Southenders Johnny Dean and Chris Gentry, who would reappear in Menswear — were among the new mods featured in that article. For Parmenter, it was the end of the line. "By the summer of 1994, there'd be queues right down the road," he says. "That was before the press or anything. It was just word of mouth, because the music they were playing was so completely different to anything else that was happening in London. But as soon as the *Select* article came out, it was all over."

For other people, however, that article was just the beginning. "When I saw that *Select* feature," says John Best, of Savage & Best, the PRs behind Pulp, Suede and Elastica, "I thought, they're really on to something here — the music might be crap, but the way they look is great. I already knew about Blow Up and I used to see Graham Coxon and Jarvis and Steve from Pulp there. They were just playing the usual Northern Soul and mod stuff but, until then, people had tended to look like they were in indie bands and suddenly there was that Steve Marriott end of it coming in and it just looked right. And by the time Blur played at Alexandra Palace about a year after Blow Up started, the whole audience looked like they went there. Pulp and Blow Up are very interrelated — not only do British bands look like Jarvis now, so do fashion models. It's global and I think it started at Blow Up."

> *"I think everybody gets something different out of Camden. For me, I suppose it's a bit like the way Paul Weller was fascinated by London and particularly by Oxford Street. In* A Beat Concerto, *there's a story about Weller coming up to London with a tape-recorder just because he wanted to record the sound of the city. And when you come from the sticks, you do have this idea of what London's going to be like and, I suppose, Camden is the nearest thing to what I'd imagined it would be like when I was 13."*
> *– STEVE LAMACQ*

Blow Up eventually moved to a new, much bigger home at the Wag Club, in Soho. The Laurel Tree is best known as a drinking joint with a 2am licence, but it also hosts a variety of different club nights, including everything from hardcore punk and metal to blues and poetry.

"The Laurel Tree used to have a gay disco on Friday and Saturday and the upstairs was shut the rest of the week," says Nick Garrard, who ran a blues club called Thursday Night At The Snakepit in 1986. "My club ran for a couple of months until the local alms house over the road complained about the noise and it was shut down. Thee Mighty Caesars did a residency and I played rhythm and blues records. The first thing I did, which was the most successful, was a poetry reading by the Medway poets, which was Billy Childish, Tracey Emin, Bill Lewis and Sexton Ming."

21. 9 GREENLAND STREET
Now the home of Food Records, and the independent film company, Solid, this building has long been associated with both the fashion industry and the music business. Sinéad O'Connor's management was based here in 1987 and this is where she did many of the interviews for her debut album, *The Lion & The Cobra*. Savage & Best, the PRs behind Pulp, Suede and many others, had an office here between 1991 and 1993, before moving to new premises in Arlington Road. "Our office was in what was really a fashion building," says John Best. "Vivienne Westwood was in there and so was Flyte-Ostell. I was really impressed that so many companies, which I considered to be glamorous, were in such a dingy building."

Savage & Best's old office was taken over by War Child, the charity set up to help victims of the Bosnian conflict, and who were behind the 1995 album, *Help*, which was recorded in 24 hours and featured tracks by The Stone Roses, Oasis, Suede and Paul Weller.

22. FOOD RECORDS LTD
9 Greenland Street, NW1. Telephone: 0171-284 2554
Best known as the home of Blur, Food Records was founded in 1984, by David Balfe, who had been an important part of the Liverpool punk scene, playing in Radio Blank, Dalek I Love You, Big In Japan and the Teardrop Explodes. He had also got together with Bill Drummond in the late-70s to form Zoo, the record label and management company behind the Teardrop Explodes and Echo & The Bunnymen.

Food's first release was the single *Soul Murder* by Brilliant, a band formed by ex-Killing Joke bassist Youth. Through Youth, Balfe met Zodiac Mindwarp, a heavily-tattooed singer from Bradford, with the rather unusual ambition of making an album which combined heavy metal and hip hop. Balfe was immediately convinced by Zodiac's vision and signed him and his band, the Love Reaction. By this time, Balfe had been joined by Andy Ross, a former member of the largely

Camden-based Disco Zombies, who also wrote for *Sounds* under the pseudonym Andy Hurt. Ross had a good understanding of the media and played an important part in raising the label's profile. "It's almost impossible to contemplate now," says Ross, "but in 1985 no one had tattoos — *no one* — if you did, then you were a sailor from the last war or very odd indeed. Then Balfy discovered Zodiac, who was covered in tattoos, and it was all very scary. It certainly scared my neighbours."

After Zodiac Mindwarp & The Love Reaction, Balfe and Ross signed Voice Of The Beehive, Crazyhead and Diesel Park West in fairly quick succession, which was enough to convince EMI Records to take a stake in the label — although the Food bands didn't exactly look or behave like the average chart acts. "In our office, there's Zodiac Mindwarp & The Love Reaction, Crazyhead and our band," said Melissa from Voice Of The Beehive in 1988, "and we're all sat there drinking or getting stoned in the closet — it's an ideal world!"

Voice Of The Beehive, who were also managed by Balfe, were Food's first pop band, and had a succession of hits in 1987 and 1988. At the end of 1988, Ross was given a tape by a band called Jesus Jones. He did what he usually did with demos, took it down to his local pub — which, at this point, was the Devonshire Arms on Kentish Town Road — played it to his mates and asked them what they thought of it. The demo of a song called *Info Freako* was subsequently released as a single and reached the Top 50. Jesus Jones went on to really establish Food's name with their 1991 album, *Doubt*, which reached Number One in the UK and hit the Billboard Top 30 in the United States.

Food signed their next band, Seymour, on the strength of a demo of the song, *She's So High*, and a gig at Islington's Powerhaus— although Ross later persuaded the quartet to change their name to Blur. When *She's So High* was released as the band's debut single, in October 1990, it entered the Top 50, while the follow-up single, *There's No Other Way*, reached Number 8 in April 1991.

In March 1992, Food relocated from Soho to an office on Arlington Road in Camden Town. "We wanted to move to a place that was a bit more vibey and less hassle than the West End," says Andy Ross. "We also wanted to be a bit more independent from the major companies that are based in Hammersmith. It was a bit of a statement as well, because Camden is where the venues are, and it seemed sensible to base a record company where the gigs and musicians are. It was cheaper, too, so it made sense all round."

At the end of 1992, Balfe rejected Blur's second album, *Modern Life Is Rubbish*, and insisted that the band wrote at least two more tracks for it. When the album was released in May 1993, the critical response was muted to say the least. It was during this period that Balfe famously declared to Ross that "Guitar music is dead" and decided to sell his shares to EMI.

By the time Balfe left Food, the release of Blur's *Parklife* was just a couple of months away and critical opinion had taken a huge swing in their favour. It was Ross — already one of the prime movers on the Camden scene — who enjoyed the first major fruits of Blur's success, and he was also MD of Food during the infamous Battle Of Britpop. Blur's *Country House*, which had been inspired by Dave Balfe's new residence, eventually beat Oasis's *Roll With It* to the Number One slot in August 1995 and their album, *The Great Escape*, also reached the top of the charts. However, Blur — like every other band in the country — had soon been pushed into the sidelines by the unstoppable rise of Oasis. "That was a great period," says Ross. "Through the summer of 1995, right up to when Blur won four awards at the Brits. I just felt so liberated and I was also having a laugh. Food, Creation and Go! Discs had all started around the same time in the mid-80s, and we had all known what it was like to be a touch and go operation, so it was a good time for everyone."

Food had also had enormous success in Japan with Shampoo and picked up new bands, such as Dubstar and The Supernaturals, while The Bluetones had signed to their publishing company. They moved from their old office on Arlington Road to Greenland Street in 1996.

23. GREENLAND STREET

Back in the 50s and 60s, this street housed an Irish dancehall called the Galway Club. It was never as popular as the neighbouring Buffalo [now the Electric Ballroom], possibly because, in a town largely populated by people from the West Coast of Ireland, its name was a little too area-specific. However, in 1951, the Irish superstar Delia Murphy, who made her name with a song called *The Spinning Wheel*, walked from Chalk Farm Tube Station, through cheering crowds of Irish men and women, to sing at the Galway Club.

Three decades later, the same hall was the setting for several warehouse parties, some of them involving Soul II Soul and the Young Disciples. "Me and my friends did three or four parties in Greenland Street and absolutely rammed the place," says Ben Jones. "We had a near riot in the street because we had a thousand people inside and about 800 outside, who we had to turn away."

"There were a lot of good parties on Greenland Street," says Paddy James. "These days, we're back to super clubs like Cream and the Ministry Of Sound, whereas the warehouse thing was much more about doing it yourself. It was a bit like jumble sales, you sussed out where the best ones were and kept going to them."

24. COLLECTORS EMPORIUM
7-8 Greenland Place, NW1. Telephone: 0171-482 5083
Part of the Vintage Magazine chain, this basement warehouse sells thousands of film posters, comics and magazines, including back issues of *NME*, *Melody Maker* and *Sounds*.

Courtney Love at the Underworld, November 1991 [Ed Sirrs]

25. TOWER RECORDS
162 Camden High Street, NW1. Telephone: 0171-439 2500
The only surprising thing about the recent arrival of Tower Records on Camden High Street is that it took so long for one of the major chains to open a store here. "I've been sat in the Good Mixer when people have come walking in with HMV bags," says Steve Lamacq. "The nearest HMV is at Oxford Street, which probably means that people are coming in from out of town, going to the West End to buy some records and then rushing up to Camden, because it's the next stop for music fans."

This is one of Tower's smaller stores, but it still houses thousands of CDs, books and newspapers, with a substantial import section. This was once the site of the first Soul II Soul shop, which sold records, T-shirts and Funki Dred paraphernalia, and where Jazzie B regularly held court on a beaten-up, black leather sofa.

26. THE UNDERWORLD
174 Camden High Street, NW1. Telephone: 0171- 267 3626
This cavernous club, which lies in the basement of the World's End pub and bills itself as 'The Home Of Rock And Indie', first opened as a venue in the autumn of 1990.

Heavenly Records did a showcase here in January 1991, which featured sets from the Manic Street Preachers, East Village, St Etienne, the Moonflowers, Flowered Up and DJ Andy Weatherall. Five months later, Voice Of The Beehive played three consecutive shows which they billed 'Orgy In The Underworld', draping the place in satin and net and covering the walls in slides of naked men and women, while transvestites wandered around the venue.

From the start, the Underworld was a good place to see visiting American bands, such as Urge Overkill and Smashing Pumpkins, who made their London debut here in September 1991. When Hole played in November, Courtney Love did an impromptu stage dive and ended up having her dress and underwear virtually ripped off by the audience. When Love got back onstage, she was so angry and frustrated that she smashed up her favourite Rickenbacker guitar and the experience later prompted her to write the song *Asking For It* on Hole's 1994 album, *Live Through This*.

"I can't compare it to rape because it's not the same," Love told Pamela Des Barres during their 1994 meeting for *Interview* magazine. "But in a way it was. I was raped by an audience — figuratively, literally, and yet, was I asking for it?"

Over the next couple of years, Screaming Trees, Soundgarden, Afghan Whigs, Bob Mould and Therapy? all played at the Underworld; and it became a favoured place for popular metal bands to do small club gigs, including Anthrax, Fear Factory and Kyuss. Suede also did one of their first big London shows here in January 1992, supporting Pulp, followed by their own headline spot a few months later.

The Underworld's weekend club nights have always been popular, frequented by bands like Blur, Lush and anyone else who happened to be in Camden, and were generally a reliable barometer of a band's social standing. Blur guitarist Graham Coxon once complained that, after the release of the band's highly unacclaimed *Modern Life Is Rubbish* album, he would go down to the Underworld and no one would talk to him. Still, that was probably better than having a handful of beer boys singing the words to *Girls & Boys* at him, which is exactly what happened following the release of *Parklife*.

These days, the Underworld is better known for its club nights than for live bands, but it is still a popular place to go.

27. THE WORLD'S END
174 Camden High Street, NW1. Telephone: 0171-482 1932
The World's End stands on the site of the late Mother Red Cap, which was the oldest pub in Camden until it finally gave way to redevelopment at the end of the 1980s.

According to local legend, the pub got its name from a woman called Jinney, the daughter of a Kentish Town brickmaker, whose parents were hanged for witchcraft and who was suspected of being a witch herself. These suspicions were confirmed when two out of three of her husbands were found burnt to death in the oven of her cottage — one might have been an accident, two was simply being careless and she was nicknamed Mother Damnable or Mother Red Cap, because of the colour of her hat. The Mother Red Cap subsequently became a stopping off point for 17th Century highway men and women and the pub and its 18th Century tea gardens were later regarded as the traditional 'halfway house to Hampstead'.

In the 1960s, Dominic Behan — who, like his more famous brother, Brendan, was no stranger to Camden Town — recommended the Mother Red Cap as one of the best pubs where you could expect to hear Irish singing in London. By the 70s, it had a reputation for being a really rough place and was also one of the few pubs around here to admit travellers. "The old Mother Red Cap was one of the biggest pubs known to humanity," says Suggs. "Yet there were only ever four people in there, at any one time."

The World's End couldn't have been more different to the old Mother Red Cap when it was finally unveiled, after two-and-a-half-years of redevelopment, in 1990. The rough old pub was suddenly transformed into an enormous modern bar with stained glass windows. The manager at the time of the opening was Mick Pearl, the former bassist in the Q Tips which might explain why the words to John Lennon's *In My Life* were etched into the wall. When the Underworld was opened in the basement in 1990, The World's End initially became a favourite drinking spot with the music biz, although most of them moved elsewhere a couple of years later.

CAMDEN HIGH STREET - SOUTH SIDE

NEWSREEL: THE 80s

The devil moon took me out of Soho
Up to Camden where the cold north wind blows

This could be our final dance
This could be our very last chance
Just the sound of your voice
Wherever I may be changes everything
And then the world's all right with me
You're my London girl

DOPE SMUGGLER GRASSED ON HEROIN GANG

SKINHEADS IN NIGHT OF VIOLENCE AT ROCK CLUBS
Saturday night violence broke out at Camden's three top rock clubs
with ugly scenes — involving skinheads

HOSPITAL QUEUES GROW

SUS ARRESTS 'LOWEST IN LONDON'

THE POPE TO VISIT CAMDEN?
IT'S ON THE CARDS,
SAY COUPLE IN THE KNOW

CHAMPAGNE HELPS TV-AM GO WITH A BUZZ...

CAMDEN HITS THE HIGH IN HEROIN ADDICTS

Three crumbling 20-storey tower blocks in Camden Town have
reached crisis point — and this week councillors were asked to
consider knocking them down after only 15 years' life

WILL CAMDEN TOWN
TURN INTO
AN ELEPHANT AND CASTLE?

A block of flats in Camden — nicknamed "Madhouse Mansions" —
was condemned at an Old Bailey hearing on Friday as "a palace of sin"

CRIME LEAPS WITH POLICE ON PICKET DUTY
Crime has shot up in Camden by 13 per cent — and police have
admitted it could be due to the Miners' Strike

THE ROCK'N'ROLL GUIDE TO CAMDEN

UNDERWEAR
'HAVOC'
IN HIGH STREET

Sid'N'Nancy, the new film telling the story of Sid Vicious, has missed
an important part of his life, according to a former flatmate.
It is the Camden connection

THE DAY BOB DYLAN
CRUISED IN

DISNEY MOVES TO CAMDEN

POLICE SWOOP IN SEARCH OF HEROIN

DON'T LET THE DEVELOPERS RUIN YOUR HIGH STREET

A simple arrest turned into a pitched battle between police and
rockabillies in Camden High Street on Saturday afternoon

'SAVE PASCAL'S CAFE' URGES PETITION

POLICE WAR ON FASHION DRUG
Six men were arrested when police discovered a large quantity of the
designer drug ecstacy in their car on Saturday night

Britain's new Foreign Secretary, John Major, fought his first
Parliamentary campaign in Camden — and was soundly defeated

POLICE FEAR 'DISORDER AND ACID HOUSE INVASION'
Heroin is killing young people throughout Camden and the Police are
turning a blind eye to the drugs dealers

GUILDFORD 4: CAMDEN ALIBI

The next time I see you we'll be down at the Greeks
There'll be whiskey on Sunday and tears on our cheeks
For it's stupid to laugh and it's useless to bawl
About a rusty tin can and an old hurley ball

Take my hand, and dry your tears babe
Take my hand, forget your fears babe
There's no pain, there's no more sorrow
They've all gone, gone in the years babe

PARKWAY
&
INVERNESS STREET

THE ROCK'N'ROLL GUIDE TO CAMDEN

"Parkway is the kind of place where Liam Gallagher can saunter down the road with his crash helmet under his arm, without anyone bothering him. It's because it's Britpap land. It's Camden and it's territory where you're not infringed upon."
— Phill Savidge, 1997

"I really noticed the demise of Camden Town when I saw Morrissey coming up one side of Parkway, Noel Gallagher going down the other, while Blur just hung around at the bottom. All in one day."
— Suggs, 1996

1. LADIES TOILETS
The Island On Parkway, NW1.
The ladies toilets, beneath the junction of Parkway and Camden High Street, are an indirect monument to the writer George Bernard Shaw, who advocated the building of public lavatories for women when he was a member of the St Pancras Vestry in the 1920s.

However, the toilets have not always been as public as Shaw would have liked. They were closed for many years during the 70s, so women were directed across the road to an orange horse box outside the Tube Station while the local winos set up a long bench in front of them and turned the site into their favourite vantage point. The toilets were eventually reopened in the early-80s and became a stopping-off point for girls who wanted to redo their make up *en route* to the Electric Ballroom or Camden Palace.

George Bernard Shaw would probably be satisfied to know that the toilets are now open between 8am and 7pm, seven days a week, and that there would be uproar among the local market traders if Camden Town ever tried to do without its famous ladies again.

2. ODEON CAMDEN TOWN
14 Parkway, NW1. Telephone: 0181-315 4229
This five screen cinema, complete with a café-bar, opened in July 1997, after a long battle to bring film back to Camden Town.

The original cinema was built in the 30s, on the site of the 19th Century Royal Park Theatre, and was widely considered to be one of the most beautiful in London. Back then, it was called the Gaumont, later changing its name to the Odeon, the Gate Three and finally the Parkway Centre, before reverting back to an Odeon.

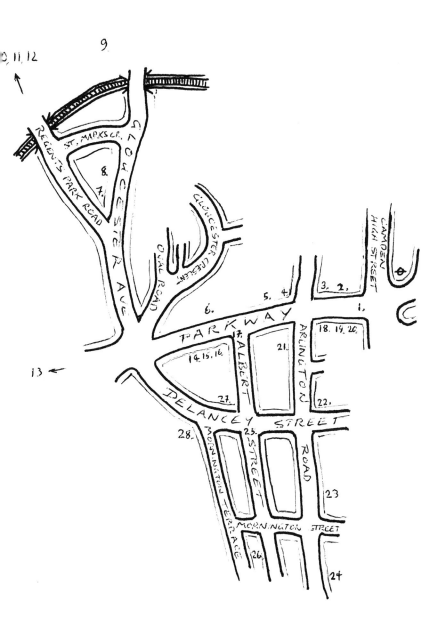

It was here, in October 1981, during the cinema's brief Gate Three period, that Madness premiered their *Take It Or Leave It* movie, which was directed by Stiff Records' boss, Dave Robinson, and told the story of the band's formation and rise in Camden. Midway through the film, the band climbed onstage in front of the screen, and started aping their own movements. Afterwards, they took their families up the road to the Dublin Castle for the official launch party.

Throughout the 80s and 90s, the cinema had to put up an ongoing fight against redevelopment and, despite the support of local celebrities like the playwright Alan Bennett, it closed down several times, most recently in 1994. Now, however, as the new Odeon, which seats 900 people, it looks like there will be a cinema in Camden Town for many years to come.

3. 172 ARLINGTON ROAD
In the early-90s, this housed both Food Records and the music PRs Savage & Best and was at the centre of the whole Britpop scene [its close proximity to the Good Mixer partly explains why that pub became so popular]. The reformed Madness had a rehearsal room upstairs and Jesus Jones' frontman Mike Edwards recorded in his own studio in another part of the building.

4, GOODFARE RESTAURANT
26 Parkway, NW1. Telephone: 0171-485 2230
Opened in 1973, this Italian caff has remained pretty much the same throughout the passing years and is one of the best place for egg and chips in Camden. It was a favourite hangout for Madness and The Pogues in the early-80s and is referred to by regulars as 'Stella's', the name of the straight-talking waitress. Bob Dylan and Liam Gallagher are among the people who have eaten here.

5. THE GOLDEN GRILL
38 Parkway, NW1. Telephone: 0171-485 7432
Better known as George & Niki's, this is the best and cheapest place to eat traditional English food in Camden Town. The restaurant has been in the same family for 50 years and has been run by George Georgiou and his wife, Niki, since 1980. However, it is George's cousin, Vange, the head waiter and a bit of an Elvis-lookalike, who gives the Golden Grill much of its character.

It is only a small restaurant — although there are more tables in the garden and an extra dining room at the back — but the walls are covered in photographs of celebrities who may or may not have eaten here, such as Desmond Lynam, Jack Duckworth, Ted Heath and Ulrika Johnsson, and bands who definitely have, including George Michael, Goldie, Björk, Jazzie B, Nellee Hooper, Tricky and Oasis.

The Golden Grill is fully licensed with decent house wine and a

selection of spirits. Back in the 80s, it was one of the few places in Camden Town where you could drink away the hours between the pubs closing at 3.00pm and opening again at 5.30pm. Not surprisingly, Shane MacGowan frequently made use of its generous licensing hours. "Shane used to come in all the time," says Vange. "He drank his own special cocktail, which was basically a shot of each of the seven spirits that we've got hanging up on the optics. We used to get lots of people coming in to drink in the afternoons, but everyone's an alcoholic these days so you can drink anywhere you like all day long."

The Golden Grill's reputation was originally based on its extensive menu which includes roast dinners, fry-ups, vegetarian dishes and a variety of puddings — one of which left Axl Rose puzzled when Guns N'Roses ate here during the band's first English dates in June 1987. "What the fuck is Spotted Dick?" cried Axl. "I can't believe you guys eat this thing called Spotted Dick!" Guns N'Roses left George slightly less bemused: they became the only band he has ever thrown out of his restaurant.

Seven years later, Spotted Dick and some of the other hangover-curing stodge on the menu was a positive attraction to the local Britpop bands, who renamed the restaurant 'School Dinners'. "The indie kids call George & Niki's 'School Dinners'," says Mary Byker, a long-time customer. "That's because most of them are young enough to remember what a school dinner actually tastes like."

Elastica ate in the Golden Grill in their early days because it was cheap, but it seems to have some sort of a Midas touch. "I think this place gives people luck," says Vange. "We've had so many bands who've started off coming in here and then gone on to do really well. I don't know what it is, maybe it's just because it's relaxed and I tell them what I think. They say, 'Vange, what do you think of my new record?'. I think it's shit. They go, 'Thank you very much' and some of them don't come back again but some of them do. I'm just straightforward with people."

Although the Golden Grill was temporarily associated with Britpop, it has a lifespan which stretches way beyond that. "This restaurant is definitely not indie, it's rock'n'roll," says Vange. "We used to have Elvis nights on Fridays and Saturdays, where that was the only music I'd play. My heart is in rock'n'roll and as long as I'm here this place is always going to be about rock'n'roll."

He's certainly got reams of rock'n'roll stories: like the day Tom Jones came in and did impromptu versions of *Delilah* and *What's New Pussycat?* Or the evening Bobby Vinton was eating in here in 1986 when the radio announced that *Blue Velvet* had gone to Number One and he immediately ordered a few bottles of champagne and treated everyone in the restaurant to a celebratory glass. Or the night Julio Iglesias came in and George told him that he wasn't allowed to leave until he'd gone down on one knee and serenaded a female customer.

Noel Gallagher occasionally ate in the Golden Grill when he lived across the road in Albert Street, and his brother has also numbered among Vange's customers. "Liam was sitting here one day having a drink with a few friends," he says "There was this girl in here, who had been to one of their concerts and was about half a mile back from the stage, and she just couldn't believe that he was sitting two tables away from her. He was drinking a pint and, when he'd gone, she asked me if she could keep the glass as a memorabilia of him being that close to her. I said, 'Don't be stupid' and she goes, 'I'll pay you.' So, for a laugh, I said, 'Give me 20 quid for it', and she gave it to me — so I took it, the stupid cow. There's some sad people out there, there really are. No wonder these pop stars go loopy. They get famous and they go all loopy, because they've got people like that chasing them about all the time."

Despite the emergence of various new cafés and restaurants on Parkway during the 90s, the Golden Grill has retained its popularity. "Family businesses are dying out, which is why people like this place," says Vange. "I'd like to open a bar in Camden one day, a little tapas bar, where people can come in and drink and have snacks and relax. I'd have good taped music and all the old film stars on the wall — Marlon Brando, Dean Martin — and a nice big screen showing old 50s movies. I think that's why we do so well here, cos we're different. Everyone knows us, whereas the other places keep changing their staff and have miserable waitresses, which makes people depressed and puts them off their dinner."

"If you come here and you meet Vange you keep coming back. It's as simple as that," says Bal Croce, another regular. "I met Vange and he became a friend — I came here the night before my wedding. It's that sort of a place."

"One of the great things about George & Niki's is that it has never changed," says Steve Lamacq. "You do wonder about people in bands who feel the need to move onto the Groucho Club or somewhere, that would just be terrible for me, to be courting press whenever you go out. Whereas the great thing about somewhere like George & Niki's is that you don't get any hassle and you don't think your menu will end up in some gossip column."

6. DUBLIN CASTLE
94 Parkway, NW1. Telephone: 0171-485 1773
Much of the Dublin Castle's reputation is based on the fact that Madness played some of their earliest and most exciting gigs here. Its rock'n'roll stature was reinforced during the summer of 1995 when Blur chose this as the venue for a high-profile 'secret' gig and Liam Gallagher made it one of his Camden Town drinking haunts.

Built in the last century, the Dublin Castle is a good-looking pub with a long bar, mirrored walls, red lamps, formica table tops, a decent jukebox and a small downstairs venue where bands play most nights of the week. It is one of the few pubs in Camden which hasn't really changed its decor since the 70s, which is probably because it has had the same landlord, Alo Conlon, since 1976.

Live music at the Dublin Castle dates back to a Monday night folk session in the late-60s. Then, in the summer of 1970, the publican of the time, Bernard Finlay, built a clubroom at the back of the pub. Despite opposition from local residents who were worried about being disturbed by the noise, Mr Finlay eventually unveiled a £22,000 banqueting hall and was granted a special-hours licence allowing him to keep the pub open till midnight six days a week. It was the first time that such a licence had been granted in England.

One of the initial big events to take place in the new banqueting hall was in December 1970 when Bernadette Devlin, the young Northern Ireland MP, did a benefit concert for someone who had been charged with exploding a CS gas canister in the House Of Commons. She sang *My Dark Rosaleen* in Gaelic and then *The Red Flag* in a duet with Dominic Behan, the brother of the writer, Brendan, who was a regular face around the Irish pubs of Camden Town.

Alo Conlon, from County Mayo in Ireland, became the landlord of the Dublin Castle in 1976, after running two previous pubs in Stoke Newington and Kentish Town. He got an unexpected slice of rock'n'roll glory when Madness asked him to introduce the video for their 1979 single, *My Girl* — a cameo he earned after giving them one of their earliest gigs, in April 1979, even though they had to pretend to be a jazz band in order to get it. "Madness were a bunch of local boys and it was the first time they had ever played on a stage for money," says Alo Conlon. "They said they were a jazz band but they turned out to be heavy rock — they'd shake the foundations of the building."

"At that time the Dublin Castle was putting on either middle-of-the-road country & western bands, or jazz-ish kind of stuff," remembers Suggs. "But we managed to get a residency for about two months and, along with the 2-Tone Tour, those gigs were probably the highlight of being in Madness. Week by week, we became more and more infamous, so there would be queues round the block. There was a genuine feeling of excitement and the Dublin Castle really would be *the* place to be on a Friday night."

During this period, Madness were asked to support their new friends The Specials at the Nashville in West Kensington — the only problem was that the date clashed with their Dublin Castle residency. They solved it by playing both gigs on the same night, and later filmed a rerun of the two shows as the climax to their 1981 autobiographical movie, *Take It Or Leave It*. "At the time, I don't think anyone realised how important the whole thing with us and The Specials was going to be," says Suggs. "I remember thinking that it was more important that we hung on to our residency at the Dublin Castle, so we ended up doing both gigs. But all those bits in the film were true — there really did end up being more people on the stage than there were in the audience."

Madness attracted a great deal of record company attention that summer, eventually signing to Stiff, rather than one of the major labels. But Camden Town continued to be a focus point for many factions of the music business throughout 1979. "We always went to the Dublin Castle on Fridays to see Madness," says Joe Dilworth. "They also had a mod night and you used to get the better bands from that scene playing, and me and my sister got into following certain bands about, like the Merton Parkas. But I went away for the summer of 79 and, when I came back, everything had completely changed. *Quadrophenia* had come out and it was suddenly really dangerous to be a mod in Camden Town. We used to get chased and beaten up all the time, just going out to gigs, and I couldn't even go and see Madness anymore cos their skinhead following had really taken over."

After the buzz surrounding Madness, the Dublin Castle reverted back to its previous policy of mainly booking R&B, country, cajun, blues and rockabilly. The house favourites included The Big Town

---

"One of the highlights of my life was to be drunk on some television show, in Dublin, all maudlin, singing about Camden Town. If I've heard one person sing about Dublin in Camden Town, I've heard five thousand." – SUGGS

Playboys, who would regularly attract Robert Plant to their gigs, the Balham Alligators, Howling Wilf and Juice On The Loose. "I remember seeing people like Alvin Crow, who was a big name in Western Swing, playing in the Dublin Castle, with BJ Cole, in a pick-up band," says Mike Hart, who was a regular here during the 80s. "Terry Allen played and Katie Webster, the blues pianist from Louisiana — there were just all sorts of people like that."

By 1994, the Dublin Castle changed its booking policy to include various indie nights, the most famous of which was Club Spangle on Mondays, which was run by Simon Williams and Chris Myhill. "In a way, the Dublin Castle was Simon Williams trying to recreate the Panic Station," says Steve Lamacq who usually went to Club Spangle. "That was partly the idea, to put a good package of bands together. It wasn't as big as the Panic Station, but it was a regular Monday gig. It's odd how you grow up going to these things and end up doing them yourself for the next generation of kids. And obviously it did work, because a lot of bands came through from there, like The Bluetones. All those Monday night shows were like A&R showcases — although, by that point, A&R was five times as competitive as it was at the Panic Station just seven years previously."

During the Britpop summer of 1995, Club Spangle was *the* place to see new bands and among those who played that year were Cast, plus Lush, Lloyd Cole and Blur who all did 'secret' gigs here — the latter's gig, which actually took place on a Saturday night, in May, was the biggest event the Dublin Castle had staged in years. "Blur fever was at its height, but that gig was a bit of a cock-up really," says Andy Ross, MD of the band's record label, Food. "It was supposed to be a secret gig, and we were only going to sell tickets in the Dublin Castle or give them to mates in the Good Mixer, but when word got around that Blur were playing at the Dublin Castle for about a fiver, it wasn't just fans who bought them. There was also a bunch of blokes who happened to be in the vicinity who were like, 'Well, I don't think much of them, but for a fiver I'll go and have a laugh', so there was a fairly hostile element watching them. Someone chucked a glass at Damon and there were people shouting at the back, so it all got a bit fractious. It was a pretty good gig, but it wasn't one of the greatest of all time."

Among those who frequented the Dublin Castle during that period were various members of the Sex Pistols, Pulp, Elastica, Ant & Dec, Paul Weller and Oasis — particularly Noel, who lived across the road on Albert Street throughout 1995. "We've had a few flyers through the door: 'Come and see my band at the Dublin Castle, two quid,'" he told Stuart Maconie in *Select* that June. "So, of course, great, I think, I'll be there."

The Dublin Castle might not be as popular a venue as it was during its Club Spangle period, but that didn't stop it from being one of the three Camden pubs where Liam Gallagher played a preview tape of

Oasis's third album, *Be Here Now*, four months before the record was released. The pub has also continued to be an essential stop-off point for visiting Madness fans — although they are unlikely to ever bump into Suggs. "I really feel uncomfortable going in the Dublin Castle now," he says. "My face is all over the place, so people double-take and go, 'It *is* him', whereas in most pubs you can blend into the background. It's a shame, cos the landlord, Alo, was great to us."

7. CECIL SHARP HOUSE
2 Regent's Park Road, NW1. Telephone: 0171-485 2206
This prominent neo-Georgian building on the junction of Regent's Park Road and Gloucester Avenue was opened in 1930 by the English Folk Dance Society and named after their founding member Cecil James Sharp. Born in London in 1859, Sharp was a music teacher who dedicated his life to the collection and promotion of folk songs. He published *A Book Of British Song* in 1902 and later allowed his quest for new material to lead him to the Appalachian Mountains, where he spent time with the descendants of a group of English settlers and wrote about the thousands of tunes and variants he discovered there in his 1919 publication, *English Folk Songs From The Southern Appalachians*.

The English Folk Dance Society have continued to promote Sharp's work, by keeping his books, manuscripts, photographs and papers in the Vaughan Williams Library at Cecil Sharp House. They also stage traditional dancing (such as Saturday night ceilidhs), singing sessions, special guest evenings and major events like the London Folk Festival. All sorts of musicians have played at Cecil Sharp House over the years, including Margaret Barry, The Dubliners and Ewan MacColl. During the 70s, many Irish musicians made pilgrimages here in order to collect obscure folk songs which they then learned and incorporated into their sets. On a different note, Morecambe & Wise once used the basement of Cecil Sharp House to rehearse for a new series of their TV series. Cecil Sharp House also houses a specialist Folk Shop [Telephone: 0171-284 0534], which is open every day apart from Sunday and sells records, cassettes, CDs, traditional music books and a wide variety of instruments, ranging from Appalachian dulcimers to acoustic guitars.

8. FILM-MAKERS' CO-OPERATIVE/LONDON MUSICIANS' COLLECTIVE
42 Gloucester Avenue, NW1.
This was once the site of the Film-Makers' Co-operative and London Musicians' Collective, where they held gigs, showed films, played records and had various facilities, such as a badge-making machine.

The most famous gig to ever take place here was on New Year's Day 1979, when Madness played for the last time under their previous name of The Invaders. They were supported by the Millwall Chainsaws, a punk trio who were making their debut appearance that night and were fronted by future Pogue Spider Stacy. "I've got a poster of that gig with 'Millwall Chainsaws' done in felt pen," says Suggs. "I thought the gig had been sponsored by Rock Against Racism, cos the monitors had RAR written on them, in fact they'd been pinched from a previous Rock Against Racism festival. I don't remember much about the actual gig, but I do remember that there were about four people in the audience — those Invaders' concerts were only really attended by our friends, we certainly didn't have any fans at that point. People were always a bit mystified by us, cos I think they were expecting a punk band, not the weird hybrid that we were at that time."

The Chainsaws set left no room for ambiguity, particularly when they did a song called *Skinhead Escapes*, which Stacy had been inspired to write after reading Richard Allen's *Skinhead* series. It began with the lines: "*Joe Hawkins died for somebody's sins, not mine/I'm buggered if I'm gonna pay this fine, one two, three, four...*"

"That was one of our best gigs," says Stacy. "We also did a song called *Fuck Off* which consisted of the, er, musicians going, 'BOOM! BOOM!' and me shouting, 'Fuck off! Fuck off!' and rolling around on the floor and generally making an exhibition of myself." The Millwall Chainsaws did seven gigs in the space of the next two-and-a-half-years and then, joined by Shane MacGowan, did a one-off gig as the New Republicans, singing Irish rebel songs at Richard Strange's Cabaret Futura in Soho. They were pelted offstage by a group of drunken squaddies, but the performance gave MacGowan the impetus to form Pogue Mahone 18 months later.

The Musicians Co-op was best known for jazz, but punk broadened the parameters so that it could cope with bands like the Millwall Chainsaws and Alan McGee also promoted shows here under the name Communication. "The Musicians' Co-op initially did a lot of jazz improvisation, with people like Evan Parker and Derek Bailey doing acoustic stuff," says Mike Hart. "But punk had a knock-on effect so, by the early-80s, you had Genesis P Orridge playing there and you could hear literally any kind of music, plus dance and all sorts of other things. In the Film Co-op, they had nights where you could bring along your own film and have it shown. I played there fairly regularly between 1982 and 1984 with a band called the House Devils, and one of the first gigs we did was improvising the soundtrack to a film that someone was showing. Quite a lot of big names played at the Co-op, people like David Toop and Steve Beresford, and I think some of Rip Rig & Panic might have come through there, too."

9. THE ENGINEER
65 Gloucester Avenue, NW1. Telephone: 0171-722 0950
Co-owned by Laurence Olivier's daughter, Tamsin, this is an upmarket bar with a separate restaurant which tends to attract lots of musicians,

PARKWAY

such as Terry Hall, and local celebs, like Harry Enfield. Back in the 60s and 70s, the Engineer was a quiet, old men's pub, with a long tradition of Sunday folk sessions. In the early-80s, it was popular with those attending the nearby Film Makers' Co-operative/London Musicians' Collective. "There was a lot of interaction between the two places," says Mike Hart. "The Co-op didn't have a toilet so you either had to use the iron staircase or go across the road and use it as an excuse to have another beer. It was just a nice pub, full of local people, and we would always end up there when the Co-op closed."

Many of those old locals have since died or moved elsewhere, and their former seating area has now been converted into a dining room, which has a reputation for being one of the best places to eat around Camden.

10. WB YEATS & SYLVIA PLATH
23 Fitzroy Road, NW1.
There's a blue plaque outside this house to show that the great Irish poet and mystic William Butler Yeats moved here as a small child in 1867 and this is where his brother Jack, the painter, was born. One of Yeats' first memories, which he described in his *Autobiographies*, is of looking out of the window of this house and seeing some boys playing in the street, one of whom was wearing a uniform, and was probably a telegraph messenger. When Yeats asked a servant why he was wearing a uniform he was told that the boy was going to blow the town up and Yeats went to bed terrified.

Over the years, Yeats has inspired dozens of musicians, most notably Mike Scott, who did an interpretation of *The Stolen Child* on The Waterboys' 1988 *Fisherman's Blues* album; Bono, who once did a live rendition of *Mad Is The Mist And Snow* at Dublin's Abbey Theatre; and Van Morrison, who has made several references to Yeats' poetry in his own songs. Scott and Morrison, plus other singers, such as Shane MacGowan, and the actor Richard Harris, did interpretations of his poetry for a tribute album called *Now And In Time To Be: A Musical Celebration Of The Works Of WB Yeats*, which was released in 1997. But it is not just Celtic songwriters who have been drawn to his poetry — Courtney Love declared her admiration for one of his later poems, *A Crazed Girl*, saying, "Patti Smith was in love with Rimbaud, I'm in love with Yeats."

The American poet Sylvia Plath was also in love with Yeats and, in 1960, was keen to buy 41 Fitzroy Road, purely because it was in the street where he had lived. However, Plath and her husband, the poet Ted Hughes, were reluctant to take on a mortgage without an assured income and let the house go. By 1962, Plath and Hughes had separated and, as Sylvia was walking through Primrose Hill one day in October, she saw a 'Flats To Let' sign in front of the house where Yeats had lived. She instantly decided it was "*the* street and *the* house" for her, persuaded some builders to let her have a look at the top masionette and, within minutes, was negotiating with the agents for a five-year lease.

Plath, and her two children, moved into the top two floors of the house that December. Although it is commonly believed that Plath wrote most of *Ariel* while she was living in Fitzroy Road, she had actually finished the majority of those poems before she moved here. However, she felt that living in Yeats's house was "a real inspiration" to her writing and it was here that she wrote 12 poems, including *Mystic*, *Words* and *Edge*. These poems reflect more than a troubled state of mind, they show the breakdown of her will to live, and it was in this house, during a particularly bad depression, that she gassed herself on February 11, 1963, aged 30. Plath's only novel, the partly autobiographical, *The Bell Jar*, was published just before her death and immediately made her a cult figure. Plath was one of Richey James's favourite writers and the Manic Street Preachers quoted some of her poetry on the inner sleeve of their 1992 *Generation Terrorists* album.

11. CREATION RECORDS
109x Regents Park Road, NW1. Telephone: 0171 722 8866
The home of Oasis, Creation Records moved from its old base in Hackney to these offices in Primrose Hill in April 1995. The label was launched in 1983, by Alan McGee, a British Rail employee who had recently moved to London from his native Glasgow and started two clubs — first, Communication, at the Musicians' Collective in Gloucester Avenue, and then the Living Room, above a pub on Tottenham Court Road. Inspired by the popularity of the Living Room, and some of the musicians he had met there — notably Joe Foster, Dan Treacy and Ed Ball — McGee decided to form his own record label and named it Creation in honour of one of his favourite bands.

Creation's first release was the single, *73 In 83*, by a fanzine editor called the Legend! [who would become more widely known as the music journalist Everett True], followed by singles from other bands, such as The Jasmine Minks and The Pastels, plus his own two groups, the Laughing Apple [which also featured future Primal Scream guitarist Andrew Innes] and Biff Bang Pow!.

However, it was the Jesus & Mary Chain who gave the label its first classic single when they recorded *Upside Down*, backed with a cover of *Vegetable Man* by Syd Barrett, in October 1984. McGee had put the Mary Chain on at the Living Room that June and offered them a one-off single on the strength of their soundcheck, while the gig was enough to convince him that he wanted to be their manager. That November, McGee's mate, Bobby Gillespie, who had gone to gigs with him in Glasgow, became the Mary Chain's drummer and, even though the band had now signed to the Warner Brothers subsidary, blanco y negro, *Upside Down* sold more than 35,000 copies when it was released in February 1985 and went on to became one of the biggest-selling indie singles of the 80s. A large part of the band's appeal was down to their early gigs, which were some of the most exciting in years. "The Jesus & Mary Chain are putting excitement back into rock'n'roll," said McGee in a statement to the press. "This is truly art as terrorism."

In October 1985, Bobby Gillespie quit the Mary Chain to concentrate on fronting his own band, Primal Scream, who released the single *Velocity Girl* on Creation in 1986. By this time, McGee had stopped managing the Mary Chain and, over the next three years, devoted himself to Creation, releasing records by Felt, The Bodines, The Weather Prophets, Momus and Nikki Sudden. In 1987, Warners gave McGee the chance to set up his own label, Elevation, which he did, taking The Weather Prophets and Primal Scream with him. Elevation fell through but, luckily, Creation had the House Of Love and My Bloody Valentine; the former received a great deal of media attention and the latter released one of the more memorable singles of 1988 , *You Made Me Realise*. Soon afterwards, however, Phonogram lured the House Of Love to a major label, while My Bloody Valentine spent much of the next three years in the studio.

Meanwhile, McGee's life had been invigorated by acid house and it was the Primal Scream single, *Loaded*, that gave Creation its first Top Ten hit in 1990, and their 1991 album, *Screamadelica*, subsequently prompted Sony to buy 49 per cent of the label in return for international rights, which gave McGee serious money to develop his label. In addition to Primal Scream, Creation's roster also included Ride and Teenage Fanclub and McGee had also picked up The Boo Radleys and Bob Mould. Then, in October 1993, Oasis signed to Creation, having been invited to do so by McGee, when he saw them supporting 18 Wheeler at Glasgow King Tut's Wah Wah Hut five months earlier. "I believe in fate and that everything's mapped out for you," says Noel Gallagher. "It's like Alan McGee being in the club that day. Five minutes before we went onstage, the promoter was insisting that we weren't going to play under any circumstances and probably at the exact moment that he was finally agreeing to let us go on, Alan McGee was walking into the club."

Within 17 months of that meeting, *Definitely Maybe* had given Creation its first Number One album followed, in the summer of 1995, by the multi-million selling *(What's The Story) Morning Glory* and 1997's *Be Here Now*. The success of Oasis has made this the label that many bands would most like to sign to — its current roster includes Super Furry Animals, The Boo Radleys, 3 Colours Red and Arnold — and turned Creation a household name.

12. PRIMROSE HILL, NW1
Primrose Hill is one of the most popular parks in London and, since it reaches a height of 206-feet, it provides one of the best views of the city. The Rolling Stones were photographed here in November 1966 for the

cover of their *Between The Buttons* album. They had spent the previous night in the recording studio, so photographer Gered Mankowitz smeared Vaseline across his camera lens in an attempt to hide the bags under their eyes. 28 years later, Mankowitz took Oasis to the same spot to photograph them for the cover of *Mojo* magazine, using the same blurred lens technique. The front cover of the Oasis single, *Wonderwall*, was also shot here, by Michael Spencer Jones, in 1995.

Various other bands have been photographed here over the years, including Madness, who had a song called *Primrose Hill* on their 1982 album, *The Rise And Fall*, and shot its front cover here. Blur also sang about Primrose Hill in *For Tomorrow* on their *Modern Life Is Rubbish* album. The place also holds a certain romance for Elastica — when they signed their publishing deal with EMI Music, they went for a meal in the West End then took a taxi up here to sign the contract on Primrose Hill.

13. LONDON ZOO
Regent's Park, NW1. Telephone: 0171-722 3333
Britain's largest zoo is populated by elephants, zebras, monkeys, bears, giant pandas, lions, birds and fish and has provided several rock'n'roll stories over the years. For instance, it was a London Zoo tiger called Raja who had a run in with Ringo in The Beatles' film, *Help*; one of the giraffes is currently sponsored by Jon Bon Jovi's son; and Rolf Harris posed here with a white rhino in 1971, when he was recording the song and commentary for a film about their importation.

On a different note, Nick Cave was a regular visitor to the Zoo when he first arrived in London from Melbourne in 1980, and often earned a tenner for a day's work of washing dishes in the cafeteria or picking up litter around the ground. "I would queue up in the early hours of the morning, with tramps and various other people who'd been out all night," he says, "and generally got picked to work every other day."

In recent years, the Zoo has been the setting for various rock'n'roll parties, including 10,000 Maniacs who launched their *Blind Man's Zoo* album at the aquarium in May 1989 — among the casualties were two prize fish who were found dead in their tanks after being subjected to a two-hour preview of the album. The following year, Happy Mondays launched their *Pills, Thrills'N'Bellyaches* LP at the same venue and caused havoc when one of the guests dropped E into a fish tank and another threw a park bench into a nearby pond.

14. HAMISH'S
85/87 Parkway, NW1. Telephone: 0171-267 3591
A small wine bar and restaurant on Parkway, whose basement has been the scene of various rock'n'roll parties during the 90s. The guests, or hosts, have included Pulp, Blur, Lush, St Etienne, The Wonder Stuff, The Mission, Gallon Drunk, Vic Reeves, Bob Mortimer and Sean Hughes.

15. SAVAGE & BEST/PARKWAY RECORDS
79 Parkway, NW1. Telephone: 0171-482 7166

Savage & Best are one of the best known PR firms in the music business, having helped to launch the careers of Pulp, Suede, The Verve, Elastica, Echobelly, Kula Shaker, The Auteurs and The Longpigs.

Originally known as Best In Press, the company was set up on January 2, 1990, by John Best, a former journalist and PR for Virgin Records. Best had become disillusioned with working for a major record label and decided to start his own company in the spare bedroom of his house in Camden Square. In September 1990, Best asked his friend Phill Savidge, who had also been a PR at Virgin, to help him out, even though Savidge had recently opted out of the music business to write poetry. Soon afterwards, Best was given his first big break when he was asked to take on the publicity for 4AD, whose roster included The Pixies, the Cocteau Twins and Lush."I had done some independent PR before I worked at Virgin," says Phill Savidge. "And it seemed to me that independent press was all about queuing up in the Post Office, while everyone cashed their Giros and OAP things, forking out about 150 quid on stamps and then spending the rest of your time licking them. And the opposite of that, as far as I could tell, was selling your soul to a major, which is why I had stopped doing PR. But then the 4AD thing came up and you no longer had to tell journalists that the bands you were doing were rubbish — which is what I had to say about most of the ones at Virgin — you could be honest."

Savidge's original two-day week increased to three days, then four and then five and, in February 1991, the two of them moved to a proper office in Greenland Street, which was where they really began to establish themselves. The first band to seriously benefit from the duo's PR technique was Curve, whose first single was sent out as a white label promo with no details apart from the office phone number. As a result, journalists wanted to find out more about Curve and their next London gig at Camden's Underworld in March 1991 was so packed that most of the people there still had no idea what the band actually looked like.

"That Curve gig was the first time I thought to myself, 'The power of the press'," says Savidge, "because there was about 50 journalists in there, and none of them could get anywhere near the stage. Curve came on and they were just laughing because they couldn't believe that everyone had turned out."

Later that year, the company took on Pulp's publicity, initially for free, following a tip from Best's then girlfriend Miki Berenyi, the lead singer of Lush, who had shared a festival bill with them in France. "I'd seen Pulp years before when I reviewed *Little Girl With Blue Eyes* for *Music Week*," says Best, "but, like most people, I'd made a decision about them, that they're kind of bleak and quirky. Then Miki came back from France and said, 'Pulp are brilliant, come and see them', so I did and I knew that she was right."

The following year, they took on Suede, who were famously billed as 'The Best New Band In Britain' on the cover of *Melody Maker* in April 1992, and went on to appear on the front of dozens of magazine covers that year, including *The Sunday Times Magazine*. Not surprisingly, the Suede campaign won Savidge the Les Perrin PR Award for that year and the band also sowed the seeds for Britpop when Brett Anderson appeared on the front cover of *Select* magazine in April 1993.

Around the same time, Best In Press changed its name to Savage & Best and moved to new premises on Arlington Road, which was next door to Food Records and round the corner from the Good Mixer pub. They were now doing publicity for Elastica — who had virtually formed in their Greenland Street office — plus Echobelly and Menswear, and had become inextricably linked to both Britpop and the Camden scene.

Aside from press, John Best was managing The Verve and, at the end of 1994, Savage & Best formed their own record label, Parkway. Their first release was a double seven-inch single by Powder in March 1995. "I don't want to be derogatory about Powder," says Best, "but by that stage people thought that if Savage & Best did something, it had a certain cachet. I saw other indie labels like Fierce Panda, and I thought we'll do a thousand seven-inch singles, get a few reviews and make our money back. But suddenly it was, 'Savage & Best are doing a label, it's got to be big, because they do Suede, Pulp and Elastica.' So there was all this intense attention and the bands suffered a bit because of it. By the time the records came out, the Camden scene had already found its stars and anybody else was always going to be an also-ran."

Parkway released other records by Sugar Bullet, Jonah and Fluffy before deciding to relaunch the label in 1997. It has now been separated into three labels: Parkway for indie and pop bands; Double Parked for dance acts; and Kahuna which will license one-off dance singles. "Camden was a bad place to be by the end of 1995," says John Best. "At that time, I was wishing that I hadn't called the label Parkway, because it immediately tethers it to the whole Camden scene. But out of bloody mindedness I'm still calling it Parkway because I'm determined that it shouldn't be sunk by somebody else's idea of what we're doing."

16. TRATTORIA LUCCA
63 Parkway, NW1. Telephone: 0171-485 6864
In the early-70s, this traditional Italian restaurant shared its site with the record shop, Blue Horizon, which was run by producer Mike Vernon who had started a label of the same name in 1967 and released the first records by Fleetwood Mac. However, by the time the Rock On record shop opened in 1975, Blue Horizon had moved, allowing the restaurant to expand into its old premises. "Trattoria Lucca was a real favourite with everyone at Rock On," says Frank Murray. "We thought that going to the Trat, as we used to call it, was the height of sophistication. Now, of course, Camden Town has restaurants of every nationality."

Even though there are many different places to choose from, some people in the music business still exercise positive discrimination in favour of Trattoria Lucca and its traditional service, complete with Italian-speaking waiters and a good, old-fashioned dessert trolley. "They opened a Café Uno across the road, so I go out of my way to take people to Lucca," says Andy Ross, who always chooses this as the venue for his monthly lunch meetings with Radio 1 DJ and journalist Steve Lamacq.

"When me and Andy first got to know each other," says Lamacq, "he had Diesel Park West on his record label and I was just some no mark at the *NME*, who couldn't get on a guest list for love nor money. And then years later, as we got a little bit of success, we started meeting up for lunchtime drinks and eventually we started going out for something to eat and it was like, 'You know what, Andy? This is what real music industry people do — they do lunch.' So we started going to Trattoria Lucca and they always gave us the same table, in the corner by the window, and we really felt like we'd moved up in the world. I mean, when you've had all those penniless days when no one's interested, and you can barely afford to go to a caff, let alone a restaurant, going for an Italian at lunchtime was really something. When we first went there, we always ordered the same kind of red wine and then, just after *Parklife*, Andy moved up a notch to Barolo. I guess it's a realism thing — I mean, you can go somewhere far flashier and eat less food for a bigger price — but I knew we'd made it when we went to the Italian and drank the poshest glass of red wine on the menu. That was it, we'd arrived! He had Blur and I was on Radio 1, Britpop had done us both proud."

17. THE SPREAD EAGLE
141 Albert Street, NW1. Telephone: 0171-267 1410
The Spread Eagle used to be a classic old men's pub, where people came to enjoy a pint of Young's beer without the interruption of a jukebox. In 1995, however, those two characteristics — plus the fact that it was Noel Gallagher's local and stands directly across the road from the Dublin Castle — suddenly made it attractive to a different generation, and it took over from the Good Mixer as the chief music business hangout in Camden Town.

Built towards the end of last century, the Spread Eagle was originally a small pub with two tiny bars on Albert Street, but gradually expanded across two adjoining shops and finally extended onto Parkway in the mid-60s. "The Spread Eagle was a favourite hangout of mine because of the beer," says Suggs. "Everyone really liked that Young's beer. In fact, some of my friends from Kilburn used to come to Camden for a pint before we went to see Chelsea. But three times out of five, we never even used to get out of the Spread Eagle. We'd just spend the whole afternoon there."

The Spread Eagle was a daily port of call for the local writer

David Thomson, who celebrated the pub in his book, *In Camden Town.* "It is now 11am. The Spread is open," Thomson wrote in a diary entry from January 1980. "The first pint delicious with one newly rolled cigarette. Both are part of a ritual with memories and sentimentalities."

Thomson's words had a big impact on the young Suggs. "The strongest bond that I had with smoking and drinking was the few lines that I read from David Thomson's book," he says. "He wrote that he wouldn't have a cigarette until he had his first pint of beer in front of him, which would more often than not be in the Spread Eagle, with the sun streaming through the dust in the air, and then he'd roll his first fag when the head had settled."

Just as the Good Mixer had filled up with people who wanted to find an alternative to the Devonshire Arms, it was the same crowd who first moved up the road to the Spread Eagle. "We'd got fed up with the other pubs in Camden," says Alie Allerton, who works in Rhythm Records. "But the Spread Eagle was good because it was really quiet and you were guaranteed a seat after work, which is a consideration when you've been standing up for eight hours. The other thing was, I'd already had eight hours of music, so I don't need to hear any more. So we started going there and everybody followed us [*laughs*]. It's true — it's funny how it happened to the Devonshire and then to the Good Mixer and now it's happened to the Spread Eagle."

Even though Noel Gallagher moved into Albert Street in January 1995, it wasn't until later in the year, when the Spread Eagle was completely refurbished, that it really started to become popular with music business types.

"Apollo 440 did this football tournament in Mile End and we won," says Mary Byker, who is the band's vocalist. "There was Blur, Pulp, Jamiroquai and The Bluetones and no one had heard of Apollo 440, but we won. It was just when the new landlords had taken over, but before they did the pub up, and we brought the trophy in to a celebratory drink and because we knew it was quiet. Then a week later, the Spread Eagle was being described as 'the new Good Mixer' and I was like, 'Oh, no, we're not going to go down that road again, are we?' The irony is that they don't play music so bands can't listen to their own records on the jukebox, like they did in the Mixer."

One of the main reasons why the Spread Eagle increased in popularity is because it was within staggering distance of the Dublin

---

"The thing about the Spread Eagle is that the people who work there still recognise their old regulars. If Jason sees me coming up the road he'll pour me a pint. While all the kids are sitting there looking at Liam, chewing gum and drinking halves of some sort of lager, I'm trying to get a bloody drink." — ALIE ALLERTON

Castle, so it was a good place to drink between bands. "It's funny to watch the people in the Spread Eagle take stock of the night before," says Nick Garrard, who has been drinking here for several years. "You can see them separating out the Dublin Castle pint glasses from their own, and sometimes there's extra bits of furniture, where someone's brought a bar stool over. I mean, even Alo, the landlord of the Dublin Castle, drinks in the Spread Eagle and so does the guy from the off-licence across the road."

By 1996, the Spread Eagle was no longer a quiet pub, it was a place where people fully expected to see a whole rake of pop stars. "I was asked to help out this Radio 4 crew who were doing a series of programmes, one of which was about A&R," says Steve Lamacq. "They wanted to come to Camden believing that it was full of members of Blur and Oasis and Elastica, they thought that everywhere you went there would be a Top 40 star casually reading a copy of *The Spectator* in the corner. And I kept saying, 'Look, it just isn't like that, but I'll take you out there.' So we picked a night when there was a gig at the Dublin Castle and one at the Falcon, in the belief that we would encounter empty pubs or pubs full of anonymous people who all want to be in bands. Our first port of call was a pint in the Spread Eagle — we went in and Liam Gallagher was just about to leave and Graham Coxon was at the bar. So I introduced the crew to Graham and they were like, 'Wow, it really is happening, isn't it? I thought you said, It's not like this, Steve?' And they just looked at me as if I'd been trying to keep it a secret, because I didn't want publicity for this little scene that I was in."

As Oasis began to saturate the front covers of the tabloids, the Spread Eagle turned into the kind of pub that could keep the paparazzi in stories for weeks. "I remember sitting in there early on a Sunday evening," says Steve Lamacq, "when this car screeched to a halt outside, followed by the slam of a door. Then one of the doors of the Spread Eagle flew open and this haze of blonde hair whizzed round the pub, looking through all the bars, and then there was the bang of the other door and the car screeched off. The whole pub went deadly silent and then everyone went, 'That was Patsy Kensit! It really *was* Patsy Kensit. I saw the myth'. Everyone wants to be a part of rock'n'roll's history and just seeing Patsy Kensit in a pub in Camden is enough to make some people feel that they are in the Oasis story."

Yet even though the Spread Eagle is now one of the most popular pubs in Camden, it is still the kind of place where even someone like Liam Gallagher can go for a drink with very little hassle. "Liam Gallagher was sat outside the Spread Eagle with a drink and a fag, at the usual height of Britpap mania," says Phill Savidge, whose PR office is round the corner from the pub. "Everyone who walked by him was going, 'Isn't that Liam? What's he doing sitting outside a pub in Camden.' But it's exactly because it *is* Camden and because it *is* the Spread Eagle that he can do that."

18. THE RAT & PARROT
25 Parkway, NW1. Telephone: 0171-482 2309

"One summer evening drunk to hell
I sat there nearly lifeless
An old man in the corner sang
Where the water lilies grow
And on the jukebox Johnny sang
About a thing called love..."

It's difficult to imagine the most romantic song to ever come out of Camden Town being written in a pub called the Rat & Parrot. However, in the days when Shane MacGowan drank here and was inspired to write The Pogues' classic, *A Pair Of Brown Eyes*, this was a big, old Irish pub called the Camden Stores.

"It's a theme pub now," says MacGowan, "but it used to be a real pub, where you could go early in the evening, in a mood, and sit on your own at the counter, drinking pints of cider. There'd be all these Paddies lined up along the bar, staring into their pints as well. It was the perfect place to go for a mournful drink, before you went somewhere more lively, where you could have a fight with someone, and take your mood out on them."

During the early-60s, the Camden Stores was one of the best Irish pubs in the area. Standing in the shadow of Our Lady Of Hal's Catholic Church, the Stores was particularly popular after Sunday morning Mass, when there would be a virtual stampede from the altar to the bar. The staff prepared for the Sunday morning scrum by lining up 30 pints of beer on the counter and continuing to serve at a rate of approximately 20 more per minute.

The Camden Stores had been taken over by Tommy Mangan in 1957, a good-natured, Behanesque figure, who held late-night singing and drinking sessions in the upstairs cocktail bar. Following his death in 1966, most of Camden's Irish community lined the streets as his funeral cortege passed through the town — a scene that was repeated when his wife Elizabeth died 13 years later, aged 43. Grace Mangan, the eldest of the couple's three children, subsequently became one of London's youngest landladies.

Before long, however, the Camden Stores had passed into new management and, in 1984, it was given a complete refurbishment. This meant a new glass frontage and abandoning records like Ray Lynam and Philomena Begley's *My Elusive Dreams* in order to accommodate the first video jukebox in the area. It was no longer recognisable as an old-fashioned bar full of life and Irish music and looked like the last pub in Camden that could have inspired *A Pair Of Brown Eyes* when it was released as a single a year later. Swapping the name the Camden Stores for the Rat & Parrot in 1995 suggests that there is no going back.

19. CHENG DU
9 Parkway, NW1. Telephone: 0171-485 8058

A Chinese restaurant with a reputation for being one of the best places to eat in Camden. Before it became Cheng Du in 1986, it was a French restaurant called Nine Parkway, which had live jazz at weekends and the added attraction of staying open after the pubs had closed. "On Saturday evenings, we'd all go to this tiny French restaurant and listen to a bit of jazz," says Alie Allerton, who would come here after finishing a day's work at Rhythm Records. "It was a place where people went to drink because it was open after the pubs had closed, and it was local guys who played there — such as, Paul Francis, a bass player who has played in quite a lot of bands round Camden, and Roger Beaujolais, who plays vibes and has worked with Fairground Attraction and Tricky."

20. THE JAZZ CAFE
5-7 Parkway, NW1. Telephone: 0171-916 6060

The Jazz Café was dreamed up in 1990 by John Dabner and Jean Marshall, who had established another venue of the same name in Stoke Newington three years earlier. They set about converting this old Barclays Bank into a jazz venue and were still carrying out essential building work when they opened for business that December.

However, by the beginning of 1992, the Jazz Café had gone into

receivership and was bought by Vince Power's Mean Fiddler Organisation. "I had my eye on the Jazz Café for a while," says Power. "I used to have a look at the building and the people who were going into it whenever I was driving through Camden. John Dabner ran it for about a year and then I went in and basically bought it from the receivers. At that time, Camden was going through a bad recession and there weren't really that many takers for anything. That was just a short time ago, but you could have bought a lot of bars in Camden back then."

Power set about refurbishing the Jazz Café, decking it out in chrome with blue neon lighting, two bars [one downstairs and a cocktail lounge upstairs] and a balcony restaurant, which overlooks the stage. "I didn't know one single thing about jazz," admits Power, "but I felt the whole concept was right for Camden and I wanted to keep it the way it was. When I took it over there were all sorts of cries about me changing it into another rock'n'roll gig or an Irish place but I never had any intention of moving away from jazz."

Among Power's Mean Fiddler employees was an avid jazz fan called Adrian Gibson and he became the booker for the venue. "One of the greatest times at the Jazz Café was when Tony Bennett played during the daytime," says Power, and among the others who have performed here are Courtney Pine, Astrud Gilberto, Dr John, Gil Scott Heron, Jools Holland, Iris Dement, Otis Rush, Emmylou Harris and Percy Sledge. Gavin Friday, who did a three-night stint in October 1995, is one of the artists who didn't quite fit into the Jazz Café's usual booking policy, but his shows attracted everyone from Siouxsie Sioux to Nick Cave and Shane MacGowan.

21. KAY'S IRISH MUSIC
161 Arlington Road, NW1.
This record shop, which closed down in the late-80s, was an Irish institution, stocking over 5,000 records by the likes of Johnny McEvoy, Big Tom And The Mainliners, Paddy Reilly, Brendan Shine and all the greats. They ran a mail order service and had one of those rare machines which cut solid centres out of singles, so that these records could be played on Irish jukeboxes all over the country. They also sold musical instruments, such as accordions, flutes and bodhrans, plus Irish cards and claddagh jewellery. "Kay's was the only place in Camden Town where you could get shamrock on St Patrick's Day," says Andrew James, who grew up in the Devonshire Arms. "We used to go round there all the time to buy Irish tapes and albums."

Shane MacGowan was also a regular. "I used to buy records in Kay's," he says. "What sort? Bloody awful ones, mostly. I just used to buy the stuff that was popular at the time, like *The Boys Of The Old Brigade* by Sean Dunphy when it was the Number One Irish record in London in the early-80s. I also bought Paddy Reilly stuff and McCormack albums. When Kay's was there, it wasn't cool to be Irish and they probably didn't realise that it ever would be. I mean, not a lot of people did. I suppose I should have gone into Kay's and said, 'Look, I've got this group and we're going to make it hip to be Irish, so hang on in there and you'll make a packet', but it didn't occur to me. Then, one day, just as The Pogues were really beginning to happen, Kay's disappeared."

22. THE CROWN & GOOSE
100 Arlington Road, NW1. Telephone: 0171-485 2342
Owned by the same people as Bar Gansa, this pub usually resembles an overcrowded living room with art deco on the walls and comfortable sofas. The room upstairs has established itself as something of a media haunt and it was here that Madness took the first step towards reforming in order to play two shows at Finsbury Park in June 1992. "I met Suggs and Carl in the Crown & Goose," says Vince Power, who promoted those shows. "I offered them X amount of money and one of them said, 'You think we can make that much? OK, we'll go for it', and they ended up making a lot more money out of it than that."

23. THE BEDFORD ARMS
80 Arlington Road, NW1.
Now the location of a Housing Association, this was once the site of the old Bedford Theatre and a pub of the same name. Both buildings were razed several years ago but, during the 50s, the Bedford Arms was the most exciting place to hear traditional Irish music in London. This was largely due to its resident musicians: the street singer Margaret Barry and the fiddle player Michael Gorman.

Margaret Barry had a highly distinctive voice and had been brought to London in 1953 to appear in a BBC TV programme by the folk archivist Alan Lomax. Instead of going back home, Barry moved to the East End of London, before moving up to Camden Town and finding a natural place for herself in the bar of the Bedford Arms. She played banjo and would defy the 'No Dancing' sign on the pub's wall by breaking out into spontaneous step dances. The thing that really made Barry special, however, was her incredible voice, which she used to great effect on traditional songs such as *She Moved Through The Fair*, *My Lagan Love*, *The Galway Shawl* and *The Factory Girl*. Sinéad O'Connor has expressed her admiration for Margaret Barry and added the latter song to her repertoire in 1997. The songs that Barry and Michael Gorman sang in the Bedford Arms in the 50s can be heard on the album, *Her Mantle So Green*, which was released on Topic Records in 1994.

24. DANTE GABRIEL ROSSETTI
38 Arlington Road, NW1.
The Pre-Raphaelite poet and painter Dante Gabriel Rossetti lived here

with his brother William and sister Christina, who were also poets, during the early 1850s. Both Dante and William were among the seven people who formed the Pre-Raphaelite Brotherhood which, although short-lived, had an enormous effect on Victorian art. Rossetti's paintings were inspired by The Bible, Arthurian literature and Dante. During Rossetti's time in Camden, he went out with Elizabeth Siddal, a Pre-Raphaelite beauty who inspired many of his paintings and who became his wife in 1860. However, Siddal died from an overdose of laudanum in 1862 and the heart-broken Rossetti interred many of his poems with her dead body — although he did take the trouble to dig them back up in order to publish them a few years later.

25. ALBERT STREET

This leafy Victorian Street is the home of artists and writers such as Beryl Bainbridge and AN Wilson, and the former residence of Noel Gallagher — although it wasn't until the property boom of the 80s that Albert Street really began to fill up with the wealthy and famous.

In 1967, this was one of Camden Town's meanest streets, filled with lodging houses and squats, and with a history of drunken brawls and fatal stabbings. That was the year that the film director Bruce Robinson moved into a dilapidated house here with several other ex-drama students and settled into a bohemian existence that would later inspire his cult movie, *Withnail & I.*

For most of the four years he lived in Albert Street, Robinson had no work and no money — apart from £11 National Assistance — and his possessions were limited to a gas oven, a bare light bulb, an Olivetti typewriter and a mattress on the floor. He did, however, have a glamorous girlfriend, the actress Lesley Anne Down, whose Jaguar car enabled him and his mate to escape from Camden Town to the Lake District in the winter of 1969, a holiday which he also recreated in *Withnail & I.*

In the days when Robinson lived in Albert Street, most of his neighbours were Irish navvies, crammed into cheap lodging houses, sometimes six to a room and two to a bed. They were told to leave their boots at the front door and were forced to wear bed caps in order to stop their Brilliantined hair dirtying the pillows — if the ever-vigilant landlady found any greasy marks, the offender was given a week's notice.

By the early 70s, Robinson had moved on and even the navvies were forced to start looking for accommodation elsewhere, as the builders moved in and began to change the old face of Albert Street.

26. NOEL GALLAGHER
83a Albert Street, NW1.

Noel Gallagher lived in the basement flat of this house from January 1995 until May 1996, and it was here that he wrote *Wonderwall*, a love song to his future wife Meg Matthews, with whom he shared the place.

During the time Noel lived in Albert Street, Creation chief Alan McGee presented him with a chocolate-brown Rolls Royce, a Christmas present and a thank you for the kudos and money he had brought to the record label. However, lots of people did not need to see the Rolls Royce stationed outside to be able to point out Noel's flat and, by the end of 1995, it had become impossible for him to carry on living here.

The moment of realisation came on the Monday morning after Oasis had played two sold-out shows at Earl's Court in November 1995 when Noel woke up to see a procession of Oasis fans trouping down the concrete steps to the flat. Having sworn that he would never refuse an autograph, he opened the door and invited them in for a cup of tea. "I swear to God, man, it was like the chimps' tea party in here, all these kids, me with the Tetley's and the kettle," he told Phil Sutcliffe in *Q*. "Then this thought comes to me. Mark Chapman. He's here. I'm gonna get shot!" He immediately pretended that a car was on its way over to take him to the airport, cleared everyone out of the flat and resolved never to hold another informal tea party.

However, Noel's departure didn't stop Oasis fans from making pilgrimages to the flat. The new occupant apparently had the suss to turn the intrusions into a money-making venture by charging an entrance fee and giving fans a guided tour of the flat, pointing out the kitchen where Noel had written *Champagne Supernova* and the chair where he used to sit and muse. The novelty may well have worn off by now, though, so don't bet on being welcome — with or without the right passcode.

27. DYLAN THOMAS
54 Delancey Street, NW1.

The poet Dylan Thomas and his wife Caitlin moved to this house from their native Wales in the autumn of 1951. As soon as they arrived, Dylan mumbled, "See you later" and disappeared to the Edinburgh Castle pub across the road, leaving Caitlin to unpack. He had written most of his play for voices, *Under Milk Wood*, in the months prior to arriving in Camden and the couple lived here until the beginning of 1952 when Dylan went on a lecture tour of America, where he was lauded as a brilliant reader of poetry and a hard-drinking bohemian. He returned to America in October and died of alcoholic poisoning, a month later, after a heavy session in his favourite New York bar, the White Horse.

When Caitlin unveiled the blue plaque on this house 30 years after her husband's death, she said of their days in Camden Town: "It was a boozy, loving, fighting time."

28. THE EDINBURGH CASTLE
57 Mornington Terrace, NW1. Telephone: 0171-387 8916

This sprawling pub had the distinction of being Dylan Thomas's Camden Town local and, in recent years, Oasis, Blur and the Monty Python crew have also numbered among its customers. "Morrissey used to drink up in the Edinburgh Castle as well," says Suggs. "His Royal Mozness. He's gone now, but I saw him on his last day in Camden before he moved to Ireland."

The Edinburgh Castle has always been quite distinct from most of the other pubs in Camden. Back in the late 19th Century, as well as getting a drink here, the customers could also visit its free curiosities museum [where the exhibits included the egg of a Great Auk bird and relics of Lord Nelson], sit in the picture gallery or library and play lawn billiards in the tea gardens.

During the 60s, the pub was frequented by actors and actresses from the BBC Studio on Camden High Street, but it also had a loyal bunch of locals, including some of the men from Arlington House. According to the local writer David Thomson, who immortalised the Edinburgh Castle in his book, *In Camden Town*, the landlord, Michael Donovan, would give free beer to his regulars on the day before pay day and always fill a pint, without charging for the extra, when someone asked for a half. It was also a great betting pub, with a continual exchange of newspapers and tips and, since those were the days before licenced betting shops, potential winners were scribbled onto pieces of paper and secretly passed to bookie's runners.

"The Edinburgh Castle was one of the places where David Thomson used to hang out," says Suggs, who has read *In Camden Town*. "I didn't know him, but I knew him to see. I was talking to some old thespian up there who did know him, who was saying they'd put tarmac around a tree in the back garden of the pub and David Thomson went out with a trowel and emptied it out so that the roots had some room left. I've got a really vivid image of him suddenly rushing out and finding a trowel, and getting the tarmac out from round this tree, between pints. I love the way that he was going to write a book about Camden Town, and he'd got all this information, but he realised that he didn't have the energy, so he just started doing it in a diary form."

In 1984, the Edinburgh Castle was completely gutted in an arson attack by a customer who had been refused service. The pub was reopened three years later, by which time the offending customer had served almost half of his prison sentence. Despite a few attempts to describe the Edinburgh Castle as "the new Spread Eagle" — in the same way that one had been described as "the new Good Mixer" — it does not seem to have done the pub any serious damage.

"There still is something going on in Camden, but since that bloody supermarket went up and they turned the Mother Red Cap into the World's End, it's never been the same. That was the beginning of all those fashion victim kids hanging out in Camden and Britpop was the end of it." – SHANE MacGOWAN

INVERNESS STREET

"I used to drink in the Good Mixer in the 70s, not because it had a special ambience, like the French in Soho, but because it was my local. In those days, the only people who drank there were Irish workers and the men from Arlington House. But now you're saying that the Good Mixer became fashionable? Good heavens, how extraordinary!" — George Melly, 1997

1. INVERNESS STREET MARKET
Inverness Street, NW1.

Much of the character of Inverness Street derives from its fruit and veg market, a daily ritual which once prompted Brett Anderson to complain: "I can't go to Camden anymore because I get Back To The Planet fans throwing rotten vegetables at me." Inverness Street is one of London's longest running markets and, aside from fresh fruit and veg, it also sells plants, household goods and souvenirs.

2. BAR GANSA
2 Inverness Street, NW1. Telephone: 0171-267 8909
A vibrant Spanish tapas bar, whose large windows and outside tables offer an excellent view of one of the most rock'n'roll streets in Camden.

Even though Bar Gansa has been popular with local media types since it first opened in 1988, it remained surprisingly unscathed by Britpop. If you do see rock'n'roll types here, they're more likely to be the enduring Camden variety, such as John Lydon, Shane MacGowan or Suggs. Lydon has been known to hangout here with his mates when he is in London, while MacGowan says, "I practically lived in Bar Gansa for a couple of years," which explains why this was the venue for The Pogues' post-Wembley Stadium *Hell's Ditch* party in 1990.

"I remember seeing Shane in here a few years ago," says Suggs, "and he just said, 'I can't talk now, I'm doing an interview with *The Sunday Times.*' The next thing I saw was a few of Shane's cronies coming in and three hours later I saw this poor bloke come staggering out, having been drowned in about 19 bottles of wine, with his bag hanging open and absolutely fuck all in his notebook."

Suggs is still a Bar Gansa regular and wrote his 1995 solo single, *Camden Town*, after years of staring out onto Inverness Street through these windows. "Part of the song is about things I've seen while just sitting here," he says. "I once saw this old drunken busker fall over and trip up these tourists, who immediately dropped their hot dogs. I've also seen lots of other surreal things, such as the geezer who comes along and empties out a tin of baked beans for his Alsatian. He does the same thing every day — empties a tin of baked beans on the pavement for his dog. He's an old dosser kind of geezer, but why it isn't dog food and why he empties it on the pavement, I really don't know. Another thing about here is that, when you go up the stairs to the toilet, you have a brilliant view of Arlington House, you see the three columns of that great massive thing which dominates the whole area."

3. BAR VINYL
6 Inverness Street, NW1. Telephone: 0171-681 7898
Extremely popular new bar and restaurant where they serve up food with loud techno music and also sell records and put on art exhibitions in the basement. "I love Bar Vinyl," says Mary Byker. "It's added a whole new aspect to Inverness Street."

4. OUT ON THE FLOOR
10 Inverness Street, NW1. Telephone: 0171-267 5989
A small, friendly shop selling a wide range of new and secondhand records, from indie and rock singles to jazz, rockabilly, country, blues, ska and film soundtracks. Out On The Floor is run by Alan Jones, a former 60s music journalist whose interviewees included Jimi Hendrix and The Rolling Stones. Jones originally started selling records on a

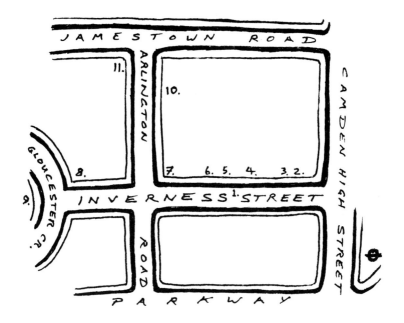

stall on Camden Market in the late-70s, later moving to a shop on the High Street and finally to these premises in Inverness Street in 1990.

"We've got a strong indie section now," he says, "plus funk-jazz, which I we didn't really do before. In the last four or five years we've got more into current things as well as retro stuff, which I personally find more interesting. It makes it more enjoyable if you've got the past and the future together."

Out On The Floor was the first record shop on Inverness Street and so it has attracted a fair number of pop stars over the years, including Graham Coxon, Bobby Gillespie and Sean Lennon. The shop was also linked to Britpop, because Paul Tunkin worked here when he started his club, Blow Up, and his band, The Weekenders, used to rehearse in the basement and also recorded demos there. "Out On The Floor is the kind of shop," says one customer, "where you get talking to the staff about a record and the next thing you know you're up the end of the road having a drink with them."

Suggs on Inverness Street, 1995 [Sean Smith/The Guardian]

5. MEGA CITY
18 Inverness Street, NW1. Telephone: 0171-485 9320
This former launderette was converted into one of London's best comic shops in 1987. It specialises in DC and Marvel, but stocks literally thousands of back issues and graphic novels. They also sell books on sci-fi, horror, film, TV and subculture and are happy to order anything that isn't in stock.

6. SHAKEDOWN II
24 Inverness Street, NW1. Telephone: 0171-284 2402
A sister to Portobello's Shakedown I, this small record shop opened in 1994 and specialises in used vinyl and CDs. They stock punk, country, reggae, 60s garage and soul, and it's a good place to find rarities.

7. THE GOOD MIXER
30 Inverness Street, NW1. Telephone: 0171-916 7929
If any one place can be singled out as a microcosm of the changing face of Camden Town in the 90s, then it has to be the Good Mixer. In the space of just two years, this was transformed from a down-at-heel boozer into the most fashionable pub in the country, where it was possible to have a drink alongside Blur, Oasis, Pulp, Morrissey, Madness, Suede, Elastica and just about every other band you care to mention.

The Good Mixer was originally called the Merry Cricketers and the bar was dominated by a huge painting of the legendary late-Victorian batsman WG Grace, and a spiral staircase which led up to a snooker room on the second floor. Like many other places in Camden, the pub was bombed during the Second World War and rebuilt in a basic working men's club style. It was at this point that it was renamed the Good Mixer, in honour of a cement mixer that the builders had left in the cellar. "I still get people asking me if it's down there," says the present landlord, Mike Hurley. "But I can't find it if it is."

Mike Hurley and his wife Pat, an Irish couple from County Cork, took over the Good Mixer in 1984, after running the Green Man in East Ham for ten years and briefly taking on the tenancy of a pub in Chelmsford. "I didn't know Camden very well," says Mike Hurley, "but this was the first pub that I got an interview for. At the time it was a notorious cider house, so the only people who were coming in were winos and drunks — it was like a Wild West show in here. If you saw a woman coming through the door, she was trouble [*laughs*]. I mean it, if you saw a woman, she had to be trouble, because women just didn't come into the pub."

The Hurleys were so keen to move back to London that they decided to take on the Good Mixer, regardless of its clientele. "We had to bar almost everyone who had been coming in," continues Mike Hurley. "I mean, half of them would be curled up on the seats asleep as soon as you'd served them, or they'd come in, ask for half a bitter, and then five minutes later they'd be tipping something from out of their pocket into their drink. So we started to change the pub — I've since heard that, if we hadn't got it right, the police would have taken away the licence."

Before Mike Hurley became a publican he had worked in Wheeler's, the famous seafood restaurant in Soho, and he decided to make cheap dinners for the Inverness Street market traders a key feature of the pub. But, appropriately enough, for a pub that would later become so inextricably linked to the music business, it was live music which initially gave the Good Mixer a new lease of life.

Above the bar, to this day, there is a framed photograph of the first person to ever play here — he lived in nearby Gloucester Crescent and everyone called him Ben, but his real name was Patrick Bergin, an actor who would make his name, playing opposite Julia Roberts, in the Hollywood movie, *Sleeping With The Enemy*. Bergin just turned up one day, in the mid-80s, and started an impromptu Irish session, but Mike Hurley immediately realised the potential of having live music in the pub. He went down to Cecil Sharp House and asked for some telephone numbers of traditional Irish musicians — they gave him just one, for Brendan Mulkere, who put him in touch with the McCarthy Family and the piper Tommy Keane. They both started doing regular sessions at the Good Mixer, and were later replaced by other Irish musicians, such as Ron Kavana and Miriam Kelly, and, by the late-80s, the Good Mixer was widely regarded as one of the best places to hear traditional Irish music in London.

Because the Good Mixer was so definitely off the main drag, famous Camden faces, such as Suggs and Shane MacGowan, were delighted to discover that this was one of the few places where they could drink in peace. "I stopped drinking in the Dev because I could no longer get to the bar," says MacGowan, "so the Mixer became the second choice."

By 1990, many people who had previously drunk in the Devonshire Arms, on Kentish Town Road, had also started to look for an alternative pub. Among them was Bal Croce, the former Sting-rays' singer who ran a video shop just off Camden High Street, with Mike Delanian, the bass player in what was then a little-known band called Gallon Drunk. It became a tradition that on Saturday and Sunday lunchtimes the two of them would get their mate Lino to look after the shop while they went drinking.

However, by this time Camden Market was so popular that a pub which you could actually squeeze your way into was becoming increasingly difficult to come by. "I'd been looking for a new pub for a while," says Bal, "and one fateful day, on our endless quest for a quiet boozer, I was walking up Inverness Street and decided to have a look in the Good Mixer. It looked exactly like what you'd expect a pub next door to a doss house to look like, and no one that I knew of ever went there cos it looked so seedy from the outside. But I went in on my own, doing a recce for the weekend, and couldn't believe it because there were just four people in the whole place and they were all really scruffy, drunken old men. It did look a bit grotty, but it had a pool table and it was empty at a time when every other pub in Camden was heaving. So I took the crew in there that weekend, ordered a drink, and then I went up to the jukebox and there was Dean Martin, Tom Jones and Elvis, plus their Irish equivalents, and some pop hits from about three years ago, which was probably the last time they'd changed the records. And it was just fab — listening to Dean Martin, while you were playing pool, with great service from the bar staff."

The Good Mixer immediately became a regular haunt for Bal and the Gallon Drunk entourage who fell in love with its free pool table, cosy backroom booth and old-fashioned Playmate Escort jukebox. After a couple of weeks, Pat Hurley invited Bal to bring in his favourite records and he happily obliged with Tom Jones' *Green Green Grass Of Home*, Dean Martin's *Little Ole Wine Drinker Me*, the Terry Stafford version of *Suspicion* plus Charlie Rich, Lee Hazlewood & Nancy Sinatra and more Elvis records. "Being allowed to stock the jukebox with our records made it an even better place to be," says Bal, "and we went from drinking in there at the weekends to being in there nearly every evening. We'd have big pool sessions — they had one pool table originally but they got another one in just to accommodate us."

Mike Hurley soon realised that the only nights that these new customers didn't stay until closing time was when he had traditional Irish music on the tiny stage in the main bar. He decided to cancel his usual live bands, the Jacket Potatoes and The Shanakies, although he still retained his music and dance licence — something which later became a key factor in the Good Mixer's popularity, because it allowed the pub to stay open until midnight.

Ironically — given that he had prompted Mike Hurley's decision to end live music in the Good Mixer — it was while Bal Croce was sitting in the pub one night towards the end of 1990 that he decided to form a glamorous drinking band called the Earls Of Suave. They took some of their songs and style from Dean Martin and Charlie Rich, two classic crooners who also happened to be legendary drinkers.

"I just remember us all being in the Good Mixer one night," says Bal, "and I said, 'Hang on a minute, we're spending £20 a night in here — I can sing a bit and you can all play different instruments, let's get a band together, then at least we'll get our beer money.' So that was when the Earls Of Suave were born, and our first gig was at the Borderline soon afterwards."

In June 1991, Gallon Drunk — who had now replaced their original drummer with Earl Of Suave Max Décharné — began to appear regularly in the music press and found themselves defiantly out of sync

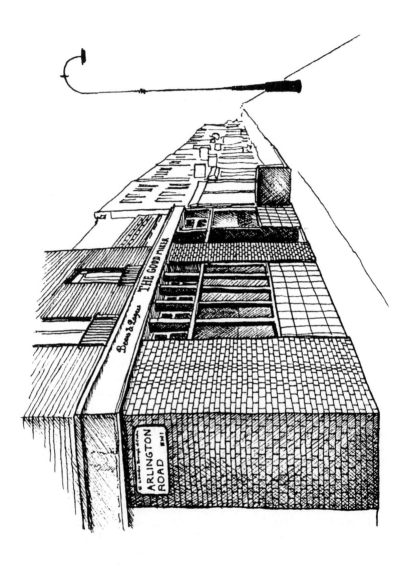

with everything else that was going at the time. "Before we started playing at the Falcon, we had absolutely no contact whatsoever with indie music," says Gallon Drunk's James Johnston. "But we gradually became aware of all that really appalling shoegazing behaviour that was going on, and the even more lamentable Scene That Celebrated Itself. Hence, the need to find somewhere that had absolutely nothing to do with indie music or shmoozing and brown-nosing, so we ended up spending all our time in the Good Mixer."

Gallon Drunk conducted all their interviews in the Good Mixer, although they always asked journalists not to reveal the pub's name — not just for social reasons but also because it was a rich source of inspiration to James Johnston. "The Good Mixer was by no means, in any way, a fashionable pub," he says. "People wouldn't be seen dead in there, unless they were the clientele of Arlington House or falling over dead. I mean, that's exactly what that pub was like — just people toppling in the door or toppling out of the door or toppling into the door."

1991 was the golden period of the Good Mixer and, in December, the Earls Of Suave played their first gig here. The Hurleys must have sensed their prime motivation for forming the band because they gave them free beer all night, while Dave Vanian and Shane MacGowan made it an even more memorable occasion by getting onstage with them. "The stage was so small that the whole band couldn't fit on it," says Bal. "There was just me and the drums and a guitarist up there, and I used to climb on the pool table and cause mayhem. On that particular night, Dave Vanian got up and did a song with us and it all got drunker and drunker. Then after we'd finished, Shane — who was completely paralytic — and Johnny, the guitarist, decided they wanted to do some Hank Williams songs. So Shane clambered up and started bashing the drums, while Johnny kept dropping his guitar on the floor and it was just this horrible, unholy din. At the time, it seemed normal, cos that's what it was like all the time — these ridiculous nights when you'd be in the Mixer until you didn't know what you were doing and you'd stumble out to get cigars from the crappy corner shop and then come back and carry on drinking yourself into oblivion."

The Earls Of Suave played their second gig at the Good Mixer on New Year's Eve 1991, attracting a surprisingly large crowd. Yet even though Gallon Drunk started to do more interviews in the Good Mixer during the first two months of 1992, it was referred to in print as The Pub At The End Of The World — a pretty good one, since the World's End was the Camden pub that the music business favoured at the time — or The Pub That Time Forgot.

"Somewhere off Camden High Street, there is the pub that time forgot," wrote Steve Lamacq in *NME* in February 1992. "The last surviving hostelry in London that hasn't yet been taken over by a CD jukebox. Some of the regulars look like they've been in residence as long as the sad threadbare carpet. This is naturally a good place to meet Gallon Drunk."

"I'd never been in the Mixer until I interviewed Gallon Drunk," says Lamacq. "It looked like they hadn't changed the decor for 20 years — it was the pub that time forgot, and it was lovely. It was the nearest thing that I'd ever found in London to the sort of pubs that Jeffrey Bernard wrote about existing in Soho in the late-60s. It was almost like a bit of Soho in Camden."

By this time, Gallon Drunk and Bal Croce's more famous friends, such as Nick Cave, The Cramps and Robert Plant, would occasionally join them for a drink in the Good Mixer. And, despite a fairly concerted effort to keep the pub to themselves, a number of other factors contributed to the pub's increasing popularity. One was that The Rockingbirds had also started to drink here and were occasionally joined by their Heavenly labelmates, St Etienne. Even though Heavenly's boss, Jeff Barrett, says he has only been in the Good Mixer once in his life, that one time happened to be on a Saturday afternoon in January 1992 when he was with The Rockingbirds and Bobby Gillespie and a journalist from *Select* magazine was also in the pub to interview Gallon Drunk.

"A viciously thin Bobby Gillespie and an equally wiry cohort are sitting by the pool table, blatantly tripping out of their gourds," David Cavanagh wrote in the March 1992 issue of *Select*. "And at the back of the pub, dripping in hair gel and supra-slick shirt patterns, we have Gallon Drunk, alchemists of holy jazz-fuelled hootenanny barbarism, maraca-driven historians of sexual treachery, flash guys, cool guys, self-styled honky white-noise boys. If this is anyone's pub, it's theirs."

More significantly, though, March 1992 was also the month that Food Records moved from Soho to new premises in Arlington Road and immediately turned the Good Mixer into an extension of their office. "I had originally thought of the Good Mixer as a dodgy Irish pub where Gallon Drunk drank because it was scuzzy, so I had deliberately avoided it," says Andy Ross, MD of Food Records. "But we moved up to Arlington Road and, instead of turning left to go to the Camden Stores, we turned right and found this place. We came in and, firstly, it

> *"I used to go in the Mixer with all the guys from the fruit market. There were all the dudes from Arlington House in there. I'm not saying they're bad people but I don't want fleas on my clothes, thanks very much. Then they'd be looking at you, you know what I mean? I went in there once with black shoes, black trousers and pink socks and it was as if I was the Frankie Howerd of Camden or something. I'm sorry, my girlfriend liked pink socks."*
> *— BARRY APPLEBY*

was empty, secondly, it had Tom Jones and Nancy Sinatra on the jukebox and, thirdly, it had two pool tables, and we just thought, Cheers! And through that summer of 1992 we had a fantastic time — it was an empty pub, with the sun streaming through the windows, and we really fell in love with it."

Ross brought all his bands to the pub and Blur, in particular, started hanging out in here all the time. Meanwhile, Gallon Drunk toured the States with Morrissey and he, too — now living locally on Gloucester Avenue — started drinking in the Good Mixer. "There was one time," says Andy Ross, "when there were two or three of Madness stood at the counter, there was Morrissey sat in the corner and I walked in with Graham from Blur, and there was no one else in the pub at all. It was incredibly natural yet totally surreal. Morrissey looked a bit surprised and then he just realised that there were musicians all over the place."

However, it was still possible to have a quiet drink in the Good Mixer. "My favourite ever Good Mixer memory was when we asked if we could shoot some of the video for the first Earls Of Suave single in the pub," says Bal Croce. "Pat told us that the best time to do it was when they closed on a Sunday lunchtime — this was when the pubs closed for a few hours in the afternoon. So we all piled up there at 2.00pm, there was about 12 of us, the band plus assorted girlfriends and mates. I thought Pat was just going to stand behind the bar while we shot the video, so we put a tiger cloth cover on the pool table and got the lights set up, but then she said, 'I'm going upstairs for my lunch now, if you want a drink just help yourself and write it down on this bit of paper.' So we all poured ourselves a pint and wrote it down, then it was, 'Who wants another drink?' and it turned into this drinking session where the video just didn't get shot and we ended up legless. Pat came back down at 5.00pm to open up the pub again and there was this sheet of foolscap paper scribbled on from top to bottom with the list of drinks that we'd poured ourselves. She added it up and said, 'Right, Bal, that'll be £150' and I was like, 'Er, unfortunately, Pat, I haven't got it, but I'll come in tomorrow and go to the bank and draw it out of my shop's account or something.' So I went in on the Monday and said, 'Look, I'm going to the bank, how much do I owe you?' And she just said, 'That's fine, forget it.' That's what I call a proper pub."

The Hurleys also made it well worth the Earls Of Suave's time of forming a pub band by giving them half a dozen bottles of champagne when they did their second New Year's Eve gig here in 1992 — this time, though, the Good Mixer had become such a popular place to be that there were almost as many people on the outside pavement as there were in the pub.

It was around this point that Gallon Drunk's James Johnston decided to get out of Camden and promptly moved to the East End. "The whole point of drinking in the Good Mixer was to stay as far away from any kind of indie scene as possible," he says. "You wanted Pat and Mike to do well because you'd become friends with them, but the whole place just became everything that you'd tried to avoid when you first went there. Once it started to get publicised it went downhill and later on it became synonymous with Britpop, and lovely-jubbly London Town and the whole flag-waving, modern Bible bullshit. And then it was definitely all over."

Even though the Good Mixer was already way too popular for James Johnston, the real change didn't actually come until the PR firm, Savage & Best, moved next door to Food Records on Arlington Road. John Best had been introduced to the pub a couple of years earlier by his then girlfriend, Miki Berenyi, the lead singer of Lush, who was friends with the Earls Of Suave crowd, but it was in 1993 that the Good Mixer went from being a pub where he and the rest of his office went for a drink after work to the place where all their bands did interviews.

"It was almost ironic to send people to the Good Mixer," says Best's partner, Phill Savidge. "To send your poncy pop stars and journalists to a pub full of serious drinkers and people who really were fucked up, just seemed like a good thing to do."

Jarvis Cocker was one of the musicians who did an interview in the Good Mixer and then started drinking here on a fairly regular basis. "I first went to it when Savage & Best moved round the corner," he says. "Because it was a quiet pub, they used to suggest it as a place to do interviews. I did one there with John Robb and I thought it was all right — not a bad pub for Camden, not too full. Obviously, it was Savage & Best's fault that it became such a well-known pub but, at the start, it was good, because there were just a few people from bands there and it was quite nice for meeting socially and they also had a licence where they could stay open until midnight."

Although Andy Ross admits that he is partly to blame for turning the Good Mixer into the most mediated pub in the country, he holds Savage & Best as even more responsible. "As soon as Savage & Best moved next door to us on Arlington Road," says Ross, "they did all of their interviews in the Mixer, *all* of them, for a period of a few months. Then those fucking journalists started hanging out there and the ones that became the most critical of the Camden scene were the ones who were most vociferously championing it at the time. It went downhill

> "Being in Camden, and particularly the Good Mixer, was very much a time capsule. Kind of like a 70s Cassavetes film or something — it was like opening the door of someone's house, looking in on it for a couple of days and then closing it again. Except we had no idea that half the bloody music industry was going to trample the door down on top of us." — JAMES JOHNSTON

because they started saying, 'Seen at the Good Mixer the other day were Pulp, Suede, Morrissey, Blur, whoever', and that was all fine and dandy until coach loads of bloody indie kids start turning up on a Friday and Saturday night."

Before the tourists arrived, though, there was a mid-period where the pub was almost entirely populated by pop stars, PRs and journalists. "The whole Good Mixer scene kind of rose and rose and rose and then fell off quite quickly," says John Best. "I must admit that I felt sorry for Gallon Drunk and the Earls Of Suave because they must have felt like Palestinians in occupied territory. I'm sure they just thought, 'Oh, leave it to the Camden indie lot' and then the Camden indie lot said, 'Oh leave it to the tourists.' I know it was our fault that people started referring to it in interviews, but the funny thing is that it worked for a while — all sorts of people seemed to come through that pub. You'd be sitting there and Matt Johnson would be in one corner and there'd be someone like Billy Childish or another one of Thee Headcoats in another and a new Camden hopeful, like Louise Wener, in another, and you'd think, 'Why is Matt Johnson here. Did he just think, I'll go to the Good Mixer tonight?'"

By this time, Blow Up, the Saturday night mod club at the nearby Laurel Tree, was in full swing and the Good Mixer jukebox was beginning to look like a Who's Who of the bands who went there — with records by Blur, Suede and Elastica. "I vividly remember Andy Ross going into the Good Mixer with seven-inch singles with their holes punched out for the jukebox," says Mary Byker, who had been drinking here since the late-80s. "He had Blur's new stuff, loads of Jam and some Madness — he was more of less laying out the Britpop manifesto."

It wasn't just Ross who was reshaping the Mixer jukebox — Savage & Best were responsible for Elastica's *Stutter* suddenly replacing Paddy Reilly's age-old *Fields Of Athenry*. Even though they had only recently formed, Elastica had already spawned the pop myth that they had signed their record deal with Deceptive on the back of a matchbox in the Good Mixer. "That's a lie, but a very good one," says Steve Lamacq, who co-founded Deceptive Records but later sold his share in it for the price of a pint. "I did meet Elastica in the Good Mixer, but we just shook hands on a couple of singles, had a drink and that was it. Sadly, the matchbox didn't come into it."

Another myth is that Oasis were thrown out of the Good Mixer and barred for life by the landlord for having a go at Graham Coxon. Oasis did visit the pub in May 1994, introduced themselves to Coxon and then insulted both him and his band, but that's as far as it went. "I've never seen Oasis in here," says Mike Hurley. "I've certainly never thrown them out. Maybe one of the lads behind the bar asked them to leave, but I honestly don't remember."

Whatever happened that night, it didn't stop Noel Gallagher occasionally drinking in the Good Mixer when he moved to Camden in

January 1995. By this time, Menswear — who had been introduced to the Good Mixer by Graham Coxon and formed the band in the pub the previous October — were hanging out here all the time. Soon their fan mail was arriving in sackloads, but their very presence was enough to scare even most of the journalists away. "I stopped going to the Good Mixer when I walked in and saw all of Menswear playing pool at once as if they'd been paid to do it," John Harris, who was then a staff writer on the *NME*, told the *Independent On Sunday* later that year. "The place had turned into a cartoon."

"In a way the arrival of Menswear kept the Camden thing going," says Steve Lamacq, "cos they were always hanging around. I mean, I didn't spend '95 in George & Niki's — it wouldn't be like, George & Niki's, then down the Good Mixer, popping your head through the door to see who was in. I'm surprised someone didn't do a version of *Private Eye*'s The Regulars, where you'd have a couple of pop stars up against the bar and, instead of it being, 'Has Jeff been in?', it would be, 'Graham been in?'"

Despite this new cartoon element, the fact that it was still possible to find Blur, and perhaps even Noel Gallagher, in the Good Mixer assured its popularity throughout the Britpop summer of 1995. "People kept on going to the Mixer because they'd heard that Blur drank in there," says Mary Byker. "And yes, Graham was always in the pub. But he used to go in there purely to drink and play pool and talk to his mates, and then the pub became a bit of a sticky subject, because people would go in there just to gawp at him. Because by that stage, it wasn't Blur, it was Graham — Damon and Alex were far too busy poncing round Groucho's or somewhere."

The Good Mixer had its busiest ever time during the summer of 1995 but, by the end of the year, some people had started moving up the road to the Spread Eagle. "There was a lot of hype during 1995," says Mike Hurley. "We had camera crews in all the time and tourists taking pictures. It's at a better level now, we still get all the regulars and a nicer type of trade. Once you start getting publicity, it brings every sort around and there were handbags being pinched left, right and centre. People write in the papers that Blur don't come in here anymore, but those people don't come in themselves — Graham has always stayed the same, he's a hell of a nice lad, and Damon still comes in for a sandwich and a cup of coffee after he's been playing football in the park."

Although the famous threadbare carpet has long gone and the Playmate Escort has now given way to a CD jukebox, the Good Mixer still exudes the same kind of Irish hospitality that made it so attractive in the first place. Bal Croce, the customer who inadvertently changed it from a quiet pub at the end of the street into the centre of the Britpop universe, tries to sum up its appeal:

"The Good Mixer was just one of those moments. It wasn't quite Daniel Farson's *Soho In The 50s*, because that involved Francis Bacon and George Melly, but it was that kind of thing on our level — not so much genius, but just somewhere you could always go where you could guarantee that something good was happening. It was just magic, strangely magic, if you were part of it. And I'm sure loads of people went in the Good Mixer in the early-90s who didn't know anyone and thought it was just another pub with a load of trendy gits who fancied themselves. But it was one of those kaleidoscopic little flashes of brilliance that only happen once and we were there and it was great. It was the pure essence of Camden at that time."

8. SOUNDS THAT SWING
46 Inverness Street, NW1. Telephone: 0171-267 4682
Opened in July 1996 by Barney Koumis, this is the coolest record shop in Camden, specialising in rock'n'roll, rockabilly, country, hillbilly, blues, doo wop and rare soundtracks. "We're basically trying to do what Rock On did in the 70s," says Koumis, which is a good enough recommendation in itself. In its previous life, this was one of the smallest restaurants in London. For years, it served traditional Greek food and was a favourite of the writer Jonathan Miller, who lives across the way in Gloucester Crescent. However, it later switched to a North African menu and this is where Dubstar were taken for a celebratory meal when they signed to Food Records in November 1994.

9. GLOUCESTER CRESCENT
There are more literati to the square inch in Gloucester Crescent than most places in London. Among the writers who populate these exclusive houses are Jonathan Miller and Alan Bennett, while previous residents include George Melly, Morrissey and the photographer David Bailey who shot dozens of famous bands in his home studio in the 60s.

10. ARLINGTON HOUSE
220 Arlington Road, NW1. Telephone: 0171- 482 3374
If any one building embodies the true spirit of Camden, then it is Arlington House, a massive, red-brick hostel for homeless men, which has been immortalised in various songs, including Madness's *One Better Day*, The Pogues' *Transmetropolitan* and Gallon Drunk's *Arlington Road*.

"Arlington House is at the core of what was good about Camden Town," says Suggs. "All those strange people coming out of that place gave the area an eccentric colour, which has kind of been swamped now. I wrote *One Better Day* after seeing this geezer lying in the middle of the road up by Camden Lock. I saw him walk over and lie down, not trying to commit suicide or anything, but just lying there because he didn't give a fuck and that's what started the song off."

Originally known as Rowton House, this was the last in a chain of six hostels which the politician and philanthropist Lord Rowton set up in London, between 1892 and 1905. At that time, there was no social security system, and lodging houses for single men were overcrowded or badly sanitised, so Lord Rowton came up with the idea of providing private cubicles instead of communal dormitories. He thought of his houses as "a hotel for working men", and each of the thousand men who lived in the Camden Rowton House had his own cubicle with his own key.

By the 30s, 'No Irish Need Apply' signs were a common sight in the windows of London lodging houses. The Irish were, however, always welcome in Rowton Houses and they quickly became the largest immigrant group at this one. The great Irish poet Patrick Kavanagh — whose most famous poem, *Raglan Road*, was set to music and has been sung by everyone from Luke Kelly and Van Morrison to Sinéad O'Connor — lived here when he arrived in London for the first time in the late spring of 1937. "There I met the artists of the *demi-monde*," Kavanagh wrote in his early memoir, *The Green Fool*. "Not all the denizens of Rowton House, Camden Town, were of this class, though. But all were quaintly individual, and these I've always loved." However, after just three nights, Kavanagh decided that he couldn't stand the institutional atmosphere of Rowton House and moved into lodgings at the Holloway-end of Camden Road, where he stayed for five months before returning to Ireland.

After the Second World War, a huge influx of Irish workers came to Britain. Many of them worked in the construction industry and, since Camden Town was one of the main pick-up points for workers, lots of them stayed here. Although none of the men were allowed to stay in their rooms during the daytime — which is why so many of them hung around in the pubs and cafés of Inverness Street — nightshift workers could get a special 'Do Not Disturb' sign for their room doors.

In the 60s and 70s, however, Rowton Houses were getting older and beginning to deteriorate, and this particular house inspired the ditty: "*Camden Town/Camden Town/Where the rough lie down...*" During this period, it was renamed Arlington House, in honour of the road it stands on, although some of the residents referred to it as 'The House' (or its rhyming slang equivalent of 'The Mickey' or 'The Mickey Mouse'), 'San Quentin', 'Dracula's Castle' or just 'The Castle'.

When Rowton Houses Ltd sold off their properties in the early-80s, Camden Council took over Arlington House. By 1988, the Council had dramatically improved conditions by doubling the size of the rooms and halving the number of tenants [thereby limiting the capacity to just under 400]. In recent years the running of Arlington House has passed over to the Bridge Housing Association.

Because alcohol is prohibited in the House, the two nearest pubs, the Locomotive and the Good Mixer, were the favourite daytime haunts of many of the residents — all that stopped in 1994, however, when the former was turned into Blakes wine bar and restaurant and the latter was taken over by the music business.

Arlington House is one of the great misunderstood places in Camden Town, even though it has given the area much of its character. In 1993, Channel 4 did a documentary on it called *What Do You Expect - Paradise?*, which gave a visual account of the men who once drank in the Good Mixer and provided at least some insight into Arlington House. "You've never seen a better doss house in your life," concluded one resident.

11. BLAKES
31 Jamestown Road, NW1. Telephone: 0171-482 2959
Blakes stands on the site of the Locomotive — one of the great lost pubs of Camden Town, which dated back until at least 1856.

When the Good Mixer became completely overrun with music business types during 1993, the Locomotive was the last refuge in town. A tatty old bar with big red booths, a pool table, a jukebox stocked with Irish and country classics — and a clientele that seemed to consist entirely of the men from Arlington House, Mary Byker and the Earls Of Suave — the Locomotive looked like the kind of place where you might expect Tom Waits to hang out.

Unfortunately, when the Locomotive's lease went up for sale in the late summer of 1994, it underwent a major facelift and was completely gutted. When it reopened later that year as a wine bar called Blakes, its stripped-down walls, cushy sofa, candle light and barmaids with 'Babe' T-shirts were about as far removed from the Locomotive as you could possibly imagine.

The men from Arlington House didn't last the new course, as Blakes evolved into an upmarket bar and restaurant. "The Locomotive was a great bar," says Shane MacGowan. "I used to drink in there a lot when a mate of mine was living in Arlington House in the 80s. It's too bad they did it up."

> *"Just before the whole Camden thing took off, The Cramps were in London to do some press and I arranged to meet Lux and Ivy so I could take them for a drink. And, of course, I took them to the Mixer. We were walking up Inverness Street and I saw these two Spanish psychobillies coming out of Out On The Floor — they had just bought this record, and they pulled it out of its bag, and it was a Cramps bootleg. They were looking at it on the doorstep and they were really excited about it, pointing to different tracks going, 'Look at this!' Then they looked up and saw Lux and Ivy walking past them and their jaws just hit the floor as they watched them disappearing into this pub on the corner. I saw them scuttle into the Mixer behind us — they didn't come up to Lux and Ivy or anything, they just sat in the corner staring at them and drinking." – BAL CROCE*

THE ROCK'N'ROLL GUIDE TO CAMDEN

"Me and my friends were trying to find somewhere to live and we eventually managed to get into this Housing Co-op in Camden. The bloke who was the kingpin in the house was away at the time, but all his mates were staying there and they got wind of the fact that the Co-op wanted to move us in and they obviously didn't want that to happen, cos it was their den. So on the night that we went to have a look at the house, they were all off their heads in the living room and there was this one bloke shagging the settee. He'd got his trousers pulled down with his bare arse showing and his knob in between the two back cushions — he was obviously doing it to scare us off and make us think, 'Oh, we can't live here', but it didn't work cos we were desperate and had nowhere else to go. As it turned out, I was the only one of us who really stayed there. It was an old Victorian house which was falling to bits and there was no central heating or anything, so it was always freezing. It became really obvious that the main bloke was a dealer and whenever I came back from college at about 5.30pm there would be a big encampment of people in the living room, waiting to score some gear off him. I'd come down and cook me dinner, a right rubbish meal of cod in butter sauce or something, and there'd be all these people lying on the settee. It really wasn't such a great audience to have watching you eating your dinner." – JARVIS COCKER

INVERNESS STREET

NEWSREEL: THE 90s

Oh yeah, the pirate radio station told us what was going down
Got the tickets from some mashed up bloke in Camden Town
Oh and no one seems to know exactly where it is
But that's okay 'cause we're all sorted out for E's & wizz

RIOT FEAR OVER £555 POLL TAX

A "Fashion Mafia" gang raided the Camden Town studios of two of
the world's top designers — whose clients include pop singers and
Hollywood film stars — stealing up to £50,000 worth of exclusive
clothing on Saturday night

FEAR OF SUMMER OF RACE-HATE

TREE OF HEAVEN — END IS NIGH

Warning that a second Hillsborough or King's Cross disaster could be
waiting to happen at the popular Camden Lock Market have been
sounded this week by the area's Chief Of Police

A chapter in Camden's musical history will come to an end
as soon as the bulldozers prepare to move in and demolish
Camden Lock's Dingwalls

DRUGS MENACE BLAMED
MARKET AT THE LOCK MAY CLOSE
A senior Tory Councillor has renewed calls for Camden Lock Market
to be closed down, saying it is the cause of an increasing drug culture

A man was stabbed in the throat and left with a
broken shoulder after he went into a Chalk Farm kebab shop
in the early hours of Sunday morning

CLAMP ROW
The tour manager of Regent's Park rock band, Flowered Up,
couldn't pay to have a clamp removed and needed his van to star in a
video. So when the clamping firm arrived on Friday to remove the
van, he tied his two rottweilers to the clamp.
A row followed and the police arrived to calm tempers

MARKET CROWD NO DIFFERENT TO FOOTBALL CROWDS

THE ROCK'N'ROLL GUIDE TO CAMDEN

A leading Civil Rights lawyer has joined a chorus of criticism of the police who allowed the British National Party to march through the Regent's Park Estate on Sunday. It is the first time since the 1950s that a Fascist group has mobilised on the streets of Camden

DEATH BY HEROIN

SHOPPERS TARGETED AS BOMB INJURES 18

Police revealed that people seeking to buy illegal drugs in Camden Town were not always getting what they bargained for. Dealers were found to be passing off anything from crushed cardboard to herbs as cannabis to gullible punters. Several were prosecuted or cautioned for deception after they tried to sell fake drugs to undercover officers

END OF LINE FOR 'DISNEY' HIGH STREET

THREE'S A PARTY CROWD
The Irish Centre in Camden Town was the scene of a huge celebration on Friday when the Bridgewater Three arrived to celebrate their first night of freedom after 18 years in prison

WHEN ALBERT STREET LOST ITS INNOCENCE

THE SHADOWS OVER TRENDYTOWN
Drugs and thugs are poisioning easy streets of Camden

RADICAL PIAZZA PLAN FOR CAMDEN

LIAM CAUTIONED AFTER CLASH
Oasis singer Liam Gallagher was cautioned by police today over a clash with a cyclist in Camden earlier this month.
Gallagher, 24, allegedly grabbed the cyclist and threw off his sunglasses after he claimed the star's Mercedes had "cut him up".
A police spokesman said after the criminal damage caution:
"There will be no further action"

In the middle of the night
It feels alright
But then tomorrow morning
Oh then you come down
Oh then you come down
What if you never come down?

Three Sides Of Camden

BRITPOP: THE CAMDEN CONNECTION

By the autumn of 1995, T-shirts bearing the words 'Fuck Britpop' were starting to appear on the streets of Camden Town. It would be another 14 months before Liam Gallagher and Patsy Kensit draped themselves in a Union Jack bedspread to appear on the front cover of *Vanity Fair* magazine, but some of the people who had been forced to live at the centre of Britpop had already had their fill of it.

The roots of Britpop can be traced back to 1990/91, when bands such as Blur, Lush and Moose would play gigs or just hang out at the Falcon pub in Camden and then spend every Thursday night at an Oxford Street nightclub called Syndrome. Even though these bands were generally lumped together as 'Shoegazers' or the 'Scene That Celebrates Itself', Syndrome attracted whichever musicians were visiting London, including Courtney Love and Kurt Cobain.

"It was Syndrome that really helped the Camden scene to develop," says Andy Ross, who coined the word 'Shoegazing' when he was writing for *Sounds*, "which is ironic, given that it wasn't actually based here. But most of the people who went on to form the Britpop scene went to Syndrome on a Thursday night."

Syndrome and the small scene that went with it was swept away by the release of Nirvana's *Nevermind* in September 1991, and the tidal wave of grunge that followed. For the next 18 months, it was American bands who ruled the airwaves and took up most of the column inches in the British music press. By the end of 1992, though, Kurt Cobain was wearing a T-shirt that said, 'Grunge Is Dead', and people were starting to look for something completely different.

Although it would take a while for someone to coin the term 'Britpop', it had its media birth in the April 1993 issue of *Select* magazine, whose cover featured Brett Anderson, draped against a Union Jack [superimposed, as it happens], with the words: 'Yanks Go Home! Suede, St Etienne, Denim, Pulp, The Auteurs and The Battle For Britain'. The feature was the result of a collaboration between its writer Stuart Maconie, *Select*'s then Editor Andrew Harrison and, perhaps most importantly, Phill Savidge, whose PR company, Savage & Best, did press for most of the bands that were mentioned.

"Britpop started as an anti-American movement, which is how that *Select* cover came about," says Savidge. "At that time American bands were everywhere and some of it felt personal. I felt attacked by something I had no control over. Suede, for me, were celebrating Englishness: they made it matter again what you looked like; they didn't do the value-for-money EP, they just released fantastic singles; they were all about being up there to be shot at. Before that everything had been so dowdy — I liked Nirvana and Sonic Youth, but the very word grunge just gave everyone an excuse not to make an effort. Obviously, the glam thing was a very important part of both Suede and

BRITPOP

Pulp and it was also about looking inward, and celebrating your own kind of music."

By this time, Suede and Pulp were among the Savage & Best acts who frequently did interviews, or just hung out, in the Good Mixer pub in Camden. Blur, whose latest album, *Modern Life Is Rubbish*, would later be recognised as the first Britpop album, also drank in the same pub, because their record company, Food, was based round the corner.

In October 1993, Camden was given an additional focal point when Paul Tunkin opened a Saturday night club called Blow Up, where he played Northern Soul and classic British rock like The Yardbirds, The Who and The Small Faces. Blow Up immediately became *the* place to be on a Saturday night and the sharply-dressed regulars usually included an array of the new Camden pop stars. Around the same time, some of the clearly punk-influenced upcoming bands, such as Elastica, These Animal Men and S*M*A*S*H, were lumped together under the banner of the 'New Wave Of The New Wave' and received lots of attention from the music weeklies during the first couple of months of 1994. "The New Wave Of The New Wave wasn't so much a forerunner to Britpop as a cul-de-sac," says Phill Savidge.

Ironically, given that it had started as an anti-American movement, Britpop really began with the death of Kurt Cobain in April 1994. Not only did Cobain's suicide mark the end of the road for grunge, it also created the need for a new icon to love. "Kurt Cobain was the John Lennon of our generation," said Noel Gallagher, in one of the early Oasis interviews, summing up the effect that his songwriting had on so many people. However, it would be another four months before Oasis released their life-affirming third single, *Live Forever*, while the release of Blur's third album, *Parklife*, almost directly coincided with Cobain's death — ecstatic reviews of it appearing just pages apart from his obituaries.

"*Modern Life Is Rubbish* had come out in 1993, but it took six months to kick in with the critics," says Andy Ross. "It got slaughtered when it came out but then there was a complete change of view by the press, so journalists wanted to say *Parklife* was brilliant before they'd heard a bloody note. There was a massive tidal wave welling up in Blur's favour and, by the time the album came out, we were riding on the crest of it."

In May, with obvious reference to *Select*'s Suede cover from the year before, Damon Albarn appeared on the front of *The Face*, against a Union Jack backdrop with the headline: Blur: Brit Up Your Ears. "If nothing else, *Parklife* suggests that we may soon once more become a righteous pop nation," concluded *Face* journalist Cliff Jones. "Britain, your wake up call is here, and its name is Blur."

If Blur were the wake up call, then Oasis went off like a loud alarm bell. Their debut album, *Definitely Maybe*, was widely hailed as the greatest British pop album since *The Stone Roses* when it was released in August. However, it would take Oasis's second album to catapult them into a different stratosphere to their Britpop contemporaries and, that November, they found themselves on a mini-French package tour in the company of Echobelly, Elastica, Shed Seven and Gene.

Back in London, Camden had become the undisputable centre of Britpop and a new breed of bands had begun to emerge. The most infamous of these were Menswear, who had originally come to Camden to hang out at Blow Up, had formed in the Good Mixer in October, were supporting Pulp by Christmas and receiving a ridiculous amount of press by the beginning of 1995.

Noel Gallagher moved into a flat in the centre of Camden Town in January 1995 and Club Spangle, at the Dublin Castle, became one of the most popular places to go on a Monday night. Blur played a secret gig at the Dublin Castle in May and several of the other places that were of central importance to Britpop — such as Food Records, Savage & Best's office, the Good Mixer, George & Niki's restaurant — were all based in Camden. Oasis's record company, Creation, also moved into new offices in neighbouring Primrose Hill.

By Easter, the whole of Camden was crawling with people who were in bands or simply wanted to form one, plus the attendant journalists, A&R men and booking agents. Britpop was much more than a Scene That Celebrates Itself, it was an Entire Industry Celebrating Itself right in the middle of Camden.

Melody Maker ran a cover feature on the area in June — slapping Menswear on the front — and followed it, a month later, with one on Britpop. "What we are seeing," wrote Paul Lester, "is the thrilling, full-blown renaissance of British pop. Truly we may never have had it so good." The main feature divided the bands into three categories. The Champions [Blur, Oasis, The Stone Roses, Suede, Pulp, Elastica, The Boo Radleys, Radiohead, Supergrass and Gene], The Contenders [Black Grape, Menswear, McAlmont & Butler, The Charlatans, Teenage Fanclub, Sleeper, Echobelly, Shampoo, The Verve and Shed Seven] and The Hopefuls [Marion, Heavy Stereo, The Bluetones, Cast, Salad, My Life Story, The Weekenders, Powder and Elcka].

During that summer of 1995, teenagers crowded into Camden from all over the country, keen to spend an evening drinking in the Good Mixer or watching a band in the Dublin Castle. Most of them were dressed in the kind of clothes that Jarvis Cocker had been wearing for years. The climax of the whole Britpop thing came when both Blur and Oasis released singles on the same day: August 14. Blur's *Country House* versus Oasis's *Roll With It* was billed as The Battle Of Britpop, which turned out to be a strong enough story to make the front pages of most of the tabloids as well a slot on the *Six O'Clock News*. Two days after the singles were released, Damon Albarn presented *Britpop 95*, a BBC2 programme about British guitar pop, which featured Blur, Pulp,

BRITPOP

Elastica, Supergrass, The Boo Radleys, Marion, Menswear and Powder. Oasis declined the invitation to appear.

As it turned out, it was Blur, rather than Oasis, who won the first round. "That summer of 1995 was an exhilarating time," says Andy Ross. "I first broke the news to Damon that we were Number One in the bar of the Good Mixer, before we went to play football in Regents Park, and that was a great moment. Then it all went horribly wrong."

Blur's victory was short-lived to say the least. Even though their album, *The Great Escape*, received a much more favourable critical response than Oasis's *(What's The Story) Morning Glory?*, the latter quickly outsold it and established itself as one of the biggest selling British albums of recent years.

By now, though, the whole Britpop thing was beginning to turn sour. Noel Gallagher was quoted in *The Observer* as saying that he hoped Damon Albarn and Alex James would catch AIDS and die. He apologised, but the animosity between him and Albarn was deep rooted.

The Britpop party was officially over. The first 'Fuck Britpop' T-shirts began to appear and most of the bands started to distance themselves from each other and from Camden. Rather than continue to be part of a scene that the rest of the country had only just woken up to, many people preferred to stay at home and turn inward.

"One of the original problems with Britpop was cocaine and just excess in general," says one interviewee for this book. "Obviously, music and drugs go hand in hand, and most people have dabbled with one thing or another. But by far the biggest, and least talked about, problem was heroin. There were a lot of people who should have been having a good time that summer who were just too fucked up to remember anything about it."

Still, there was some mileage left in the Camden scene yet. Suggs released his first solo album in October — which included a song called *Camden Town* — giving most of the national newspapers an excuse to write about the home of Britpop. "I'd been talking about writing a song about Camden Town for ages," says Suggs. "So I finally wrote one, but it was also about the tourists, who had become a metaphor for everything that was going on here."

However, by the time Suggs' single was released, the first Camden obituaries were being formulated. "Camden was shit," said *Vox* in January 1996. "It smelt of piss, you needed a bank balance the size of Mars to live there and, besides, Blur drink in Soho now. The place died on its arse when they started selling Good fucking Mixer T-shirts." [That kind of missed the point of Good Mixer T-shirts — which had been available over the pub counter since the late-80s when the only people who were there to buy them either couldn't afford them or simply weren't interested.]

"Britpop was almost like a cake that was taken out of the oven before it had been baked," says Mary Byker. "It was growing and there was the possibility that it might have grown into something that wasn't just about retro behaviour. But, instead, the media jumped ship because they realised that they had created a monster which actually wasn't as great as it had been made out to be. They just came to Camden, set their movie there, sucked a lot of the life out of the area and then decided to start looking for somewhere else to go."

The leading Britpop players had gone their separate ways — Elastica spent months on the road, Damon Albarn went into temporary exile, Jarvis Cocker became a national hero and Oasis quickly moved on to the kind of megastardom that Noel Gallagher had always predicted — leaving the minor characters to suffer the backlash. Inevitably, it was those who had made themselves most visible who were treated the harshest. "For me, Menswear were a lot better than people made them out to be," says Phill Savidge, whose company is responsible for their press. "But, initially, they were probably pawns in a post-modern experiment between a PR company and the music press. As people, because they were young and glamorous, they fitted into our ethos. I was pretty aware that some people thought they were vacuous and that they might think that Savage & Best were vacuous because of it — that's why I said they were probably a post-modern experiment, because you could see how far you could take a notion without being rumbled. But when you're playing with people's lives or careers, and are watching them grow up in public, it was a fairly humbling experience."

In addition to Menswear, Savage & Best had to further atone for the perceived sins of their own record label, Parkway, which had launched both Powder and Fluffy. "I think people thought we were having a joke with Fluffy," says John Best. "They thought we were thinking, 'What can we get away with now?' And to an extent, I suppose we were. But I feel a bit aggrieved, because I do have some scruples. I know that some people were saying at the beginning of 1996 that Britpop's dead, so therefore Savage & Best are dead. But I knew a good band before Britpop existed and I'll know a good one afterwards."

Although Britpop was over as far as the music press were concerned, the rest of the media were only just waking up to the idea of some kind of swinging London scene and welcoming the opportunity to stick the Union Jack on their front covers. The big summer hit of 1996 was *Three Lions*, the England football team's official single for Euro 96, and a Britpop record in the sense that it was sung by Ian Broudie, from the Lightning Seeds, and written by the comedians Frank Skinner and David Baddiel. It became an instant anthem.

It took Andrew Innes, from Primal Scream — a band who were never in any danger of being labelled 'Britpop' — to draw a direct parallel between Britpop, British football and the recent Beef Crisis. If Britpop and Euro 96 weren't exactly the revenge of the Beef Crisis, then they were at least a diversion from it. "Britpop's just a sad little dream in certain people's heads," he told Ben Stud in *Melody Maker* in June

BRITPOP

96. "Britpop is wimp pop. Just a bunch a fuckin' bed wetters wettin' their fuckin' beds."

"The thing I hate about it," continued Bobby Gillespie, "is all that Union Jack shit. When Pete Townshend chopped up a Union Jack to have a suit made of it, it was treason and art. It had fuck all to do with fuckin' nationalism. This lot, though, these bedwetters, they mean it."

Yet as far as the general public were concerned, Britpop's star was still in the ascendant — and Tony Blair was smart enough to hitch his wagon to it. He had already aligned himself with both Oasis and Blur and realised that the music industry could play a very important part in Labour's election campaign. "The one thing the British music industry is crap at is appreciating just how much it actually means for tourism," says Andy Ross. "It's absolutely immense. From the Good Mixer comes the Britpop scene and from the Britpop scene comes loads of tourism. Tony Blair realised that it was a great idea to get the music industry to say, 'We vote Labour', which is fair enough. The irony is that being in a band, or being on an independent record label, is the most Thatcherite of all industries. If you don't sell records, or you don't have people turning up at your gigs buying your CDs, then you go out of business. Every band is a small industry and Camden is a hotbed of Thatcherite Conservatism masquerading as right-on Labour voters."

Nevertheless, Britpop did play a significant role in electing the new Labour government — it had also spawned new buzz words in other areas of the arts, such as 'Britart' and even 'Britlit'. Tony Blair acknowledged the role that the arts had played in both Labour's victory and in Britain's future by inviting a number of leading musicians, writers, comedians, actors and artists to Downing Street, in July 1997, for a showbiz reception — top of the guest list was Noel Gallagher, his wife Meg Matthews and Creation chief Alan McGee. The event was held in the early evening but probably wasn't that dissimilar to the afternoon tea party that Mary Wilson held at Number Ten in 1967 to talk about raising money to turn the Roundhouse into an arts palace for the people.

"The cultural ramifications of Britpop are enormous," says John Best. "Almost the whole of swinging London is built on 15 or 20 people who were around in Camden in the early-90s — I honestly believe that. I think fashion has fed off Britpop in all forms, so that it starts off with Jarvis Cocker down at Blow Up in 1993 but then it goes out into New York fashion society and mushrooms. I'm not sure how much money has actually come back to the people who were the progenitors, but the ripples that they created were huge. And I think that the overall influence of Britpop is almost immeasurable."

Britpop is now a tag that no one wants anything to do with, but the place that spawned it is too resilient to be killed off by one little scene. "Today, thank God, Britpop is over and service is back to normal," says Mary Byker. "I would have moved out of Camden at the height of the media frenzy if I had honestly thought that we were going to be locked in a Britpop timewarp forever. But the storm has passed and you can still have a good time here. You can go to the Camden Palace on a Tuesday night and see a techno band one week, then a hip hop band, then an indie band, then something else. Britpop made it harder to get a seat in the Spread Eagle, but that's about it."

CHISWICK RECORDS

CHISWICK: THE FIRST RECORD LABEL

When Ted Carroll and Roger Armstrong set up Chiswick Records, in the upstairs room of the Rock On record shop on Kentish Town Road, in December 1975, they created the first proper rock'n'roll scene in Camden Town.

The idea to form a low-budget record company was inspired by great American labels, such as Chess and Sun, which had provided a platform for the first rock'n'roll bands. Plus the fact that Carroll — who had opened a record stall in Golborne Road in 1972 and one in Soho a couple of years later — could see there was a gaping hole in the market. "Lots of people wanted to buy stuff that sounded a certain way but which didn't seem to exist on record," he says. "So that's how we started recording contemporary bands. We just went round the pubs looking for someone with the kind of style that we thought would appeal to other people."

Chiswick's first A&R mission was to see a band called Chrome, at the Lord Nelson pub on the Holloway Road, after Carroll had spotted their name in the back pages of *Melody Maker*. However, the first band to record a demo for Chiswick were the Hammersmith Gorillas, who had impressed Carroll with their 1974 version of The Kinks' *You Really Got Me* and whose singer, Jesse Hector, was one of his customers.

"I used to go to Ted's record stall to buy rock'n'roll records," says Hector. "We were the first band to be taken into the recording studio and we made two tracks in about four hours."

By this time, Carroll and Armstrong had invited Trevor Churchill to be the third partner in Chiswick. Churchill had worked for various record companies, including EMI, and had helped to set up the label Rolling Stone, working with the Stones on records such as *Exile On Main Street* and *Sticky Fingers*. "Ted and I thought that if we were going to start a label, we needed somebody who actually knew how the structure worked," says Roger Armstrong. "Trevor was moving to Hamburg to work for Polydor Records and we met him just before his leaving party and asked him if he wanted to get involved. He said, 'Give me ten per cent and I'll be your adviser' but we said, 'No, we'll give you a third.' The theory was that, if it worked, we needed somebody like him and we wanted him as a partner. If it didn't, he had a third of nothing and ten per cent of nothing is the same as a third."

In the meantime, Chrome had unexpectedly evolved into the Count Bishops. "This guy called Mike Spencer turned up at the Soho stall, straight off the plane from New York, and asked me where he could find bands to go and see," says Armstrong. "So I told him about various places, including the pub on the Holloway Road where we'd seen Chrome. The next time we went to see Chrome, their roadie, which is what Mike Spencer started off as, got up at the end and sang three or four numbers and played harmonica. And before too long he'd taken them over and rung up a friend of his in New York and said, 'I've joined this band and we've got a record deal and we're playing gigs.' So the guitar player flew into town not knowing that the deal was with two guys just starting a record company, whose entire financial base was a couple of record stalls and the gigs that they had were in bars!"

The Count Bishops' *Speedball* EP, which was recorded for £92 at Pathway Studio, above the Hope & Anchor pub in Islington, became Chiswick's first release in December 1975. It was a noisy, hard-edged R&B record which sounded like a punked-up version of the early Stones. Even though the Count Bishops were right on the edge of what was going on at the time — they were initially regarded as rivals of the Sex Pistols — Chiswick's next release was a reissue rather than something recorded especially for the label.

"I had always wanted to do a reissue label, because I could see that there were all these obscure 1950s 45s that people were going crazy for," says Carroll. "One of the best known ones was *Brand New Cadillac* and people were paying about £5 or £10 for a copy whenever one turned up, which was hardly ever. I knew the majors weren't interested in reissuing that stuff because they were busy doing triple albums by Yes. So I figured you could license it, put it out, sell a few thousand copies and everybody would make some money."

Trevor Churchill managed to get Chiswick a licensing deal with EMI and Vince Taylor's *Brand New Cadillac* became the label's second release. The third was by the 101'ers, whose singer Joe Strummer would later cover Taylor's song when he was in the Clash.

It had been a gig in Camden, at Dingwalls in October 1975, that prompted Ted Carroll to offer the 101'ers a one-off single deal with Chiswick. Four nights after the Dingwalls show, Carroll took Roger Armstrong to see them play at University Of London Students' Union. "It wasn't even like a gig," says Armstrong. "They were playing in the bar, with no stage, and then there was Ted and me and about three students, standing there with our arms folded, while Joe Strummer, who was wearing a suit, went beserk. Ted and I immediately thought, 'We've got to do something with these guys.' I mean, there were five people watching and everyone else was getting drunk, yet Joe was full-tilt, like he was playing Wembley Stadium or something. So we made a record with them and, just before we were about to put it out, I was over at the Red Cow in Hammersmith waiting for the Jam to come onstage, when someone banged me on the shoulder. I turned round and it was Joe Strummer, with this weedy little kid standing behind him, a Keith Richards-lookalike, who turned out to be Mick Jones. Strummer was very twitchy in those days and his opening gambit was, 'Have I done the right thing?' and he hasn't even told me what he's done. So I'm going, 'What do you mean?' And he's like, 'Well, I've left the 101'ers, I've joined a band with him', pointing to Mick. I was thinking, 'Well, thanks a fuckin' lot, Joe — we haven't put the record out yet, but you've broken the band up and now you want me to tell you if you've done the right thing'."

Chiswick were directly involved in Mont de Marsan, the first European punk festival which took place at the end of August 1976. The festival was organised by Marc Zermati, who was a regular at Ted Carroll's stall on Golborne Road and had set up his own record label, Skydog. Originally, both the Sex Pistols and the Clash were meant to play, but the Pistols pulled out because they didn't want to be on the same bill as Eddie And The Hot Rods and the Clash followed. Among the bands who did play were The Pink Fairies, the Damned, the Count Bishops and the Gorillas, who dropped the original prefix from their name. The Gorillas then became the first band to actually sign to Chiswick and *She's My Gal* was the label's fourth release.

Carroll and Armstrong also came close to signing the Jam — Paul Weller was another regular at the Rock On stall in Soho — but were beaten to them by Polydor in January 1977. "We had been going to see the Jam and talking to John Weller about recording them," says Ted Carroll. "We worked out a deal for a one-off single, and then Polydor came in and signed them. We'd actually agreed a deal and then John Weller came up to see me at my flat in Camden one night — I think Paul was with him — and said they were afraid that if they signed to Polydor they might get lost in the rush. I told them that they should really do a single with us because they had enough of a following to create a bit of a stir and then they might get a better deal from another record company. But Polydor upped the offer and gave them six grand in cash, which was a lot of money at that stage, so they went for it."

Soon afterwards, however, Chiswick were presented with a punk band unlike any other: Motorhead. "Lemmy used to come to the stall in Golborne," says Ted Carroll. "He'd always be looking for obscure records but he never had any money and then suddenly he was playing bass in Hawkwind, so one day Lemmy had a cheque book [*laughs*]. I was interested in him because he was a nice guy and all the records that he would buy were things I liked myself. Then one day he came in with Larry Wallis and Lucas Fox and he said, 'I've left Hawkwind, I'm forming my own band called Motorhead.' He told me he'd actually been chucked out of Hawkwind, which he was — he got busted for speed and they slung him out so they didn't get thrown out of America."

The original Motorhead line-up recorded the album, *On Parole*, for United Artists, but they shelved it [eventually releasing it on the back of the band's commercial success in 1979]. After replacing the original guitarist and drummer with 'Fast' Eddie Clarke and Phil 'Animal' Taylor in 1976, Motorhead recorded their debut single, *White Line Fever*, for Stiff, only to have it withdrawn [again, it eventually saw the light in 1979]. And one day early in 1977, Lemmy phoned Carroll to tell him that the band were splitting up and invited him to record a live album of their final show at the Marquee. Carroll persuaded Lemmy not to split the band immediately but to record two farewell gigs and, in the meantime, cut a single for Chiswick.

"I sent them down to this studio in Kent to do a single but, when I went down the next day to see how it was going, they had virtually completed an album," says Carroll. "I went into the house first of all and there were various members of Motorhead and their entourage of chicks, all with the cartridge case belts and black leather jackets and tight black jeans, strewn around on those big cushions, asleep. Then I went out to the studio and they had taken these big studio speakers down from the ceiling and put them on two little tables on either side of the desk, physically about three feet away from their ears, and Speedy Keen, the producer, and the engineer, John Burns, were sitting there playing this backing track at ear-splitting volume while Lemmy was doing vocal overdubs in a booth, and there was all this speed chopped out — you can imagine the scene. I told them that since they had started to record an album, they might as well carry on and they finished it the next day. We put *Motorhead* out as a single and it sold really well, and the album was our first to chart."

"Ted sent us off to Escaped Studios," remembers Lemmy, "with Speedy Keen — and, believe me, that was a fucking apt description, the trouble was it was all our speed he was taking — and John Burns. We did 11 backing tracks and no vocals, right, and then Ted came down on the second day and was standing there listening and he goes, 'What about the vocals?' and I said, 'Not on this track, on the next', and it got to track four and he said, 'Oh, all right, you bastards, you can finish the album', and that was *Motorhead*."

Meanwhile, Chiswick was developing its roster to include the Radiators From Space [which featured future Pogues guitarist Philip Chevron] and also helped to kickstart the careers of Billy Bragg [in a band called Riff Raff], Kirsty MacColl [then known as Mandy Doubt — *mandied out* — in Drug Addix] and Shane MacGowan [they released the Nips' third single, *Gabrielle*]. But the best story concerns Jim Kerr, whose band Johnny & The Self Abusers released a single, *Saints & Sinners*, on Chiswick.

"Before the Johnny & The Self Abusers record was released," says Roger Armstong, "they split into two groups, one of whom wanted their name on the record. Ted told the manager we couldn't change the name on the label, because we'd already printed it. The truth was that we'd pre-sold the record on the name, without people hearing the actual record. In the punk days, people thought, 'Johnny & The Self Abusers? We'll buy that', so there was absolutely no way we were going to change it. Then the band sent us their new demos and I remember saying to Ted, 'They sound great, but they'll never get anywhere with a stupid name like Simple Minds'."

In 1978, Chiswick was baled out of financial difficulties by signing a distribution deal with EMI — the major didn't want to deal

CHISWICK RECORDS

with the reissue side of Chiswick, so Carroll and Armstrong started a separate label, Ace Records, and their earliest reissues were the Hollywood Rock & Roll and Link Wray albums. Meanwhile, the Damned became the first band to benefit from the new EMI distribution deal. The Damned had officially split in February 1978 but, within seven months, Dave Vanian, Rat Scabies and Captain Sensible were playing a reunion gig, as the Doomed, at the Electric Ballroom, with Lemmy on bass. They asked Chiswick's press officer, Rick Rogers, to manage them and he sent them out on a UK tour.

"In order to publicise the tour," says Rick Rogers, "the band recorded a demo of *Love Song*, which we gave away as free, white label singles on something which I had put together called the Dodgy Demo label. We needed to sell some to pay for the cost of it, so I put an advert in the back of *Sounds*, with Chiswick's address. All of a sudden there was loads of mail coming through the door and Chiswick ended up offering the Doomed a deal."

By April, the Doomed had become the reformed Damned, signed to Chiswick, re-recorded *Love Song* with Roger Armstrong and had their first Top 20 hit. Its success was partly down to a marketing ploy of releasing the single in four sleeves with a different member of the band on each. The original Dodgy Demo of *Love Song* had proved that they had a hardcore fan base and Chiswick subsequently released the single in coloured vinyl, so some people ended up buying eight copies. They followed this chart success with *Smash It Up* and the *Machine Gun Etiquette* album.

At the end of 1981, Chiswick parted company with EMI and sorted out a series of new distribution arrangements. During this period, they also set up a new label called Big Beat in order to release old Chiswick tracks and record new bands that EMI would definitely not be interested in. Among those who released records on Big Beat are The Cramps and a whole host of Camden-linked garage/psychobilly bands, such as The Meteors, The Milkshakes, The Sting-rays, The Prisoners, the Tall Boys and The Vibes. It was Big Beat that was to carry on the original spirit of Chiswick because, by 1982, Carroll, Armstrong and Churchill had decided to start winding Chiswick down and concentrate on Ace Records, which they then adopted as their company name, and which has gone on to become one of the biggest and best reissue labels in the world.

BILL FULLER: THE MAN WHO BUILT THE BALLROOM

Bill Fuller is a rock'n'roll legend and one of the central figures in the history of Camden Town. He took over a run down ballroom on the High Street in the late-30s, built it up into one of the most famous Irish dance halls in London, and then transformed it into the Electric Ballroom in 1978.

Fuller – a contractor and amateur wrestler as well as an astute businessman — built a chain of ballrooms across England, Ireland and the United States, enabling many Irish couples to meet and marry. His ability to erect such places, virtually overnight, has inspired many stories over the years. "There used to be a saying about him in the 50s," said one interviewee for this book. "'What Hitler didn't knock down in London, Bill Fuller did.'"

"Fuller was a legend round Dublin and further afield," Eamon Dunphy wrote in his 1987 biography, *Unforgettable Fire: The Story Of U2.* "He did business with a handshake, which made it difficult to sue him when later on he told you to, 'Fuck off, boy, and don't annoy me.'"

At one point, Fuller owned 23 ballrooms around the world, including San Francisco's legendary Fillmore West. He also promoted jazz concerts, including several by Billie Holiday, at New York's Carnegie Hall; helped to break Patsy Cline on the East Coast; ran a booking agency for country heavyweights, such as Johnny Cash, Jerry Lee Lewis, Willie Nelson and Buck Owens; and was the only man well connected enough to get Irish showbands into Las Vegas.

You could also say that without Bill Fuller, Oasis might never have existed – because, among his ballrooms was The Astoria, on Plymouth Grove in Manchester, which is where Peggy Sweeney met another Irish immigrant called Thomas Gallagher. A quarter of a century later, on May 29, 1989, Noel Gallagher returned to the ballroom where his parents had first laid eyes on each other to celebrate his 21st birthday. [By this time, Fuller, who still owned the building, had changed The Astoria's name to The Carousel and, more recently, to the International 2.] Noel Gallagher was there to see The Stone Roses, who were supporting James at an Anti-Clause 28 Benefit gig, and was blown away. "The Stone Roses made me want to be in a band," he says simply. For Liam Gallagher, who had been watching the Roses downstairs, seeing Ian Brown perform for the first time was almost a Damascene moment. "I just went, 'Yeah!'" he says. "I thought, 'It's here, today, in my face. I can go with that.'"

Bill Fuller smiles when he hears about Oasis and his latest part in rock'n'roll history. "Oasis?" he asks. "Are they the boys who sound like The Beatles?"

A lunch date with Bill Fuller in his adopted hometown of Las Vegas has turned out to be the crock of gold at the end of the Camden Town rainbow. "Would you like a glass of champagne?" he asks, as he settles himself into a big booth in the Country Star bar and restaurant. "Go on, have one, it's a Sunday." A gospel group, in long white cassocks, are onstage, as if to emphasise his point. And, while they sang *Oh Happy Day*, Bill Fuller started telling me a small part of his life story.

He was born in County Kerry, shortly before the Irish Civil War broke out in December 1921. In that county, the conflict between the Free Staters, who supported the Anglo-Irish Treaty, and the Republicans, who did not, was more intense than in most other parts of Ireland.

By 1923, Bill Fuller's cousin, Stephen Fuller, was among a number of Republicans who had been arrested and imprisoned in Tralee. In the early hours of a March morning, nine of them were taken to Ballyseedy Cross, where there was a mine on the road. Each prisoner had his hands tied behind him and then all nine of them were roped together in a ring, with their backs to the mine, which was deliberately detonated. Eight of them were instantly blown to pieces. The soldiers presumed that all the prisoners had been killed and, after collecting fragments of bodies from trees and bushes, distributed the remains into nine coffins. There was almost a riot in Tralee when it was discovered that one of the prisoners had escaped and the relatives of the dead insisted on opening all the coffins.

The survivor was Stephen Fuller, who was blown some distance from the mine into a nearby wood, managing to escape with minor injuries. Fuller lived to make the details of the story known and to become a powerful political figure [he also taught the writer Brendan Behan at a Republican 'Training College' near Dublin in the late-30s].

"Stephen got blown up in the air and he came down in his all together," says Bill Fuller, managing to make the Ballyseedy massacre sound amusing rather than horrific. "He was a bit shocked, but he survived. Anyway, he ran for politics and when I was going to school we used to do different things to get funds for his election campaigns. I was only a kid then, 12 years of age, but I started running dances all around Kerry. I used to charge a shilling admission and I made him £900, in shillings, for his campaign. But it was because of Stephen Fuller that I got into the ballroom business — I thought there was money in it, so that's what I decided to do when I got to England."

Initially, though, Bill Fuller had not set his sights on the ballrooms of England, much less the world. He wanted to be a farmer and his driving ambition was to own a place of his own in Kerry. By the time he was 17, he had a steady girlfriend, who he was about to marry, and he had managed to put a substantial deposit down on a farm worth £2,800. "I had bred a greyhound and managed to sell it for a lot of money," he says. "A friend of mine owned a farm in Kerry but he got a bigger farm from the Land Commission up in Dublin. So I made a deal with him: I bought the place in Kerry off him for £2,800 — I put down

£600 and arranged to borrow the rest from the National Bank in Listowel. I hadn't told my father about the deal, but he heard about it anyway and went to the bank and objected. Some solicitor had told him that he would be liable if I defaulted in the payment, because I was underage. So my old fellow objected to the deal and the bank then said, 'Sorry, we can't give it to you.' I used to ride a BSA motorbike — I was a handyman then at poaching the river for salmon — and I remember well, I got on the old motorbike and rode it into Listowel town. I went to see a fellow in Listowel, called Derby Briggs, and I said, 'Derby, there's the bike, now. Keep it, I'm going.' And then I turned around and got the train to Holyhead. And that was it, I'm gone ever since."

Once in England, Bill Fuller found work on the building sites. He was lucky enough to be taught the tricks of the trade by a Scottish man called Bob Young, who was one of the main men at McAlpine's at the time. Soon after he had first arrived in London, Fuller teamed up with Paddy Casey, to open an Irish club in Queens Road, Bayswater. Paddy Casey was one brother in a large family of Irish wrestlers and they allowed Fuller to train with them. "In my young days I was a pretty lively guy," he says. "The Caseys taught me a lot about wrestling and boxing. One of them was a champion wrestler, known as The Crusher Casey, but it was Micky Howard — who was married to one of the Casey girls — who really showed me how to wrestle and how to counter hold. If a fella puts a hold on you, you always have a counter hold, and you can break him. The Caseys were strong and tough, but I was able to counter them. I could hold my own with them, but I didn't want to wrestle professionally because I was too busy with the club."

All this physical training came in useful when Fuller took over The Buffalo Ballroom in Camden Town in the late-30s. It was such a rough Irish dance hall that it had recently been closed down by the police, but Fuller persuaded the local Chief Of Police to let him reopen it, promising to man the door himself — which he did for a number of years. He also started his own contracting business and ran it from an upstairs room of The Buffalo. "When the Second World War was on," he says. "Irish men didn't have to join up if they were from the South, it was up to them. So I started a contracting business, and I had the Borough Of Stepney and the Borough Of Islington, with about 2,000 men working for me. During the day, I ran the building business and in the night time I moved on to entertainment."

Before long, Bill Fuller had built The Buffalo up into a ballroom that could accommodate 2,000 people. He then set his sights on building or buying other ballrooms in Ireland and England, initially going to Dublin, where he built The Crystal Ballroom, and then to Belfast, where he bought The Mecca. He also started to run his own management and promotions company, looking after big band leaders, such as Jack Parnell and Joe Loss, who would tour the West Country and also play in Fuller's own venues.

BILL FULLER

In 1950, Fuller went to the United States for the first time and returned to New York soon afterwards to open a ballroom called City Centre. On subsequent trips, he travelled around the rest of the country, exploring different cities and picking up the new records of the time. According to Fuller, some of these records played a major role in the rise of the Irish showband phenomenon.

By 1953, the Clipper Carlton, from Strabane in Northern Ireland, had begun to deviate from the usual big band sounds of the time, by moving around the stage, rather than sitting at their bandstands, and incorporating various routines into their set. One night towards the end of 1954, Fuller, who had been in Derry promoting a show at the Guildhall, took his girlfriend of the time on a moonlight drive by the Atlantic.

"We went about 20 miles out of Derry into Donegal," he recalls. "And, lo and behold, there was a marquee set up on the ground, and there was a band playing, which turned out to be the Clipper Carlton. I had just been over in Nashville and I had brought back several records by different bands. One of them was Bill Haley And His Comets, who had two fantastic records out at that time, *Crazy Man Crazy* and *Rock Around The Clock*. Anyway, I had these records in the back of my car, and when your man Mickey [O'Hanlon], the drummer, got up and did his Louis Armstrong routine, he got a great hand. Cheers, I thought, I'll bring my records in to the boys. Anyway, I brought in the Bill Haley records and a couple of others, and I said to the lads, 'Now, instead of Mickey just doing Louis Armstrong, maybe Fergie [O'Hagan, vocals] and Hughie [Tourish, piano] should start doing records by other people.' And I told them to take one record each. And it came to New Year and I said, 'You can play at the Guildhall on Tuesday week.' And they brought the house down, and the next time they played they brought in 600 people of their own."

By 1955, the Clipper Carlton had decked themselves out in shiny suits and were imitating everyone from Nat King Cole to Elvis Presley, with various comedy routines thrown in, and were packing out dance halls across Ireland. Soon dozens of other bands were following the Carlton's style, but the most successful of all were The Royal Showband. When the Irish ballrooms closed down during Lent, the showbands toured England and Bill Fuller was able to help them out by booking them into The Buffalo in Camden Town or his other ballrooms in Birmingham and Manchester.

By the early-60s, the Royals had become Ireland's number one band and Bill Fuller had opened clubs in whichever American city had a large enough Irish population to make it worth his while — including Boston, Chicago, Cleveland and San Francisco. "I was travelling an average of 6,000 miles a week," he says. "My beat then was San Francisco to London, and I lived in San Francisco for 12 years. At one time, I had 23 places around the world. I even had a club down in the

Bahamas called the Cat & Fiddle. The fella who was running it got mixed up in drug dealing so he had to move out fast and I bought it off him very reasonably."

In 1966, Bill Fuller managed to get The Royal Showband an audition in Las Vegas — an unheard of feat for someone who wasn't a member of the Mafia. They were subsequently given a four-week stint at the Desert Inn that autumn. Two years later, they had a six-month contract at the Stardust, which was pretty spectacular for an Irish showband. Fuller even introduced some of the band to their hero, Elvis Presley. "I met Elvis a couple of times," he says. "I brought [Royal singer] Brendan Bowyer in one time to meet him. In those days, you'd know people and wouldn't really think of them as being famous."

Around the same time, three of the ballrooms in Bill Fuller's great chain were renamed 'The Carousel'. "I was never fussy about names," he says. "But there was a girl from Cavan working for me, called Peggy McCabe, and she liked the name Carousel." Coincidentally, the three Carousel Ballrooms turned out to be the jewels in Fuller's crown: the former Buffalo in Camden Town, the one-time Astoria in Manchester and a ballroom in San Francisco.

By 1968, though, Bill Fuller's attention was firmly focussed on one of his greatest dreams yet: building an Irish village in Galway Bay. While he was doing this, the American rock promoter Bill Graham flew to Ireland in a desperate attempt to obtain the lease on The Carousel Ballroom in San Francisco. It was easier than Graham had imagined: Fuller was waiting for him when he arrived at Shannon Airport at 8am, ordered a bottle of bourbon, shook hands on a deal, finished the remaining shots of liquor and then announced that he was going back to work on his building site. By 5pm, Graham was on a flight home, all set to turn The Carousel into the legendary rock venue, the Fillmore West.

Unfortunately, Bill Fuller's own dream did not go as smoothly. "I always had a great relationship with people from the West, both in Connemara and Mayo," he says. "But I had a lot of bad friends there in the Irish Government and they wouldn't give me proper planning permission. I wanted to build an Irish village — I had good ideas and I had contact with a lot of Irish-Americans, such as the Kennedys, and other men who had yachts down along the East Coast. Galway Bay was always a big thing with Americans and I bought that site because there was nine fathoms of water in the bay. It's so deep you could bring the Queen Mary in there. Anyway, I was going to build a big pier out into the Atlantic and a boatel out on the rocks, but I couldn't get planning permission. The people in Galway City got jealous, because I was an outsider and I was building this big thing outside the city. I built the whole lot in about 12 weeks, but they wouldn't give me final planning permission to build the pier out into the sea. I was promised everything, but given nothing. Delay was bad for me because I was building another place in a different part of the world and I had to move on."

BILL FULLER

During the 70s, he sold many of his ballrooms but adapted others into rock venues. These included The Crystal in Dublin (which became McGonagles), The Carousel in Manchester (the International 2) and The Carousel in Camden Town (the Electric Ballroom). He made a point of turning up at the latter five months after it had opened to see Thin Lizzy play with Bob Geldof, Paul Cook and Steve Jones.

"Phil Lynott was good, he worked for me a lot," he says. "And what's the other boy called? A big tall boy from Dublin who played rock — Bob Geldof, that's it! I remember one night, there was Phil and Geldof and some other lads, there were three famous groups and I put them all together and I said, 'How much do you want?' They said they wanted 75 per cent of the door and I said, 'You're a right crowd of greedy bastards!' When I went back to the Ballroom, there was a big poster with 'The Greedy Bastards' written on it. I could handle the contrariest of musicians, you know. I remember Jack Parnell wrote a jazz tune one time called *The Fuller Bounce*. He had the greatest bunch of musicians, but they were all headers in those days, and he used to reckon I was the only man who could run his tour. I'd look after the band and I'd roadie myself. After the show, we'd have a great party and then the following morning we'd pull out at round 8 or 9 in the morning, which is a hard thing for musicians. But I'd get them into the groove."

Asked about the secret of his success, Bill Fuller smiles and says: "I worked with the trends of the people. I gave them what they wanted and I gave them the best of it. It meant a lot to me to see people enjoying entertainment at a decent price. And I never went in for any hocus pocus. But any fellas arguing with me about money, I'd stick it up his jumper [*laughs*]."

By the late-80s, Bill Fuller had decided to focus most of his attention on rock mining in Las Vegas. "I came out here and got an old mine going up the hill," he says, "and decided to turn my life around another bend."

The nearest thing that Camden Town has to a Bill Fuller these days is Vince Power, a one-time antiques dealer from Waterford who owns nine bars and live music venues in London and also organises five annual outdoor festivals, including Reading and the Phoenix. A big fan of country music, Power went to Nashville in the 70s and dreamed of building his own honky tonk in North London. That dream became the Mean Fiddler in Harlesden, which opened in 1981, after Power had spent a year building it himself.

"It was a later version of Bill Fuller," says Power. "Do everything yourself, because you really haven't got the money or the know-how. I just knew that I wanted my own honky tonk — a really nice, clean place with cold beer, good music and a band playing at the end of the bar. The original drawing to get licensing was done by an architect, but after that we made it up as we went along."

By the late-80s, Power's expanding empire had crossed circles with Bill Fuller's decreasing one. Power had set his sights on Fuller's Dublin club, McGonagles, and — like Bill Graham before him — realised that the only way to do a deal was by flying halfway across the world to meet the owner.

"I got into Las Vegas at about 11pm at night," says Power, "went to a dodgy hotel, because for some reason the place was booked out and I couldn't find a decent one, and then I met Bill Fuller for breakfast at 9am in the Desert Inn. He came in and we started talking about everything apart from the deal. He told me about his mine and wanted to bring me out to have a look at it. Then when we eventually got around to talking about a deal on McGonagles, he just said, 'How much?' I mentioned a figure of what I thought the place was worth and he jumped about three feet off the ground and said, 'If I was a young man I'd hit you' — and he walked off. I had just spent 12 hours on a plane to see him, and that was the end of Bill Fuller. He didn't even pay for the breakfast!"

The deal came to nothing, but there were no hard feelings on either side. "I usually bump into Bill Fuller in Camden or Dublin," says Power. "He treats me like a young lad and tends to give me advice. He says, 'When I was your age' or 'You should eat better and look after yourself' and all that business. He's a great character; he's unique."

Although Bill Fuller now feels at home in the other rock business — "up in the mountains, with the rattlesnakes" — he hasn't ruled out the possibility of returning to rock'n'roll, even though it is now 60 years since he took over The Buffalo Ballroom on Camden High Street.

"I might make a comeback in my old age," he says. "I'd still like to build four or five big places — maybe in Seattle and in Portland, and then I'll come down again to San Francisco and LA. I'll set those places off again, before I kick the bucket."

And what about his ballroom in Camden Town?

"Oh, I'll keep Camden until I move out of this world," he says. "It was the first place of my own that I had, so I wouldn't dream of parting with it. Camden will never be sold."

SOURCES

Interviews

Alie Allerton	June 24, 1996, Dingwalls, Camden Town
Barry Appleby	April 29, 1996, Ruby In The Dust, Camden Town
Roger Armstrong	May 22, 1996, Trattoria Lucca, Camden Town
Mrs Bellamy	December 14, 1996, Pret-a-Manger, Camden Town
John Best	April 25, 1997, Camden Brasserie, Camden Town
Mary Byker	March 8, 1997, The Spread Eagle, Camden Town
Ted Carroll	June 11, 1996, Pierre Victoire, Camden Town
Jarvis Cocker	October 16, 1996, Limani, Primrose Hill
Alo Conlon	June 18, 1996, The Dublin Castle, Camden Town
Bal Croce	April 18, 1997, George & Niki's, Camden Town
Paul Cwynarski	June 5, 1996, Rock On, Camden Town
Dempsey	March 13, 1997, Café Toto, Camden Town
Joe Dilworth,	May 22, 1997, At home on Camden Road, Camden Town
John Fitzgerald	June 10, 1996, St John's Tavern, Archway
Bill Fuller	November 17, 1996, Country Star, Las Vegas
Nick Garrard	April 28, 1996, The Monarch, Chalk Farm Road
Frank Giromano	October 29, 1996, Holt's, Camden Town
Mike Hart	May 14, 1996, The Spread Eagle, Camden Town
Jesse Hector	June 4, 1996, The Spread Eagle, Camden Town
Mike Hurley	April 7, 1997, The Good Mixer, Camden Town
Andrew James	May 8, 1996, The Engine Room, Chalk Farm
Paddy James	May 13, 1996, The Albert, Camden Town
James Johnston	April 26, 1997, The Edinburgh Castle, Camden Town
Alan Jones	June 25, 1996, Le Bistroteque, Camden Town
Ben Jones	July 4, 1996 Le Bistroteque, Camden Town
Sylvia Keogh	March 13, 1997, Café Toto, Camden Town
Steve Lamacq	May 20, 1997, The Good Mixer, Camden Town
Lemmy	February 11, 1997, The Spread Eagle, Camden Town
Shane MacGowan	November 25, 1996, Filthy MacNasty's, Amwell Street, EC1
Mouse	June 11, 1996, The Elephant's Head, Camden Town
Frank Murray	May 3, 1996, Belgo, Chalk Farm Road
Philippe	April 28, 1996, The Monarch, Camden Town
Vince Power	May 28, 1997, Soho House, Soho
Rick Rogers	June 11, 1996, The Spread Eagle, Camden Town
Andy Ross	December 18, 1996, The Good Mixer, Camden Town
Nick Roumana	November 4, 1996, Holt's, Camden Town
Phill Savidge	June 11, 1997, Café Delancey, Camden Town
Ski	June 5, 1996, Rock On, Camden Town
Suggs	September 10, 1996, Bar Gansa, Camden Town
Vange	March 26, 1997, George & Niki's, Camden Town
Anne Wellstead	December 9, 1996, Quinn's, Camden Town
Brian Wheeler	June 3, 1996, The Electric Ballroom, Camden Town

THE ROCK'N'ROLL GUIDE TO CAMDEN

All quotes come from the Interviews section on previous page unless listed below:

INTRODUCTION
"*The Pogues are the Camden...*" From 'Get Your Yeah Yeahs Out!' by Bill Graham, *Hot Press*, December 15 1988
"*A generous man never...*" Qtd in **Jack Doyle: Fighting For Love** by Michael Taub [*Stanley Paul & Co Ltd, 1990*]

CAMDEN HIGH STREET — NORTH SIDE
3. ELECTRIC BALLROOM
"*I thought it was...*" Herbie Armstrong qtd in **Van Morrison: Too Late To Stop Now** by Steve Turner [*Bloomsbury, 1993*]
"*Spit on me, Dickie*" Qtd in **Send 'Em Home Sweatin': The Showbands' Story** by Vincent Power [*Kildanore Press, 1990*]
"*I saw Ian Curtis...*" Shane MacGowan qtd by Jon Wilde in 'The Liver Man', *Loaded* 1994
8. MTV (EUROPE)
"*That Disneyland...*" JM qtd in 'Jonathan Miller... On Camden Town' by Andy Glyn, *Camden New Journal*, May 23, 1985
11. COMPENDIUM
"*Do you have any books on Lou Reed?*" Qtd in 'I Remember' by Nick Kimberley from **The First Twenty Five Years Of Compendium Bookshop: 1968-1993** Produced and edited by Chris Render and Phillip Derbyshire [Aldgate Press, London, 1993]
12. GEORGE'S CAFE
"*I still come to this café...*" Qtd in 'The Clash' from **1988: The New Wave Punk Rock Explosion** by Caroline Coon [Omnibus Press, 1982 Edition]
19. CAMDEN PLAZA
"*We didn't want to replicate...*" Alex Cox to AS, 1986
50s NEWSREEL: From the *North London Press*

CHALK FARM ROAD
"*Sooner or later...*" **From Revolt Into Style: The Pop Arts In Britain** by George Melly [*Penguin, 1972*]
2. THE ROUNDHOUSE
"*The minute they walked...*" Will Birch in 'The Clash: On Broadway' review, *Mojo*, August 1994
4. REHEARSAL REHEARSALS
"*Put your hands...*" Steve Barnacle qtd by Marcus Gray in 'Eyewitness: The Clash Pigeon Shooting Incident', *Q*, December 1994
5. CAMDEN MARKET
"*We're broke, man...*" Joe Strummer qtd in 'A Clash Of Interests?' by Miles, *Time Out*, December 15-21, 1978
7. DINGWALLS
"*Dingwalls is...*" Commander Cody qtd by Roy Carr, *NME*, June 24, 1978
"*They were strange...*" Adam Clayton to AS, 1987
"*In the States...*" Boss Goodman qtd by Roy Carr, *NME*, June 24, 1978
"*I went to see The Stone Roses...*" Mark Morriss qtd by Lisa Verrico, *Vox*, September 1995
"*Dingwalls was one...*" Andrew Lauder to AS, 1997
22. THE MARATHON
"*The Marathon is where...*" Steve Earle to AS, 1996
23. KYPRIANA HOTEL
"' *Phil said...*" Joe Elliott qtd in 'Grave On!' by Andy Strickland, *Loaded*, March 1996
24. THE ENTERPRISE
"*I keep seeing James Joyce...*" Suggs qtd in 'Ska Face' by Roger Morton, *Loaded*, December 1995
60s NEWSREEL: From the *North London Press* and *North London Press [Camden Edition]*

SOURCES

KENTISH TOWN ROAD/CAMDEN ROAD
"*The dark end of the street...*" Shane MacGowan to AS, 1991
1. ROCK ON
"*Working at Rock On...*" Philip Chevron to AS, 1986
2. AH HOLT'S
"*When I was...*" Marc Bolan qtd in **The Marc Bolan Story** by George Tremlett [*Futura, 1975*]
6. DEVONSHIRE ARMS
"*Other groups take...*" Philip Chevron qtd in 'Was Moses A Pogue?' by Di Cross, *Record Mirror*, March 29, 1986
11. SAINSBURY'S
"*You get people...*" Noel Gallagher qtd in 'The Black Sheep Boy' by Stuart Maconie in *Select*, August 1995
20. RIMBAUD
"*When I first read...*" Marc Bolan qtd in **The Marc Bolan Story** by George Tremlett [*Futura, 1975*]
"*I got Rimbaud...*" Patti Smith qtd in **From The Velvets To The Voidoids: A Pre-Punk History For A Post-Punk World** by Clinton Heylin [*Penguin, 1993*]
"*Like A Season...*" Ibid
"*For two whole days...*" Letter qtd in **Arthur Rimbaud** by Enid Starkie [*New & Revised Edition, Hamish Hamilton, 1947*]
70s NEWSREEL: From the *North London Press [Camden Edition]*

CAMDEN HIGH STREET — SOUTH SIDE
1. THE BLACK CAP
"*The Mother Black Cap...*" George Melly to AS, 1997
6. SOUNDS
"Sounds *was the only...*" Kurt Cobain to AS, 1991
10. THE CAMDEN PALACE
"*We were all wearing...*" James Fearnley to AS, 1986
20. THE LAUREL TREE
"*Paul used to...*" Todd Parmenter to AS, 1997
"*From a Southender's...*" Ibid
"*By the summer...*" Ibid
22. FOOD RECORDS LTD
"*In our office...*" Melissa Beehive to AS, London, 1988
26. THE UNDERWORLD
"*I can't compare...*" Courtney Love to Pamela Des Barres in 'Rock'N'Roll Needs Courtney Love', *Interview*, March 1994
80s NEWSREEL: From the *North London Press [Camden Edition]* and *Camden New Journal*

PARKWAY
5. GOLDEN GRILL
"*What the fuck...*" Axl Rose qtd in **Guns N'Roses** by Paul Elliott [*The Hamlyn Publishing Group Limited, 1990*]
6. DUBLIN CASTLE
"*We've had a few flyers...*" Noel Gallagher qtd in 'The Black Sheep Boy' by Stuart Maconie, *Select*, August 1995
8. FILM-MAKERS' CO-OPERATIVE/LONDON MUSICIANS' COLLECTIVE
"*That was one of our...*" Spider Stacy to AS, 1986
10. WB YEATS & SYLVIA PLATH
"*Patti Smith was in love...*" Courtney Love qtd in 'The Girlie Show-Off' by Peter Relic, *Vox*, February 1997
"*The street and the house...*" Letter from Sylvia Plath qtd in **Bitter Fame: A Life Of Sylvia Plath** by Anne Stevenson [*Penguin, 1990*]
"*A real inspiration...*" Ibid

11. CREATION RECORDS
"*The Jesus & Mary...*" Alan McGee statement qtd in **The Jesus & Mary Chain: A Musical Biography** by John Robertson [*Omnibus, 1988*]
13. LONDON ZOO
"*I would queue...*" Nick Cave to AS, 1995
17. THE SPREAD EAGLE
"*It is now 11am...*" From **In Camden Town** by David Thomson [*Penguin, 1985*]
26. NOEL GALLAGHER
"*I swear to God...*" Noel Gallagher qtd in 'Top Of The World, Mam!' by Phil Sutcliffe, *Q*, February 1996
27. DYLAN THOMAS
"*See you later...*" Qt attrib to Caitlin Thomas in **Caitlin: The Life Of Caitlin Thomas** by Paul Ferris [*Hutchinson, 1993*]
"*It was a boozy...*" Caitlin Thomas qtd in *Camden New Journal*, January 12, 1984

INVERNESS STREET
"*I used to drink...*" George Melly to AS, 1997
1. INVERNESS STREET MARKET
"*I can't go to Camden...*" Brett Anderson qtd by John Harris, *NME*, November 1993
7. GOOD MIXER
"*Somewhere off Camden...*" Steve Lamacq, *NME*, February 1992
"*A viciously thin...*" From 'Bladdered!' by David Cavanagh, *Select*, March 1992
"*I stopped going...*" John Harris qtd in *Independent On Sunday*, September 1995
10. ARLINGTON HOUSE
"*A hotel for...*" Qtd in **What Do You Expect — Paradise?** [*Channel 4 Documentary, 1993*]
"'*No Irish...*'" Qtd in **The Irish In Britain** by Kevin O'Connor [Sidgwick & Jackson, London, 1972]
"*There I met the artists...*" Qtd in **The Green Fool** by Patrick Kavanagh [*Penguin, 1975*]
"*Camden Town/Camden...*" Ex-Rowton House resident to AS, 1994
90s NEWSREEL: From *Camden New Journal, Camden & St Pancras Chronicle, The Times* and *The Evening Standard*

BRITPOP
"*If nothing else ...*" Cliff Jones in 'Looking For A New England', *The Face*, May 1994
"*What we are...*" Paul Lester in 'Britpop', *Melody Maker*, July 22, 1995
"*Camden was shit...*" '95 Reasons Why '95 Was... Total Rock'N'Roll', *Vox*, January 1996
"*Britpop's just a...*" Andrew Innes qtd by Ben Stud, *Melody Maker*, June 1996
"*The thing I hate...*" Bobby Gillespie qtd by Ben Stud, *Melody Maker*, June 1996

BILL FULLER
"*Fuller was a legend...*" From **Unforgettable Fire: The Story Of U2** by Eamon Dunphy, [*Viking, 1987*]
"*The Stone Roses...*" Noel Gallagher to AS, 1994
"*I just went...*" Liam Gallagher to AS, 1994

SOURCES

BOOKS, ETC

Bacon, David & Maslov, Norman **The Beatles' England** [*Columbus, 1982*]

Camden History Society **Primrose Hill To Euston Road: A Survey Of The Streets Of West Camden** [*Camden History Society, 1982*]

Clarke, Ross **Led Zeppelin: Breaking And Making Records** [*Kingsfleet, 1992*]

Coon, Caroline **1988: The New Wave Punk Rock Explosion** [*Omnibus, 1982 Ed*]

Cronin, Anthony **Samuel Beckett: The Last Modernist** [*Flamingo, 1997*]

David, Lester & Robbins, Jhan **Richard And Elizabeth** [*Star, 1977*]

Davies, Hunter **The New London Spy** [*Corgi, 1967*]

Dunphy, Eamon **Unforgettable Fire: The Story Of U2** [*Viking, 1987*]

Elliott, Martin **The Rolling Stones: Complete Recording Sessions 1963-1989** [*Blandford, 1990*]

Elliott, Paul **Guns N'Roses** [*The Hamlyn Publishing Group Limited, 1990*]

Ferris, Paul **Caitlin: The Life Of Caitlin Thomas** [*Hutchinson, 1993*]

Frame, Pete **Rock Family Trees** [*Omnibus, 1993*]

Flood, Adrian **The Irish In Camden** [*London Borough Of Camden, Leisure Services Dept, 1990*]

Gallagher, Paul & Christian, Terry **Brothers: From Childhood To Oasis** [*Virgin, 1996*]

Graham, Bill & Greenfield, Robert **Bill Graham Presents: My Life Inside Rock And Out** [*Doubleday, 1992*]

Gray, Marcus **Last Gang In Town: The Story And Myth Of The Clash** [*4th Estate, 1995*]

Green, Jonathon **Days In The Life: Voices From The English Underground 1961-1971** [*Minerva, 1989*]

Green, Johnny & Barker, Garry **A Riot Of Our Own: Night And Day With The Clash** [*Indigo, 1997*]

Hall, Reginald Richard **Irish Music And Dance in London 1890-1970: A Socio-Cultural History** [*A Thesis Submitted At The University Of Sussex, 1994*]

Heylin, Clinton **From The Velvets To The Voidoids: A Pre-Punk History For A Post-Punk World** [*Penguin 1993*]

Hewitt, Paolo **Getting High: The Adventures Of Oasis** [*Boxtree, 1997*]

Jeffares, A Norman, **WB Yeats: Man And Poet** [*Routledge & Keegan Paul Ltd, 1949*]

Jackson, John Archer **The Irish In Britain** [*Routledge & Keegan Paul Ltd, 1963*]

Kavanagh, Patrick **The Green Fool** [*Penguin, 1975*]

Kavanagh, Peter **Sacred Keeper: A Biography Of Patrick Kavanagh** [*Goldsmith, 1986*]

Litton, Helen **The Irish Civil War: An Illustrated History** [*Wolfhound Press, 1995*]

Nuttall, Jeff **Bomb Culture** [*Paladin, 1970*]

Manso, Peter **Brando** [*Orion, 1994*]

McCool, Jim [Ed] **One Better Day: A Profile Of The Irish Tenants Of Arlington House** [*Bridge Housing Association, 1997*]

Melly, George **Revolt Into Style: The Pop Arts In Britain** [*Penguin, 1972*]

Norman, Philip **The Stones** [*Penguin, 1993*]

O'Connor, Kevin **The Irish In Britain** [*Sidgwick & Jackson, London, 1972*]

O'Connor, Ulick **Brendan Behan** [*Evergreen Black Cat, 1973*]

Power, Vincent **Send 'Em Home Sweatin': The Showbands' Story** [*Kildanore, 1990*]

Render, Chris & Derbyshire, Philip [Eds] **The First Twenty Five Years Of Compendium Bookshop: 1968-1993** [*Aldgate Press, London, 1993*]

Richardson, John **Camden Town And Primrose Hill Past** [*Historical Publications, 1991*]

Robertson, John **The Jesus & Mary Chain: A Musical Biography** [*Omnibus, 1988*]

Savage, Jon **England's Dreaming** [*Faber & Faber, 1991*]

Starkie, Enid **Arthur Rimbaud** [*Hamish Hamilton, New & Revised Edition, 1947*]

Stevenson, Anne **Bitter Fame: A Life Of Sylvia Plath** [*Penguin, 1990*]

Storey, David **Flight Into Camden** [*Longmants, Green & Co Ltd, London, 1960*]

Taub, Michael **Jack Doyle: Fighting For Love** [*Stanley Paul & Co Ltd, 1990*]

Thomson, David **In Camden Town** [*Penguin, 1985*]

Tremlett, George **The Marc Bolan Story** [*Futura 1975*]

Turner, Steve **Van Morrison: Too Late To Stop Now** [*Bloomsbury, 1993*]

INDEX

INDEX

INDEX

INDEX

INDEX